The LEGENDS

VOLUME II

The LEGENDS
VOLUME II

Ohio State BUCKEYES

THE MEN, THE DEEDS, THE CONSEQUENCES

MARK REA

ORANGE *frazer* PRESS
Wilmington, Ohio

ISBN 978-1949248-623

Published by:
Orange Frazer Press
37½ West Main St.
P.O. Box 214
Wilmington, OH 45177

For price and shipping information, call: 937.382.3196
Or visit: www.orangefrazer.com

Book and cover design by: Orange Frazer Press with Catie South

Library of Congress CIP Number: IN PROGRESS

First Printing

DEDICATION

TO MATTHEW,

WHOSE TWINKLE IN HIS EYE

REKINDLED THE TWINKLE IN MINE.

AND ESPECIALLY FOR KELLY JO,

WHO REMINDED ME THERE ARE ALWAYS

BEAUTIFUL CHAPTERS REMAINING TO BE WRITTEN.

ACKNOWLEDGMENTS

This is my second collaboration with Orange Frazer Press, and it was once again my privilege to work with such experienced and talented professionals. From the first relaxed chat in publisher Marcy Hawley's office about writing a sequel to *The Legends* to marveling at the savvy marketing mastery of inexhaustible project manager Sarah Hawley, the oftentimes laborious process of transforming an idea into a finished book was made so much easier.

As for Orange Frazer editor John Baskin, he challenged me years ago to adopt a more literary style with my writing, and to paraphrase a well-worn saying, it's never easy to teach an old dog new tricks. But I like to believe the old dog met that challenge, going beyond simple scores and statistics to add more depth and substance to the subjects in this book. Even between book projects, John often offers notes of praise and encouragement, and I could not be more appreciative of his friendship.

Photos that appear within these pages were accumulated from a variety of sources, but three individuals are due special thanks.

I have worked on several projects over the years with Michelle Drobak at OSU Photo Archives, and I continue to appreciate her preparedness, professionalism, and attention to detail. I have known Sonny Brockway of Brockway Photos for more than thirty years, and he has been a patient and willing participant with each of my book projects. Finally, Becky Roberts at *Buckeye Sports Bulletin* took time away from her other duties at the newspaper and was extremely helpful in procuring photos from recent issues.

While on the subject of *Buckeye Sports Bulletin*, it has been my pleasure to have been affiliated with publisher Frank Moskowitz and his company since 1988. It was Frank who gave me my first opportunity to cover the Buckeyes on a daily basis, and he shares with me a love and passion for the history and tradition of Ohio State football. I have been able to spend a sizable chunk of my professional life doing what I love, and for that I will always be grateful to Frank.

Jack Park and Rex Kern are my most reliable go-to sources when it comes to Ohio State football history, and they once again came through for me during this project. Jack possesses an uncanny memory of all things Buckeye, while Rex is an endless fountain of funny stories and entertaining anecdotes of his time in and around the Ohio State program. I am honored beyond description that each considers me a friend and colleague.

Thanks to the countless Ohio State football players and coaches with whom I have interacted over the years. They provided not only insight and colorful background information for these pages, but hours upon hours of entertainment on cool and crisp autumn afternoons. It goes without saying, but I'll state the obvious anyway: Without their contributions, this book would never have been possible.

My family has always been basecamp for me, and no peak seemed too high to climb with them in my corner. My late parents were each school teachers who provided nothing but encouragement when I decided I wanted to pursue a writing career. My older brothers, twins who likely would just as soon have remained the only offspring in the family, have been rock-solid in their support, especially during these past few years when I have needed it most.

I am forever indebted to my daughter Jessica, who remains the crowning achievement of my life, and her husband David, who gifted me four years ago with my first grandchild, a curly-topped, inquisitive, enchanting, perpetual motion machine named Matthew, who seems to believe Grandpa is a pretty cool guy. I hope the little boy I refer to as Grandpa's bestest little buddy always feels that way.

Jess also graciously served as one of two proofreaders on this project. The other was Kelly Elliott, who in addition to unselfishly sharing her grace, kindness, wisdom, and love with me, also managed to rekindle a fire I thought had burned out. Kelly was an unflagging champion of this project, and her words of faith and encouragement helped me to see it through.

It has been eight years since I last published a book, and I honestly thought I would never write another. My wife, Lisa, passed away unexpectedly in 2015, and my passion for writing seemed to die with her. She was the light of my life as well as the keeper of my dreams, and I struggled not only with sorrow and loss but the memories of everything we shared.

But one realizes there is a period of healing you must endure, and with help from aforementioned friends and family members, as well as love and understanding from those closest to you, the realization slowly sinks in that you are still here, and your departed loved one would want you to continue to do what you do best. This book is the result of that realization.

Benjamin Franklin once wrote, “Either write things worth reading, or do things worth writing.” Each of the subjects in this book has accomplished things that were well worth the writing. I hope I have done their stories justice with a book you will deem as enjoyable to read as it was to write.

CONTENTS

The LEGENDS

VOLUME II

FREDERICK PATTERSON

OSU HALFBACK 1890—1891

NICKNAME: Fred

HOMETOWN: Greenfield, Ohio

HEIGHT: 5 ft 10 in **WEIGHT**: 175 lb

Roots of the Ohio State football program as we know it today began to take hold when Woody Hayes was hired as head coach in 1951. But those roots began as seedlings when the university fielded its first football team in 1890, a rag-tag group of students who gathered to take on Ohio Wesleyan in a May contest that ended with the Buckeyes earning a 20–14 victory.

That stands as the first official game as well as the first win in program history, but apparently the participants didn't think much of it at the time. The "team" disbanded, and not until the following November did a different collection of players get together to lose three straight games and "complete" the 1890 season.

The following autumn, the Buckeyes resembled much more of a real team although calling it a team by today's standards would be somewhat of a stretch. Most history books indicate that former Princeton quarterback/fullback Alexander Spinning Lilley returned for a second season as head coach in 1891, but recent research projects claim Lilley did nothing more than stop by practice a time or two—usually on an afternoon pony ride—to offer advice. That advice, according to one former team member, amounted to very little, saying, "About all we got was that eleven men played on a side."

Regardless of who or who wasn't coaching the team, the roster was an eclectic mix of farm boys, pre-law and pre-med students, and those just curious about the relatively new sport of football. One of those was Fred Patterson, a light-skinned African American who was the son of a former slave-turned-blacksmith from Greenfield, Ohio, a rural dot on the map in northern Highland County that was once an important hub along the Underground Railroad.

Fred's father, Charles Richard Patterson, was a native of Virginia, where in 1833 he had been born into slavery. His owner had young Charles apprentice as a blacksmith and he quickly became adept at the trade, earning the reputation as the finest blacksmith in the region. But growing increasingly resentful that his owner profited from his skill while he did not, shortly before the 1861 outbreak of the American Civil

War, Charles joined several other members of his family to make their way along the Underground Railroad to a variety of points throughout the free states, scattering into Ohio, Indiana, Illinois and New York. Charles went only as far as Greenfield, where he applied the skills he had acquired as a slave and soon became foreman for a local carriage manufacturing firm.

After becoming established in the small village, he married Josephine Utz, a sixteen-year-old Virginian who was the daughter of a former slave and her German husband. The couple married on Independence Day in 1864, and immediately started a family with daughter Mary born in 1868 and Nellie following two years later. Their first-born son, christened Frederick Douglas Patterson after the famous writer, orator and abolitionist, was born September 17, 1872, and would eventually be joined by siblings Samuel, Dorothea and Catherine.

Fiercely proud and determined that his son would get all of the education opportunities that were denied to him, Charles was prepared to send young Fred to high school in the fall of 1885. But Greenfield High School, then located on the west bank of Paint Creek, was for white children only, and Superintendent William Moler met Fred at the door and refused to let him enter the school. Each weekday morning, Charles would send his son to school, and each time the youngster was turned away because of the color of his skin. Not until attorney and former Ohio state senator Mills Gardner successfully sued the Greenfield School Board was Fred permitted to attend classes.

In 1889, he became the first African American to graduate from Greenfield High School, and then he enrolled at Ohio State, where he found the atmosphere much more welcoming. Patterson participated in a variety of campus activities, and held membership in a number of clubs, including the prestigious Horton Literary Society. He was elected class president during his junior year and also spent some time as editor of *The Lantern*, the university's student newspaper. Fred also found time for athletics, dabbling in a little baseball and answering a call in 1890 for students to form a

Fred (top row, third from the left) was a member of the 1891 Ohio State Football team.

"scrub team" that would scrimmage against the varsity football squad.

The Buckeyes were scheduled to play Kenyon College on Thanksgiving Day in 1890, but starting halfback Hobart Beatty had stopped showing up for practice and second-stringer Walter Landacre had left the team following the sudden death of his mother. OSU captain Paul Lincoln—likely the real head coach of the team—asked Patterson if he wanted to play on the varsity team against the Lords. Not only did Patterson play, he scooped up a fumble late in the game and ran it into the end zone to become the first African American to score a touchdown for the Buckeyes.

By the time the 1891 season began, Patterson was asked to become a full-fledged member of the varsity team, and became the first African-American football player to earn his letterman's jacket.

The Buckeyes played four times that year, including twice within a four-day span. The season began on a Wednesday with a 56–0 loss at home to Western Reserve, and continued the following Saturday with a 26–0 defeat at Kenyon. According to reports of the day, the team was unhappy with the trip to Kenyon, claiming the playing field was in poor condition and the official assigned to the game clearly favored the home team.

After two weeks of practice, the season resumed November 28 with an 8–4 win against Denison and concluded with a 6–0 shutout of Akron on December 5. It was the first regular-season December game in program history, and there wouldn't be another for more than a century when the Buckeyes took a 52–12 win against Michigan State on December 5, 2020, as part of a schedule jumbled by the COVID-19 pandemic.

Fred was invited back to play another season with the Buckeyes in 1892, but he accepted a teaching job in Louisville, Kentucky, with the intention of making some money before returning to school. He wrote to a university friend, "I am down here in this land of good whiskey, fast horses and fair women, and to tell you honestly, I am making hay in a way that is pleasant to me.…I am trying my hand at experience, and let me tell you it is the best of teachers."

While living in Kentucky, Fred met Bettie E. Postell, a school teacher and one of nine children of a former slave and Union Army soldier. Fred taught history in Louisville until returning to his hometown in 1897 to help with his family's buggy manufacturing business. His younger brother, Samuel, was battling an illness and his father needed help running the operation.

A year later, however, Fred answered a call to volunteer for Army duty during the Spanish-American War. He was among those sent to Tampa to meet their regiment in preparation for an invasion of Cuba, but the war ended before the regiment was activated. Fred returned to Greenfield to work with his father, now grief-stricken after Samuel had been found dead in Paint Creek, the victim of an apparent suicide.

C.R. Patterson & Sons was a thriving enterprise whose integrated workforce at times numbered more than 50 people. Most of the 28 high-quality models the company produced were sold in the $125 to $150 range, and Patterson & Sons rivaled every other buggy manufacturer in the Midwest in terms of sales and customer satisfaction. Meanwhile, Fred and Bettie were married in 1901 and gave birth to sons Frederick in 1903 and Postell in 1906.

After Charles died in 1910, Fred took over the everyday running of the business, including accompanying sales manager Charles W. Napper, the son of Fred's older sister Mary, on trips around the country to secure orders. During those travels, Fred began to notice the growing number of automobiles appearing on the road, instantly recognizing the future of the transportation industry. By 1914, Fred had transformed the buggy business into an automobile manufacturing firm with Fred designing and building a vehicle he called the Patterson-Greenfield Automobile. Equipped with a 30-horsepower, four-cylinder engine, the auto came in either a closed touring model

The son of a former slave, Fred was a pioneer with the Ohio State football team and later as a successful businessman.

or a convertible roadster and sold for between $685 and $850.

The Patterson-Greenfield still remains as the only automobile built by an African-American owned company. Estimates differ on how many cars were actually produced, but the number is likely between thirty and 150. Unfortunately, the company could not compete with larger manufacturers, but in the 1920s, Patterson changed course again and began building school bus and truck bodies on chassis purchased from other manufacturers. He changed the name of his business to the Greenfield Bus Body Company, and it flourished as the top supplier of school buses to Ohio school districts. According to one estimate, nearly half of the school buses on the road in Ohio in 1929 had been manufactured in Greenfield.

That same year, the stock market crashed in October, an event that signaled the beginning of the end for many small businesses around the country. It was a fate that also befell the Greenfield Bus Body Company although its doors remained open until 1939. Fred, however, would not live to see his family business shuttered. Anxious from the looming financial ruin, Frederick Douglas Patterson suffered a heart attack and died on a snowy January 18, 1932, at the age of sixty.

Patterson's death notice was published in the *Ohio State Monthly*, calling him "one of the most widely known African-American leaders in southern Ohio." Unfortunately, no mention was made of his time on campus, either as student or athlete. For while Patterson might have been an African-American trailblazer as far as the Ohio State football team was concerned, that trail grew decidedly cold after he left school. Julius B. Tyler, the son of a prominent Columbus businessman, played for the Buckeyes in 1896, but he left the team after only one season, and it wasn't until 1929 when Ohio State would have another Black player on its roster.

JOHN SIGRIST

OSU CENTER 1897–1901

HOMETOWN: Congress, Ohio

HEIGHT: 5 ft 10 in **WEIGHT**: 185 lb

Wearing the uniform of the day, complete with woolen turtleneck sweater with a block "O" squarely emblazoned on the chest, the young man bends at the waist, hands on his knees, and offers a sardonic smile from more than a century ago. On one level, it is a mesmerizing portrait of a young man entering the prime of his life. On another, especially if you know the story of the photo's subject, it is a tragic reminder of just how violent the game of football can be.

The subject of the black-and-white photograph is John Sigrist, a football player for the Ohio State University at the turn of the twentieth century. Sigrist never scored a touchdown for the Buckeyes, never earned All-America honors, and never played on a national championship team. Yet his legacy is one that is much more than statistics, awards or a granite gravestone in a small community on the edge of Amish country about ninety miles northeast of Columbus.

John Larkum Sigrist was the son of Swiss/German immigrants, Christian and Madeline Kampt Sigrist, a farmer and homemaker who lived just outside Congress, Ohio, a tiny town in the northwestern corner of Wayne County. John was born in 1873 with his actual date of birth a bit fuzzy due to the sporadic bookkeeping methods of the day. Some records have the Sigrist family containing as many as ten children with John and sister Caroline sharing the same birth year (although they were not twins).

Like most others who were raised on a farm during the latter part of the nineteenth century, young John learned the importance of hard work at a young age. Unlike others, however, he wasn't only interested in the crops that he and his siblings helped their father grow. John was interested in how corn, soybeans, wheat and hay were grown, from planting through harvest, and was determined to make the study of agriculture his life's work.

John attended nearby Oberlin Academy Preparatory School, a secondary school located on the campus of Oberlin College. It was at Oberlin Academy where John got his first taste of competitive football, but rather than follow most academy grads to Oberlin College, he instead enrolled in the School of Agriculture at Ohio State at the age of twenty-two. In those days, Oberlin had a much better established football program than Ohio State, and the Yeomen had won each of their six meetings with the Buckeyes by a combined score of 200–14. But the lure of OSU's agriculture school was just too great, and John moved to Columbus where he easily entered campus life that included joining a fraternity and going out for the football team.

He was forced to sit out the first three games of the 1897 season because of a faculty policy forbidding first-year students from competing in varsity athletics. But when that policy was suddenly rescinded, and John was permitted to play, he started in the center of both the offensive and defensive lines and became what many historians describe as the cornerstone for Ohio State's first successful teams. His leadership qualities were so impressive that his teammates elected him team captain for the 1898 season.

Success didn't come quickly, however. The Buckeyes were a program-worst 1–7–1 in 1897 and followed that with a 3–5 record in 1898, but their fortunes began to turn when the university hired John B.C. Eckstorm as head coach prior to the 1899 season. Eckstorm, a graduate of Dartmouth College, guided the team to its first-ever unbeaten season that year, a 9–0–1 finish that included wins against Oberlin and Western Reserve for the first time in program history. The only blemish was a 5–5 tie at Case in mid-October.

Ohio State's success during the 1899 campaign was attributed to the strength of its line play, which the student newspaper, *The Lantern*, exalted as "almost invincible both in offensive and defensive work." The linemen on that team had similar backgrounds as Sigrist—strong, muscular country boys born in bucolic settings and raised on the discipline and work ethic of their fathers, most of whom were turn-of-the-century dirt and dairy farmers.

Homer Wharton, known for a powerful voice and splendid physique, was a law student from Guernsey County, so named for the granite-rich Isle of Guernsey in the English Channel from which many of the county's rock-hard early settlers emigrated. Wharton manned one of the guard positions along with Josephus Tilton, whose sinewy arms and brawny torso were the result of growing up on his family's livestock farm near Jelloway in Knox County. Left tackle was the domain of Delbert Sayers, a Morrow County native whose natural athletic talents also made him the team's most accomplished goal kicker. John's younger brother, Charles, a taller and more lithe version of his older sibling, held down the position of right tackle.

With the turn of the century, the Ohio State football program seemed to get even stronger. The Buckeyes began the 1900 season with six consecutive shutouts before an 11–6 loss to Ohio Medical and an 0–0 tie with Michigan in what was described in *The Lantern*, as "the best game ever played by an Ohio State eleven."

The team finished the season with an 8–1–1 record, thanks in no small part to Sigrist, who was "always in the thick of the fray," according to *The Lantern*, and described as "perhaps without exception the finest specimen of strength and physical competence" the Buckeyes had ever had.

Interest in the program began to grow as the victories started to mount. While crowds to Ohio State football games had never numbered more than a few hundred, university officials were forced to rent temporary bleachers from the Sells Brothers Circus that wintered across the river from campus in order to boost University Field's seating capacity to 1,500.

Under today's eligibility rules, Sigrist's collegiate career would have ended after the 1900 season. But because the rules of that era were based more on academic standing, if a student-athlete was still enrolled at the university as a student, he could continue to participate in athletics.

Even so, the 1901 season began without Sigrist in the lineup because he had not yet returned to Ohio from a summer job at a logging camp in Olympia, Washington. Perhaps his absence—along with his brother, who joined John at the Washington logging camp—was a reason behind a 0–0 tie with Otterbein in the season opener.

But after the Sigrist brothers returned, the Buckeyes rolled to shutout wins against Wittenberg, Ohio University, and Marietta to set up an October 26 battle with old foe Western Reserve.

Warm temperatures accompanied the multicolored fall foliage that greeted a sellout crowd of 1,500 who paid 50 cents apiece to jam into University Field to watch a nip-and-tuck game. *The Lantern* described the crowd filled with coeds who would wave "scarlet and gray pennants one moment and crumble score-cards in nervous hands the next. Meanwhile, the gentlemen in the stands found constant employment for the strongest epithets which their vocabulary contained—profane or otherwise."

Ohio State scored a touchdown midway through the first half on a 75-yard punt return by fullback Elwood "Laffy" Bulen, and held a 6–0 lead at halftime.

Early in the second half, though, tragedy struck. On a simple pileup in the middle of the field, Sigrist locked up with the player opposite him, and as *The Lantern* reported, "(He) struck the man opposite him with his head. He was bent backward and went to the bottom of the pile with all the other players on top." Sigrist, who only briefly lost consciousness, was carried from the field and taken to the nearby Armory where he waited nearly an hour before a doctor arrived to examine him. Meanwhile, his teammates eventually hung on for a 6–5 victory against Western Reserve.

When medical help finally arrived, Sigrist was determined to have sustained a serious neck injury. He was quickly transferred to Grant Hospital, where surgeons advised immediate surgery to determine the extent of the injury. But because Sigrist was awake and in such good spirits, doctors decided to delay the surgery until X-rays could be taken to determine exactly what had happened. Those X-rays were delayed until the following afternoon, and they revealed the worst possible outcome—a fracture and dislocation of the cervical vertebrae at the base of Sigrist's neck. The dislocation had crushed his spinal cord and produced paralysis from the neck down.

Doctors prepared for delicate spinal surgery, but again delayed, this time while university authorities sought to obtain permission from John's parents. Meanwhile, Charles remained at his brother's bedside, trying to comfort John but also gently stressing the graveness of the situation. "He replied with that smile, so characteristic of him," Charles said later. "Then he said, 'All right. Perform the operation and I'll pull through it."

Remaining conscious and offering little evidence of the extreme pain he must have been suffering, John's condition deteriorated quickly and he died at 1:30 p.m. on Sunday, just one hour before his surgery was to begin and approximately twenty-four hours after his limp body had been carried off the field by his Ohio State teammates. Set to graduate the following spring from the School of Agriculture, his senior thesis, "The Influence of Rainfall and Temperature on the Production of Hay and Oats in the United States," was found at his desk in his dormitory room, where he had been working on it the morning before the game.

A memorial service was held the following Tuesday in the University Chapel with more than 1,500 mourners gathering to pay their respects. Afterward, the casket was loaded into a hearse and taken to Union Station for John's final journey home. A

"John Sigrist's life was fraught with principle and with charity....He had a smile for everyone. He has left us that most precious of memories—that of a thousand little, nameless, unremembered acts of love....Mankind has lost an honest helper and Ohio State University a heroic son. May he live forever in the memory of this institution, once blessed with his presence."

—Charles C. Poindexter

day later, he was laid to rest on the family farm near Congress.

The agriculture professor, Billy Graves, perfectly captured the somber mood around campus when he wrote, "The death of so excellent a player, so good a student, so honorable a man, fills us all with a kind of horror that will not be shaken off.... His honest candor, his modest demeanor, his devotion to clean sport has endeared him to all of us; and his death has given a shock to the life of the University from which it will not soon recover."

Charles C. Poindexter, an African-American classmate in the School of Agriculture who would later become a professor of agriculture and biology at Fisk University in Nashville, Tennessee, memorialized his friend by saying, "John Sigrist's life was fraught with principle and with charity....He had a smile for everyone. He has left us that most precious of memories—that of a thousand little, nameless, unremembered acts of love....Mankind has lost an honest helper and Ohio State University a heroic son. May he live forever in the memory of this institution, once blessed with his presence."

But even as condolences and eulogies were being offered, critics almost immediately began to call for the discontinuation of football at Ohio State. The game the following week against Ohio Wesleyan was canceled, and there was talk of suspending the season out of respect for Sigrist.

Amid a national debate, during which one newspaper used the tragedy of Sigrist's death to opine that "the price paid was too high for the satisfaction that is to be gained from the game," the OSU Faculty Council established a committee to examine the risks of continuing the football program. And it might well have ruled for abolition of the sport until Charles Sigrist came forward. Charles had withdrawn from school following the death of his brother and returned to the family farm, but he sent word to university officials to say that it was his wish, as well as that of his family, that football continue at Ohio State. Shortly after that, the committee voted 18–8 to continue the football program.

The 1901 season resumed, but to say the players' hearts weren't in it would be an understatement.

The Buckeyes lost their next three games, salvaging a 5–3–1 record with a Thanksgiving Day win against Kenyon in the season finale. Eckstorm left Ohio State after the season, and the program drifted for the next eleven years under six different head coaches.

Charles Sigrist returned to the Pacific Northwest and enrolled at the University of Washington, where he completed his football career as a standout lineman for the Huskies. He also earned a law degree and maintained a successful practice in the Seattle area until his death in 1956.

At least two attempts to establish a memorial to John Sigrist were attempted. In 1908, members of the Alumni Association requested a bronze memorial to be placed at Ohio Field during the official dedication of the Buckeyes' new home stadium. The same request was put forward some twelve years later when the campaign was underway to raise funds for construction of Ohio Stadium.

In neither case did a memorial ever materialize, leaving generations of fans never knowing about Sigrist or his legacy with regard to Ohio State football. And in perhaps one final bit of ignominy, Sigrist's name is misspelled "Segrist" in most university record books, including the official *Ohio State Football Media Guide*. That apparently stems from the fact newspapers during his era frequently misspelled his name and Sigrist never bothered to correct the mistakes.

"We once asked John why he didn't tell someone," Tilton said years later. "He said it didn't matter. He said getting written up was OK with him no matter how they spelled his name."

ERNIE GODFREY

OSU END, CENTER 1912–1914 **ASSISTANT COACH** 1929–1961

HOMETOWN: Dover, Ohio

COLLEGE FOOTBALL HALL OF FAME: 1972

Hushed tones greeted the old man as he shuffled his way through the old North Facility, the football complex that was later expanded into the Woody Hayes Athletic Center on the outer northwest region of the sprawling campus at The Ohio State University in Columbus.

Slightly stoop-shouldered but eyes still sparkling, the man held a cane in one craggy hand and reached out with the other to shake hands with coaches and old acquaintances as he was treated like royalty. One person whispered, "That's the greatest line coach who ever lived." Another shook his head and said, "No, he was the greatest kicking coach ever." Truth be told, they were both correct as coaches and staff members who knew their Ohio State football history paid homage to longtime assistant Ernie Godfrey as he paid what would be his final visit to the practice facility where he had spent much of his adult life.

Now in his late eighties, Godfrey could reflect and reminisce about when legendary Notre Dame head coach Knute Rockne referred to him as "the best line coach in America," the time Paul Brown credited him with helping the Cleveland Browns win a National Football League championship, and the praise heaped upon him by Woody Hayes, who called Ernie "a true legend."

Had he wanted to, Godfrey could have been head coach of the Buckeyes at some point in history. He watched from the sideline as the university changed coaches seven different times, and on more than one of those occasions had more than enough support to make a run for the top spot himself. He had been a head coach before, and had been an extremely successful one. But after seeing the view from the top of the mountain, he had been content to let someone else worry about the schedule-making, the gladhanding of influential boosters and the sometimes-contentious interaction with members of the Board of Trustees. Ernie just wanted to coach football, and he did it well enough to earn enshrinement in the College Football Hall of Fame.

Ernest R. Godfrey was born April 19, 1892, in Canal Dover, Ohio, so named due to its location and origins along the Ohio and Erie Canal. Although in recent years the town now known simply as Dover has nearly equaled the size of nearby New Philadelphia just to its southeast, Canal Dover was dwarfed by its Tuscarawas County neighbor during Ernie's childhood.

He was one of six children born to Andrew Godfrey and his bride, the former Christiana Dorothea Lahmers, people of German descent, sturdy stock and an unyielding work ethic. When Ernie was a youngster, his father was a butcher while his mother looked after the family's house on Second Street, which was known to have a boarder or two under its roof from time to time.

As Ernie grew into a teenager, the family moved to Front Street on the west bank of the Tuscarawas River, an important link in the Ohio and Erie Canal. Never one to miss an opportunity to better himself and his family, Andrew secured a position with the local teamsters and spent the next several years as a boatman along the canal, helping barges navigate their way along the waterway from New Philadelphia toward Lake Erie until floods forced much of the canal to be abandoned in 1913.

By that time, young Ernie had already graduated from Dover High School and begun his studies at Ohio State. He apparently had little time for anything but athletics and academics, playing football and basketball while securing his Bachelor of Arts degree. He played end for the football Buckeyes in 1912 under the tutelage of John Robertson Richards, a season in which the team won an Ohio Athletic Conference championship with a perfect five league wins in as many games. But the 1912 season also featured an ugly 37–0 loss to Penn State, a game in which Richards accused the Nittany Lions of dirty play and pulled his team off the field.

Several newspapers statewide ridiculed Richards with commentary from the *Toledo News-Bee* offering, "Coach Richards of Ohio State, who took his team off the field Saturday because he declared Penn State too tough, evidently was never on Lake Erie on a choppy sea." Incensed by the criticism, Richards resigned after the 1912 season and didn't coach again for five years.

In his place, the university hired Dr. Jack Wilce, who helped shepherd the program into a new level of greatness, beginning with entry into the Western Conference (later the Big Ten) beginning in 1913. The former University of Wisconsin star fullback and assistant coach produced winning records in eight of his first nine seasons with the Buckeyes, including three conference championships.

Playing end as well as center for Wilce's first two Ohio State teams, Ernie was an important part of the 1913 team that finished with four wins and a tie in seven games as well as the 1914 squad when the Buckeyes lost only twice during a seven-game schedule.

Ernie was also a guard on the OSU basketball team under the guidance of head coach Lynn St. John, who was also the director of university athletics. The basketball Buckeyes finished just one game out of first place in the conference standings during the 1913–14 season with only a loss at Chicago preventing them from taking the title.

After graduation, Ernie returned to Dover for the summer before securing a job teaching history at Wooster High School, just about thirty-five miles northwest of his hometown. The teaching job carried with it an extra stipend for helping to coach the school's football team, and Ernie was immediately hooked. With the exception of a two-year stint as a U.S. Army first lieutenant in World War I, he would spend the next forty-eight years as a football coach.

He spent only one season at Wooster before landing his first college job. With most young men headed off to military service in the first world war, Wittenberg University in Springfield, Ohio, was in need of someone to run its football program. Few other options seemed available, so the school hired young Ernie Godfrey, who had turned just twenty-four the previous spring and was only a few years older than most of his players.

To say his first taste of head coaching was palatable would be an overstatement. The Tigers won only two games and tied two others while suffering five losses and finished in last place of the Ohio Athletic Conference standings in 1916. That showing apparently did not dissuade Wittenberg officials on Ernie, however. After his stint in the Army, the school rehired him as head football coach and the program enjoyed varying degrees of success over the next decade.

The Tigers celebrated Ernie's return to campus with an undefeated season in 1919 and repeated the feat the following year in 1920. During that decade-long run, Godfrey's teams won 61 times, lost only 19 and had six ties. The Tigers also won the OAC championship in 1927, and when they moved to the Buckeye Athletic Association the following year, they won the title there. Meanwhile, Ernie was also coaching the Wittenberg basketball team, a squad that won nearly sixty percent of its games while he was at the helm.

By the late 1920s, Ernie had caught the attention of Ohio State head coach San Willaman, who had been an assistant on Wilce's staff. When Wilce resigned following the 1928 season and Willaman was promoted to replace him, the new coach drove to Springfield to make an impassioned plea for Ernie to join his new staff. Eager after ten years for a new challenge, Ernie agreed and began a stay in Columbus that would last for the remainder of his life.

Beginning with Willaman, he served under seven head coaches—Francis A. Schmidt, Paul Brown, Carroll Widdoes, Paul Bixler, Wes Fesler and Woody Hayes—spending nineteen years as line coach, four seasons in charge of defensive backs, ten years as freshman coach,

On game day, Ernie would observe the game from his perch in the Ohio Stadium press box and telephone his observations to Schmidt, who sat on the bench. Schmidt would listen to Ernie for a minute and then yell into the phone, "Goddammit, Ernie, tell me something I don't know!" and throw down the phone.

and nearly all of that time as the team's kicking coach.

When Willaman resigned following the 1933 season and Ohio State hired the mercurial Schmidt away from Texas Christian University, Ernie played the role of trusted friend and confidant to the paranoid new head coach who believed everyone was trying to steal away his good ideas. The deeply religious Godfrey, who never swore, also played good-naturedly foil to the foul-mouthed Schmidt.

On game day, Ernie would observe the game from his perch in the Ohio Stadium press box and telephone his observations to Schmidt, who sat on the bench. Schmidt would listen to Ernie for a minute and then yell into the phone, "Goddammit, Ernie, tell me something I don't know!" and throw down the phone. Once in a while during practice when a lineman wasn't using a proper blocking technique, Ernie would pull him out for some one-on-one instruction until Schmidt would yell, "Goddammit, Ernie, put him back in there and let him learn some football."

Godfrey had some unusual character traits in his own right. His passion for the game was evident in his periodic halftime speeches, some of them featuring heartfelt tears and others provoking unintentional laughter such as when Ernie yelled, "So, let's stay in here and get those guys!"

In fact, Ernie seemed to be Ohio State's answer to Yogi Berra, uttering such malapropisms as "Scatter out in bunches" or "Let's pair off in threes." He also had a heart of gold, on full display during an outbreak of the Asian flu in 1957. For several days, Godfrey personally delivered orange juice and toast to quarantined freshmen to help them recover.

Ernie continued his full-time coaching duties until an inoperable cyst on his brain forced his retirement in 1962 at the age of seventy. Still, he continued to serve as a kicking consultant for both Hayes and Paul Brown, who founded the Cincinnati Bengals in 1968 and spent the first eight years of the franchise's history as head coach.

It was Brown who always gave Ernie credit for helping refine the kicking talents of Lou Groza when all three were at Ohio State in 1942. Groza was a freshman that season and kicked five field goals in the three games the freshmen played that season, including a 48-yarder against Pittsburgh that would have been the longest three-pointer in program history at the time.

Groza was drafted into military service in the spring of 1943 and never resumed his college career, but when World War II was over, and Groza's service in the South Pacific was behind him, he joined the Cleveland Browns. And when the Browns defeated the Los Angeles Rams, 30–28, to win the 1950 NFL championship, it was Groza's 23-yard field goal with just sixteen seconds remaining in the game that proved to be the difference.

After the game, Paul Brown said of Groza's game-winner, "I would say that Ernie Godfrey had a lot to do with Cleveland winning the championship." The coach could also have been referring to the two field goals Groza kicked to beat the New York Giants in the Eastern Conference title contest that gave the Browns an 8–3 victory and got them to the championship game.

In addition to his coaching career, Ernie served as longtime president of the Columbus chapter of the National Football Foundation, a chapter that was later renamed the Ernie Godfrey Chapter in his honor. Then on the eve of his eightieth birthday in 1972, he was elected to the College Football Hall of Fame in the pioneer coach category.

Other awards and honors came his way as he enjoyed retirement with his wife Betty at their Clintonville home near campus before Ernie suffered a heart attack in June 1980 and died a few days later at the age of eighty-eight.

GOMER JONES

CENTER, LINEBACKER 1933–1935 **ASSISTANT COACH** 1936–1940

33

HOMETOWN: Cleveland, Ohio

HEIGHT: 5 ft 7 in **WEIGHT**: 219 lb

ALL-AMERICAN: 1935

COLLEGE FOOTBALL HALL OF FAME: 1978

Gomer Jones never talked much about his days playing college football. He never was a big talker about anything concerning himself.

"There are very few coaches you can go through life and never hear anybody say a bad word about," former University of Oklahoma center Harry Moore once said. "Gomer was one of those people. He was a professional guy, and he had the respect of everybody."

Jones was an assistant coach at Oklahoma through three decades and helped the legendary Bud Wilkinson build a football dynasty in Norman. Between the years 1947 and 1963, the Sooners won fourteen conference championships, three national titles and at one time won forty-seven consecutive games, a mark that still stands at the highest level of college football.

While serving as offensive line coach for Wilkinson, Jones regularly conducted summer clinics, including one that was attended by a young Woody Hayes, who used what he learned at the clinic to formulate his famous "three yards and a cloud of dust" mentality.

But before all that, Jones was a decorated lineman at Ohio State, although you'd never have known it. "Gomer was not a self-centered guy," said Leon Cross, who played for OU in the early 1960s and then began a long career as a coach and administrator at his alma mater. "He didn't talk about his success, but I knew he was a real successful player. We just heard it mainly from the other guys on the coaching staff."

Longtime Ohio State football historian Jack Park said simply, "Gomer Jones, without question, was one of the greatest centers to ever play at Ohio State."

Gomer Thomas Jones was born February 26, 1914, in Cleveland, then the fifth-largest city in the United States. He was born the last of six children to a pair of European immigrants. His father, David William Jones, a stout man with short brown hair and steely gray eyes who came to America with his family from his native Scotland, was foreman at a Cleveland-area machine shop. His mother, the former Mary Hannah Bowen, was born in Wales and worked as a stenographer and bookkeeper.

The family moved around quite a bit during Gomer's childhood, finally landing in a narrow two-story house on East 114th Street, a dwelling with a sharp-angled roof situated just north of the Garfield Heights section in southern Cleveland. It was a perfect neighborhood for a large family with its mix of European and Slavic ethnicities and equally large families. The smell of sausages, pork, fish and freshly baked breads, cakes and pies filled the summertime air while every able-bodied man pitched in to clear neighborhood sidewalks of snow in the winter.

Gomer's mother Mary, was an accomplished cook and baker, and kept her family fed with such Welsh delicacies as Glamorgan sausage, laverbread (cooked seaweed), and, of course, Welsh rarebit as well as enough Scottish staples as bangers and mash (sausage and potatoes), neeps and tatties (a turnip-based dish) and haggis to satisfy her husband's cravings from childhood. Young Gomer was a benefactor of his mother's culinary talents, and packed more than two hundred pounds onto his squatty five-foot-eight frame. That rotund body topped by a full moon-shaped face sometimes gave neighborhood bullies license to test the youngster's mettle. But anyone who dared challenge Gomer to a fight soon discovered an immovable object with a powerful left cross. Later in life, he said, "I never started a fight but I might have ended one or two."

Jones attended old South High School just a few city blocks north of his house and was an immediate star on the football team, anchoring both the offensive and defensive lines for the Flyers. Gomer entertained dreams of attending college and perhaps continuing his football career, but when the darkness of the Great Depression began to fall over the country, there was no way his family could afford to continue his education.

While most of the rest of the country suffered from the financial collapse, major college football programs continued almost unabated during the Depression years, and Ohio State head coach Sam Willaman had no intention of missing out on the talented young lineman from Cleveland South.

Gomer reported for duty on the OSU freshman team in the fall of 1932 and graduated to the varsity the following season. But he lost his benefactor when Willaman resigned following the 1933 season and was replaced by Francis A. Schmidt, a hard-boiled coach known as much for his bow ties and foul mouth as he was for being far ahead of his time in terms of offensive philosophy.

With Schmidt at the controls of a high-powered attack, the Buckeyes won fourteen games and lost only twice during the 1934 and 1935 seasons. Meanwhile, Gomer became a star center on offense and outstanding linebacker on defense. He became the first Ohio State player ever named team MVP twice and was a consensus first-team All-American as a senior.

Jones once said his greatest thrill as a player was in Ohio State's 1935 victory against the University of Chicago. Thanks to the exploits of halfback Jay Berwanger, who later would be awarded the first-ever Heisman Trophy, the three-touchdown underdog Maroons jumped out to a 13–0 lead. But the Buckeyes came back to tie the score in the fourth quarter, and then won a 20–13 decision with a fifteen-yard touchdown from "Jumping" Joe Williams with four minutes left. The TD, Jones said, involved perfect blocking by the entire team.

Playing the center position during the Schmidt era was incredibly important. Ohio State's offensive attack called for airborne (shotgun) snaps on nearly every play. That was tricky enough, but in Schmidt's system, with its multiple formations and hundreds of variations off those formations, the length and direction of the snaps changed frequently. With accuracy and timing being so crucial to the success of each play, Gomer had to be perfect with his snap every time. It was sometimes akin to something of a carnival stunt, but somehow the 200-pounder, with most of that bulk residing in his midsection, mastered it.

After graduating with a degree in industrial arts, Gomer's talents seemed to be in high demand with professional football teams. The Chicago Cardinals made him the fifteenth overall player selected in the inaugural NFL draft, but Jones decided to play for the Cleveland Rams, a new team founded by former Ohio State teammate Buzz Wetzel that was part of the fledgling American Football League. The Rams were wildly successful, both on the field and at the ticket gate, but unfortunately the rest of the league was not and it folded after the 1936 season.

The NFL, eager to tap into the solid franchise in Cleveland, invited the Rams to become part of the more established league in 1937. But the invitation did not extend to such players as Jones and his former Ohio State teammate Sid Gillman, who had spurned NFL offers to play for the Cleveland upstarts. As a result, both men turned to coaching and careers that were wildly successful.

Each man returned to Ohio State where Schmidt gladly put them on his full-time staff. After the university failed to renew Schmidt's contract following the 1940 season, Gillman left for a job at Denison University while Gomer found work at Martins Ferry High School before joining the U.S. Navy during World War II. But that also led to a coaching job at St. Mary's Pre-Flight, where he crossed paths with Wilkinson, who had been an assistant coach at Iowa Pre-Flight. After the war, Wilkinson took a job as an assistant on Jim Tatum's staff at Oklahoma while Gomer joined Bernie Masterson as an assistant at Nebraska. When Wilkinson was promoted to head coach of the Sooners a year later, he brought Jones to Norman, beginning an era of unrivaled success for the Oklahoma program.

Over the next thirteen seasons, the Sooners won a conference championship every year and also captured three national titles, including back-to-back crowns in 1955 and 1956. Also during that era, the Oklahoma campus had become a mecca for other college coaches who sought wisdom and guidance from the most successful program in the sport. In the spring of 1952, a young coach from the Midwest made his pilgrimage to Norman, and paid special attention to the way Jones coached his offensive linemen. Since the coach was from his alma mater, Gomer decided to hold nothing back and proceeded to show Woody Hayes the kind of philosophy and technique he used to produce All-American linemen.

"Gomer Jones, who had been an All-American at Ohio State, was extremely helpful to me along with the rest of the Oklahoma staff," Hayes later said. "I came back to our spring practice and put in the Split-T (formation) exactly the way it had been explained to me. Going out to Oklahoma in the spring of 1952 (was) where I really learned the basis of our running game which to this day is the hub of our offense."

Hayes used the Split-T formation to win national championships in 1954 and '57, and a form of that running style—which later became known as "three yards and a cloud of dust"—can be traced back to what Jones taught the Ohio State coach in the spring of 1952.

Jones and Wilkinson continued to form a nearly unbeatable alliance until Wilkinson stepped down following the 1963 season. Gomer was immediately named Wilkinson's successor as head coach and director of athletics, but after just two seasons as head coach, he resigned to devote his full-time attention to the university's growing athletic department.

It was a job uniquely suited to the man once dubbed "the little round coach." Always a people person, Gomer enjoyed the daily interaction with student-athletes as well as the camaraderie of fellow athletic directors during travels to tournaments, bowl games or conference meetings.

In March 1971, Gomer and his wife Jeannette were in New York, accompanying the Oklahoma basketball team that was playing in the National Invitational Tournament. They were on their way back to their hotel after dinner when Jones collapsed and died from a massive heart attack at the 34th Street subway station. He was just fifty-seven.

"He wanted every guy he coached to love him like a brother or a dad," former Oklahoma player Norman McNabb said during a eulogy of his old line coach. "And we all did."

One profile of Jones written more than three decades after his death perhaps best summed up a life well-lived: "He was a fisherman, a Presbyterian, a cabinet-maker. A devoted friend and husband. And a coach. Gomer Jones was many things, but he was all football coach. And before he was a football coach, Gomer was a football player. One of the best Ohio State ever had."

JACK GRAF

OSU QUARTERBACK, FULLBACK 1939—1941

HOMETOWN: Columbus, Ohio

HEIGHT: 6 ft 1 in **WEIGHT**: 200 lb

ALL-AMERICAN: 1935

NFL DRAFT: 1942, Cleveland Rams

44

You could likely use the fingers of just one hand to count the number of legacy football players at Ohio State that lived up to the exploits of their father. Even fewer for those who equaled their father's success. Then there is Jack Graf, son of a three-sport star for the Buckeyes and the 1914 football team captain. Jack spent more than a quarter-century on campus, first as a star football player who won the Big Ten's highest individual honor and then as a player and assistant coach with the men's basketball program.

Jack was born April 19, 1919, in Columbus and officially christened John Richard Graf, but the youngster quickly adopted the nickname "Jack" and used it formally for the remainder of his life. His father was of Prussian descent and well-known around the community as a local football hero.

Campbell "Honus" Graf was a star player at Ohio State during the early part of the twentieth century, captaining the 1914 Buckeyes to five wins in seven games during the program's second year as members of the Western Conference (later the Big Ten). Jack was the firstborn child to Honus and his wife, the former Estella Rogers, and he would soon be joined by sister Marilyn and brother Campbell Jr.

The Graf children grew up in a comfortable two-story, brick-and-stone home on Berkshire Road, a tree-lined side street in the upper-class Columbus suburb of Upper Arlington. Growing up within easy walking distance of Ohio Stadium, it made perfect sense that once young Jack finished his exploits as a track, basketball and football star at Upper Arlington High School, he would continue his athletic career at Ohio State. It also didn't hurt that his father was a close friend and confidant of university athletic director Lynn St. John.

When Jack showed up for his first practice, it was plain that he was going to have to fight to keep from getting lost in the shuffle. Before the 1938 season, more than two hundred freshmen hopefuls reported to frosh coach Fritz Mackey in September. By the end of November, that number had been whittled to sixty, and of those, only about half performed well enough to earn letters. Those lettermen were generally invited to join the varsity the following spring, but irascible head coach Francis A. Schmidt offered no guarantees. One of the privileged few was Jack, who would have been invited as a legacy recruit anyway. But his outstanding play made it a no-brainer that he would become a full-fledged member of the 1939 varsity squad.

Once the toast of the town due to his multiple victories against Michigan, Schmidt was beginning an unfortunate downward spiral as coach of the Buckeyes. His foul mouth and paranoia regarding keeping his plays locked away from even his own players and coaching staff, sluffed off as lovable peculiarities when the team was winning, were now being used against Schmidt as championships continued to elude his teams.

Still, away from the pressures of coaching, Schmidt was at his best. "When you were with him at a party or something, he played the banjo, sang and all of that other stuff. He was one of the guys," Jack once said. "But on the field, he was all business, and if you messed up, you were a horse's ass."

Another remembrance: "We would be practicing on the old field out behind the stadium, and his wife Evelyn would sometimes show up to watch. He'd gather the players together and tell us, 'Mrs. Schmidt is here, so everybody watch their language.' And he was serious. We just looked at each other because he was the only one who ever did any swearing, and lots of it."

Jack's younger brother Campbell, who was a reserve lineman at the time, remembered one of the coach's favorite lines repeated constantly to those who botched their assignment: "If brains were shit, you wouldn't even stink."

That sometimes-prickly character still didn't stop his players from pranking their coach. Ohio State is home to an honorary group for juniors called the Bucket & Dipper Society, and initiation into the group (at least in those days) involved running around after midnight and dousing new members with buckets of water. Each year, a staff or faculty member was included, and in 1940 the special honoree was Schmidt.

Graf, who was involved in the society and knew the Schmidts well, contacted the coach's wife and told her what was happening. "We're coming to initiate Coach Schmidt at midnight," he told her. "When we ring the bell, you get him and have him answer the door."

When the late hour arrived, and Schmidt answered the door as planned, the boys doused him with two buckets of water. "Goddamn it!" he yelled. After laughing at his response, the boys told him of the honor to which he replied, "An honor, my ass!" His wife was left with the unenviable task of explaining to her water-logged husband just exactly how he had been "honored."

Getting drenched by a couple of buckets of cold water was nothing compared to the rest of 1940 for Schmidt. Of the five quarterbacks on the roster to begin spring ball that year, two were academically ineligible, one was off playing on the university golf team, starter Don Scott was a starting shortstop for the baseball Buckeyes, and Graf was sidelined due to offseason knee surgery.

OSU won its first two games, but then lost three in a row—the first three-game losing streak in sixteen years—and capped the disappointing season with a 40–0 loss to Michigan, the most lopsided defeat handed the Buckeyes by their archrivals since an identical final score in 1905. That signified the end of Schmidt's tenure after seven seasons, and the university hired as his successor Paul Brown, a coaching wunderkind of thirty-three who had won five state championships and four national titles in nine seasons at Washington High School in Massillon.

Brown soon transitioned from Schmidt's razzle-dazzle, shoot-from-the-hip style of play to a program built upon organization and fundamentals, and Jack was a cornerstone of that new philosophy.

Ohio State opened its 1941 season against Missouri with Brown still untested at the college level. Meanwhile, the Tigers were coached by Don Faurot, a square-jawed veteran of six seasons in Columbia and nine before that at Division II Kirksville State. It was also Faurot who coincidentally was among the four finalists for the Ohio State job that eventually went to Brown.

Graf, who had spent the previous two years as a backup quarterback, moved into the starting lineup at both fullback and linebacker, position changes that had an immediate effect on the Buckeyes. During an eventual 12–7 victory, Jack scored both of his team's touchdowns—a fourth-down, two-yard run in the second quarter and a one-yard plunge with about ten minutes remaining in the final period.

The second touchdown gave Ohio State a 12–0 lead, but the game wasn't decided until Jack's interception of a desperation Missouri pass in the final seconds near the OSU goal line. Additionally, Graf starred on special teams, kicking a wind-aided, 73-yard punt as well as a 48-yarder against the wind to help the Buckeyes win field-position battles.

But in the longer view of what promise the Brown era held, the key moment might have arrived early in the game. Ohio State took the opening kickoff and netted only nine and a half yards in three plays. Brown eschewed the punt and Graf bulled through the line to gain a first down with room to spare.

By the end of the season, the Buckeyes had finished with a 6–1–1 record that included forging a 20–20 tie with fifth-ranked and heavily favored Michigan. Jack had a hand in all three Ohio State touchdowns against the Wolverines, scoring twice on short plungers and throwing a 52-yard TD strike to Dick Fisher for the tying score in the game.

Jack had been the team's leader and star player, accounting for ten

"He is a triple-threat fullback, captained the basketball team, had a trophy presented in his name to the outstanding sophomore basketball player, is an active fraternity man, doesn't smoke or drink, likes smooth music best, and hasn't gotten to 'thinking seriously' about any girl, yet."
—*Harvard Crimson,* 1942

touchdowns on offense and thwarting almost as many on defense. His performance earned him All-America second team honors, and he was voted by sportswriters at *The Chicago Tribune* winner of the annual Silver Football Award, symbolic of the Big Ten's most valuable player.

A year later, Brown guided Ohio State to the program's first national championship. But Jack had used up his football eligibility, and after serving as captain of the OSU basketball team in 1941–42, he graduated with a degree in business. The Cleveland Rams, coming off a record of two wins and nine losses in 1941, needed backfield help and selected Graf in the 1942 NFL draft. But they waited until the 162nd overall pick in the eighteenth round, and it didn't take the business major long to figure out the financial situation of being such a low priority for one of the league's lowly franchises.

That, along with the balky knee injury that continued to bother him since before his junior year at Ohio State, made the decision easy for Jack to eschew a career in professional football and instead seek acceptance to the prestigious Harvard Business School. Always excellent where academics were concerned, he was accepted and the school was quick to notice its newest student with his long, lean frame, dark complexion, and shock of curly jet-black hair.

A short entry in the *Harvard Crimson*, dated April 22, 1942, noted the enrollment in the Quartermaster Corps at the Business School, entering in June, "Jack Graf, the 200-pound, 6-foot-1 athletic hero and campus leader at Ohio State University. According to *Look*, the weekly picture magazine, he has an easy-going, friend-winning personality, leads a sober, early-to-bed, social life, has been elected to most of the prestige organizations on campus, and is an all-around good-guy."

The *Crimson* continued, "He is a triple-threat fullback, captained the basketball team, had a trophy presented in his name to the outstanding sophomore basketball player, is an active fraternity man, doesn't smoke or drink, likes smooth music best, and hasn't gotten to 'thinking seriously' about any girl, yet."

That last part was apparently true in the wake of a national wirephoto taken just a month before that appeared in newspapers across the country. The caption read, "Jack Graf, star athlete from Ohio State University and elected 'the male animal' by a campus-wide vote, is shown as he proves his right to the title by charming five of New York's better looking sub-debs, at the Stork Club." The photo shows Jack sitting inside the notorious Manhattan nightclub with a broad smile and his arms around two of the young beauties.

Back in Ohio, it's not known how Catherine "Kay" Marie Schroeder took to Jack's newfound fame. The pretty young coed, who had been Homecoming Queen at Ohio State, was preparing to graduate in 1944 and had been dating Jack. Apparently, Kay wasn't bothered too much since the couple became engaged and were married in 1945.

That same year, Jack received his MBA from Harvard and returned to Columbus with Kay to start a family. He joined his father's electrical engineering company, and along with younger brother Campbell, helped form Graf and Sons, Inc.

Jack also spent some spare time assisting his college coach, Harold Olsen, with the basketball Buckeyes. That began a two-decade "side career" as an Ohio State assistant, serving Olsen as well as his successors William "Tippy" Dye, Floyd Stahl and Fred Taylor. With Graf on staff, the Buckeyes won seven Big Ten basketball titles, made it to five Final Fours, and captured the 1960 NCAA Tournament championship, still the only one in program history.

Along the way, Jack found time to serve as president of the Upper Arlington School Board as well as the Varsity "O" Association, and help Kay raise their family in their sprawling Coventry Road home that included three children and nearly a dozen grandchildren.

He remained active with such activities as golf and mentoring projects until his death in September 2009 at the age of ninety.

GENE FEKETE

OSU FULLBACK 1942

44

NICKNAME: Geno

HOMETOWN: Findlay, Ohio

HEIGHT: 6 ft 0 in **WEIGHT:** 195 lb

ALL-AMERICAN: 1942

NFL DRAFT: 1945, Detroit Lions

Each year, players, coaches and support staff members of the team that wins the title game of the College Football Playoff receive an official national championship ring. The face of the ring features the word "National" at the top and "Champions" at the bottom surrounding a golden CFP football logo. Each side is then customized to include players' names, their school, and the final score of the game.

National championship programs are also in the habit of designing their own rings, often much more opulent than the ones awarded by the College Football Playoff. For example, Alabama produced a diamond-encrusted ring in 2020 commemorating the Crimson Tide's third national title won under the current playoff format. Ohio State did likewise after winning the 2014 championship, producing a ring that featured one diamond for each of the eight national titles claimed by the school.

The first of those national championships came in 1942 during the early part of the United States' involvement in World War II. Ohio State kicked off that season with a 59–0 blowout victory against Fort Knox, and topped it off with wins against Michigan and a star-studded lineup of former college and professional players called the Iowa Seahawks.

Afterward, while several players and coaches were preparing to enlist in the armed forces, the Buckeyes held a quick awards banquet to honor the season's outstanding performances. Lineman Chuck Csuri was voted MVP by his teammates, guard Lindell Houston, halfback Paul Sarringhaus and end Bob Shaw were recognized for playing their way onto the All-Big Ten first team, and Csuri, Houston, Sarringhaus, Shaw and fullback Gene Fekete were lauded as first-team All-Americans. Fekete was also singled out by head coach Paul Brown for finishing 10th in the annual balloting for the Heisman Memorial Trophy.

Each player on the team also received a miniature gold football suitable for placing on a charm bracelet. Such extravagances as gaudy national championship rings remained nothing but futuristic dreams.

"It was 1942 and the war was hot and heavy," Fekete said. "All we got was a little gold football, but we were proud of that. We didn't know any better."

Some sixty years later, another version of the Ohio State football team won the national championship with a thrilling, double-overtime victory against the defending national title-holders from the University of Miami. Led by head coach Jim Tressel, the Buckeyes remained undefeated through fourteen games in 2002, a program-record number of victories that gave the university its first consensus national championship in more than three decades. Understandably, the team needed something befitting its accomplishment and a championship ring was commissioned, replete with a diamond-filled number "1" in the middle of a scarlet background.

Fast forward to the following fall and a golf outing during which Tressel and Fekete crossed paths. While Fekete admired Tressel's ring, the coach inquired about the 1942 team. When Fekete told him of the gold football charm the '42 team had received, Tressel formulated a plan to honor the players who had first blazed the national championship trail at Ohio State.

One of those long-ago players was Fekete, born August 31, 1922, and christened Eugene Howard Fekete into the large family of Alex Fekete and the former Vera Bogdon, immigrants who grew up just a few villages from one another in Somogy County in Hungary, which was still a monarchy well into the twentieth century.

Alex had left Hungary to avoid military conscription into the Austrian-Hungarian army just before the outbreak of World War I. He first settled in the Akron area, then the nation's fast-growing city, and went to work for the Goodrich Rubber Company. But with the onset of the Great Depression, the plant was closed and Alex was left without a way to provide for Vera and their rapidly growing family. Seemingly the only jobs available were in the coal mines of southeastern Ohio, so Alex moved to the Athens area and worked at that backbreaking job, nearly ruining his lungs as well as his eyesight before family members who lived in the northwestern portion of the state told him of employment opportunities at the Cooper Tire and Rubber Company in Findlay.

Unlike the rolling hills of the Ohio River valley honeycombed by coal mines and the accompanying thick, black smoke that belched into the sky, Findlay offered fresher air, friendlier people and the laid-back atmosphere of the old standard "Down by the Old Mill Stream," penned by songwriter Tell Taylor while fishing along the Blanchard River that travels through the heart of the town.

By the early 1940s, Alex was entrenched at Cooper Tire while his growing family occupied a two-story brick house on tree-lined Summit Street less than a block from the tire plant. Gene was finishing his high school days as an all-state performer in football and basketball at Findlay High School while older brother John was a star halfback at Ohio University in Athens and made the Little All-America first team among small college programs around the country. It must have been that longtime Bobcats head coach Bob Peden, whose teams won seven conference championships during a decade-long span between 1929 and 1938, assumed Gene would follow his brother to Athens because he made no official contact with the younger Fekete, something that grated on Gene. Notre Dame, Michigan, Ohio State and nearly every other Midwestern power program stepped into the void, and by the time Peden made any official contact, it was too late.

Michigan head coach Herbert "Fritz" Crisler thought perhaps he held an ace in the hole while recruiting Fekete since the Ohio Oil Company was headquartered in Findlay and its corporate office was filled with U of M alumni. But Gene remembered being offput by what he described as their "aura of grandeur and wealth" in contrast to the Ohio State recruiters and their "warm and homey approach."

Fekete's first season at Ohio State was as a freshman in 1941, and in sharp contrast to predecessor Francis A. Schmidt's cattle call often involving hundreds of players, new head coach Paul Brown had carefully recruited a much smaller crop of players, each with a specific responsibility in mind. Primarily,

Brown was looking for young men who could not only learn but understand what he wanted to teach them. Secondly, he wanted speed at every position.

One of the players Brown had recruited for expressly that purpose was catlike lineman Bill Willis from East High School in Columbus. Gene played against Willis in high school, offering, "The only recollection I have of that game is that we seemed to have a fifth man in our backfield all game, and it was Bill."

Because Brown and his assistants had carefully picked their first freshman class at Ohio State, with several of them hailing from Massillon, where Brown won a string of state titles, there was plenty of competition at every position—so much so that midway through the season, Fekete joined teammates Dante Lavelli and John White in initiating a rebellion of sorts.

Rather unhappy about toiling as fourth- and fifth-string team members, the trio went to assistant line coach Hugh McGranahan with an ultimatum. The only way to demonstrate their skills was to participate in full-team scrimmages, and the only way to participate in the scrimmages was to move up the depth chart. If that was not going to be possible, the boys told the assistant coach they intended to transfer as a group to Ohio University.

McGranahan asked the trio to wait through the weekend until Brown returned from Los Angeles, where the Buckeyes had just administered a 33–0 beating to the University of Southern California. The coach sat down, listened to the boys' plea for more scrimmage time (they left out the part about transferring) and began to slowly work them into the practice games.

The following year, Fekete moved into the starting lineup at fullback and enjoyed one of the most spectacular seasons in Ohio State football history. In addition to earning All-America honors and finishing among the top ten in the Heisman Trophy balloting, he had a signature moment during an early November contest against the University of Pittsburgh. On a cool, crisp Dad's Day afternoon, when players' fathers were honored guests of the university at Ohio Stadium, Gene established a program record that stood for nearly six decades.

With the Buckeyes holding a 27–0 lead in the first quarter, Brown sent in a play called "Fullback Spinner Trap," a simple trap play featuring a little razzle-dazzle off the snap. With three men in the backfield, Fekete took the shotgun snap (known in those days as an airborne hike), faked a handoff to backfield mate Paul Sarringhaus, spun around counterclockwise 360 degrees and then exploded through a sizable hole in the thoroughly confused Pittsburgh defense.

"It just opened up for me," Fekete said. "I broke a tackle and then cut down the sideline. It was Dad's Day in the stadium, and all the dads of all the players were lined up along the sideline and I felt like I could have reached out and touched my dad as I went by him. I will never forget that feeling," Gene added.

The Buckeyes went on to a 59–19 victory with Gene's 89-yard touchdown bolt the longest run from scrimmage in Ohio Stadium until it was equaled in 2010 by Daniel "Boom" Herron.

The following year, like millions of other able-bodied young men and women, Gene enlisted in the U.S. Army and reported for basic training at the sprawling Fort Bragg military installation in North Carolina. Six weeks later, he was sent to the Pratt Institute in Brooklyn, New York, to be trained as an Army engineer before another transfer to the Manhattan Induction Center, this time interviewing new recruits as an assistant psychologist.

In 1944, selections for the annual College All-Star Game were being held and organizers decided to dip into the military ranks to build a team that would take on the NFL's Chicago Bears. Gene was chosen to participate, a true honor for an Army man since the proceeds from the game were to be donated to various service organizations that entertained servicemen overseas. Except that Gene's immediate superior officer didn't think much of the honor and refused to grant Private Fekete permission to play in the game. A few weeks later, when his superior officer's superiors caught wind of the refusal, an official order straight from Army

Headquarters was issued, granting Fekete enough leave time to get to Chicago and participate in the all-star game.

Due to the delay, he was nearly two weeks late reporting for practice, and feeling the need to fit in immediately, Gene began full-speed workouts with his fellow all-stars. During his first day of practice, he took a handoff from Northwestern quarterback Otto Graham and started to cut up the field. Just as he planted his left foot into the ground to make the cut, Gene crumpled to the ground in a heap. He had shredded the ligaments in his left knee, an injury that today would have been easily repaired through surgery. In 1944, however, it was a catastrophic injury that nearly ended Gene's career in football.

After World War II, he returned to Ohio State and eventually earned a Master's degree in physical education. Part of his thesis was centered on a service manual he had written for the Air Force Conditioning Program. He joined his old coach Paul Brown and several former Ohio State teammates on the 1946 Cleveland Browns team that won the All-America Football Conference championship.

Fekete alternated at fullback with future Hall of Famer Marion Motley through the midway part of that season until it became clear his knee would not hold up to the rigors of professional football. He was limited to just six of the fourteen games the Browns played that season, but after the team won the AAFC title game in late December, Gene's teammates voted him a full share of their postseason bonus money.

Shortly after the season, Gene married his wife, the former Dorothy Helen Krick whom everyone called "Dottie," and then accepted a coaching position at Northern Illinois University. In 1949, he returned to his alma mater as a member of Wes Fesler's staff and then stayed on when Woody Hayes was hired as head coach of the Buckeyes in 1951. Wishing to spend more time with his family, Fekete left Ohio State following the 1959 season, trying his hand at selling insurance for a short time before becoming a high school teacher and coach.

When Briggs High School opened in Columbus in 1962, Gene

was appointed principal of the new school. As the chief administrator at the school, he was responsible for developing all of the programs for nearly 1,000 students, a position he held for thirteen years until his retirement in 1975.

In his later years, Gene remained a larger-than-life figure around the Ohio State football program. He attended alumni reunions, was inducted into the university's athletics hall of fame in 1998, and even once served as the guest speaker at the annual Senior Tackle. And then there was that chance meeting with Jim Tressel at a golf outing in the fall of 2003.

"Coach Tressel said to me, 'I'm going to make sure every one of your team members gets a ring,'" Gene remembered. "He told me all I had to do was get the sizes and he'd take care of the rest." Gene tracked down information from the team's living members and hand-delivered their ring sizes to Tressel's office. The following fall, the 1942 Ohio State football team was finally honored with its long overdue national championship rings.

It was that gesture from a modern-day coach that Fekete cherished for the remainder of his life. Shortly after Gene's death in 2011 at the age of eighty-eight, son Steven said, "I think, in part, it defined who Coach Tressel is as a man and as a human being. I know my father appreciated it very much. I can tell you that ring was a tremendous source of pride for him. I guarantee it will stay in the family forever."

Gene led the Big Ten in rushing and scoring in 1942, his only season at Ohio State.

CECIL SOUDERS

OSU HALFBACK, END 1942–1944, 1946

82

NICKNAME: Cy

HOMETOWN: Bucyrus, Ohio

HEIGHT: 6 ft 1 in **WEIGHT:** 210 lb

ALL-AMERICAN: 1946

NFL DRAFT: 1945, Washington Redskins

Cecil Souders never dreamed his life would wind up the way it did. A northern Ohio native and son of hard-working parents, he was a high school football star who was good enough to earn a letter for his play in 1939 with the Ohio State freshman team. With designs on continuing to play for the Buckeyes and getting his degree, a pretty young cheerleader from Chicago entered the picture and that's when things took a decidedly different turn.

"We decided we wanted to spend the rest of our lives together," Souders said, "and we ran away to Kentucky and got married. The following year, after our baby was born, I dropped out of school and went to work in a steel foundry. In the merry-go-round of life, one would be hard put to predict a smoothly running course toward success when a boy falls in love, marries and has a child by the time he is 21 years old, but I wouldn't trade my merry-go-round for the experiences of any other man."

Souders eventually returned to Ohio State, putting himself through school by working numerous jobs but leaving enough time for an All-America football career that was followed by a short stint in professional football and more than a quarter-century of success in the business world, all with that pretty young cheerleader by his side for nearly eighty years.

Cecil Belvedire Souders was born January 3, 1921, in Bucyrus, Ohio, to Calvin Souders and the former Margaret Ruth Wilson, who owned and operated Souders Hatchery, a small facility on the edge of town that kept the handful of area poultry farms supplied with live chicks. Cy was the second of three sons in between Hylen (named after his maternal grandfather) and baby brother Eugene.

Times were not as difficult in Depression-era Bucyrus as they were in other parts of the country due mainly to such established businesses as Picking and Company, a coppersmith founded on South Walnut Street in 1874 that continues today as the Bucyrus Copper Kettle Works. Cy and his family also got by with the hatchery sometimes providing enough barter material for farm-fresh meats and dairy products.

As a boy, young Cy took full advantage of wide-open spaces and nearby forest lands to perfect his rock-throwing skills, chase rabbits, play "kick the can," and occasionally hide out to avoid taking piano lessons. He played first base for the local YMCA team, but admittedly always had his eye on football.

Cy began his football career at the age of nine when he and a group of neighborhood boys would get together and play what they called football. He got permission from the Kearsley Elementary School principal to organize a small football league with a few other area schools, such as the Norton school, to play against each other. Later, when he was in junior high, the game so fascinated him that he would crawl out of the dormer of an abandoned home on the west side of Lane Avenue, climb on the roof and catch a glimpse of Bucyrus High School football games. "It was just easier," Cy said of his rooftop view. "I tried climbing over the fence a time or two, but I never went through the gate because I didn't have the twenty-five cents it cost for a ticket."

When he became a freshman, Cy went out for football and played all four years for Bucyrus, who played in the rough-and-tumble North Central Ohio League that included much bigger schools such as those from Mansfield and Marion. But the Redmen held their own in the league with Cy serving as team captain during his senior season in 1938.

Playing fullback, end and linebacker, he earned all-state honors that year and was chosen for a team of Ohio high school all-stars that was scheduled to play a similar team of Florida prep stars the day after Christmas. It was the first time Cy had ever been out of his home state, and the first sight of palm trees and white, sandy beaches in late December are enough to catch the attention of any young Midwest native. But what floored him most were the cost of accommodations. The round-trip ticket price for the train ride to Florida was $34.05 while the hotel cost $2.35 per day, including meals.

"That was a whole lot of money in those days," Cy remembered.

Facing off at the old Kumquat Bowl in St. Petersburg, the all-star teams fought to a scoreless tie. But

Cy, who had been elected captain of the Ohio squad, distinguished himself enough that future College Football Hall of Fame coach Bernie Moore offered the youngster, now 6-foot-1 and about 170 pounds, a full scholarship to play football at Louisiana State University. Moore's offer included books, tuition, room and board, and a little spending money.

With older brother Hylen already in college, Cy agreed to accept the LSU offer and told Moore to expect to see him in Baton Rouge the following fall.

When he returned home, however, Ohio State assistant coach Ernie Godfrey was waiting for him with a scholarship offer of his own. Cy not only informed Godfrey of the pledge he made to Moore, but also that he meant to honor that pledge. No amount of pleading or cajoling from Godfrey about staying home to play for the Buckeyes seemed to have an effect. But the longtime coach still had one more trump card left to play.

Godfrey went to the high school principal and found out Souders had a steady girlfriend, a

Cy's start-and-stop career with the Buckeyes included a national championship and All-America status.

pretty blonde named Jean Hoover, who was also a cheerleader. Jean had moved from Chicago to Bucyrus the year before and had immediately caught the eye of the school's football star. Godfrey went to one of Jean's classes and convinced her that the southern belles in Louisiana might never let Cy come back north, so after a little talk between the young sweethearts, Cy at least agreed to go to Columbus and take a look at Ohio State.

When he arrived in Columbus, he was met by head coach Francis A. Schmidt, a man with reputations for everything from offensive wizardry on the football field to offensive language off it. Schmidt also had a penchant for reckless driving, which Cy soon discovered when the coach picked him up in his roadster at the train station and drove him through the streets of Columbus to the Ohio State campus.

"The car was careening wildly in his favorite sport of passing streetcars on the wrong side of the street and disregarding all of the oncoming automobiles," Souders remembered. "All the while, he was screaming, 'Come to Ohio State! Come to Ohio State!' Apparently, Schmidt was once an Army major and used that stunt to demonstrate courage. Between him, Ernie Godfrey and Jean, I slowly began to realize LSU was never going to happen for me."

As a member of the Ohio State freshman team in the fall of 1939, Cy quickly separated himself from the nearly one hundred and fifty other young men who came out for the team. He made first string, and one afternoon during a scrimmage against the varsity, he distinguished himself to his new head coach. After Cy made tackles for loss on nine consecutive plays, Schmidt blew a gasket. After letting loose with a stream of obscenities, the coach erupted, "Get this (bleeping) kid out of here! I don't want to see any more of him today!!"

Later that fall, Jean and Cy could stand to be apart no longer and they eloped to Kentucky. In those days, married men could not be a member of the Ohio State football team, so Cy left school and began work in a steel foundry. The following year, the couple welcomed daughter Sharon into their family.

Thinking his football days were over, Souders, now twenty-one, began to focus on his nineteen-year-old wife and infant child, and went on a number of job interviews. But in the spring of 1942, at the suggestion of Ernie Godfrey, new Ohio State head coach Paul Brown reached out to Souders. Brown, who had taken over the program following Schmidt's dismissal after the 1940 season, informed Cy that the university had dropped its rule about married men participating in intercollegiate athletics, and wondered if Souders would like to return to the Buckeyes.

There was only one catch. There would be no scholarship money available. Money was tight, but the young couple worked a number of odd jobs, including a short time running a boarding house, and Cy went back to Ohio State and returned to play the game he loved so much.

He was a backup end behind All-American Bob Shaw in 1942 when the Buckeyes captured their first-ever national championship, and was an honorable mention All-American himself as a two-way starter on the undefeated 1944 team that won the civilian national championship. After that season, he played in the East-West Shrine Game before reporting for duty with the U.S. Navy. While in the service, he played football at the Great Lakes Training Center outside Chicago as a member of the team stationed at the Bainbridge, Maryland, naval base.

After World War II ended, Souders returned to Ohio State to finish his degree work and discovered he still had one year of athletic eligibility remaining. He returned to star for the Buckeyes in 1946, earning all-conference and All-America honors as well as the *Chicago Tribune* Silver Football Award as the Big Ten Conference's Most Valuable Player.

During his time in military service, Souders had been drafted in the 25th round of the 1945 NFL draft by the Washington Redskins. But the Redskins traded his rights to the Detroit Lions, and he joined a number of former Ohio State teammates when he showed up for Lions training camp in the fall of 1947.

During his rookie season, he played in 11 games (including four starts) and totaled 15 pass receptions for 184 yards and his only career touchdown. The following year, he appeared in 12 games for the Lions and started six times, but the team was more interested in his blocking skills than his receiving. He caught only two passes for 19 yards. Souders played in 12 games again in 1949, but had no receptions and decided at the age of twenty-eight that maybe his best years in football were behind him.

During his second season in Detroit, Cy had answered an ad for part-time work with the Suburban Motor Freight Company, which had offices in Detroit and Columbus. The job eventually morphed into a full-time sales position, and after only two years, Cy was promoted to manager of the company's Detroit terminal. A few years later, another promotion elevated him to district manager of all the firm's terminals in Michigan and Indiana. Finally, he was named executive vice president of the company and remained in that capacity until his retirement in 1984 after thirty-eight years with Suburban Motor Freight.

Like so many others, Cy and Jean enjoyed retirement in Florida, settling in Avon Park, a rectangular wisp of sand situated among more than a dozen named lakes in the central part of the state. There, they enjoyed fishing, boating and a host of friends while escaping the harsh winters of Columbus and Detroit. As they aged well into their nineties, however, the couple returned north as a nod to their roots. "We're gonna be buried back there anyway," Jean said with a laugh. "So, why not be a little closer when the time comes?"

That time finally came for Cy Souders on August 20, 2021, when he passed away peacefully in his hometown at the age of 100. At the time, he was the oldest living ex-NFL player as well as the oldest living former Ohio State football player and the final link to the first national championship in the history of the university football program.

WARREN AMLING

OSU GUARD, TACKLE 1944–1946

90

HOMETOWN: Pana, Illinois

HEIGHT: 6 ft 0 in WEIGHT: 197 lb

ALL-AMERICAN: 1945, 1946

NFL DRAFT: 1946, New York Giants

COLLEGE FOOTBALL HALL OF FAME: 1984

Warren Amling was perhaps the unlikeliest two-time All-American in the history of Ohio State football. The son of an Illinois rose producer, Amling once described his athletic exploits in high school as "nothing special," winding up in Columbus only because he wanted to become a veterinarian and Ohio State was one of only three Midwestern schools who offered such studies. Then there was the fact that he decided to go out for the football team mostly to have something to fill his spare time, and a world war that interrupted his grid career almost as soon as it began.

Once he returned from a two-year stint of military service, Amling became an integral part of the youthful 1944 team, called the "Baby Bucks," who were awarded the Civilian National Championship, before going on to win All-America accolades at different positions during his junior and senior seasons. And when he had some spare time over the winter, he went out for the university basketball team and became a standout on the hardcourt as well, achieving a feat no college athlete before or since has accomplished—membership in the College Football Hall of Fame and starting in a Final Four game in the NCAA Men's Basketball Tournament.

"You never really thought much about what you were doing when you were doing it," Warren once said. "For instance, I went to Ohio State to become a veterinarian and just thought going out for the football team would be a fun thing to do. It certainly was much different then. If recruiting was as simple today as it was for me, they wouldn't have to spend a cent on it."

Warren Eugene Amling was born December 29, 1924, in Pana, Illinois, a leafy, brick-lined town of about six thousand located near the geographical center of the state. Once a center for coal mining crisscrossed by intersections of north-south and east-west railroads, Pana transformed itself at the beginning of the twentieth century. Warren's father built one of the town's first commercial greenhouses and began the wholesale production of flowers. Pana was the perfect place for greenhouse construction because of a quirk in the climate that made it one of the least likely places in the country for a hailstorm.

Martin Charles Amling, along with brothers Herbert and Walter, founded the Amling Rose Company in Pana in 1921, which marked the beginning of the rose industry in Pana. At one time, there were more than one hundred greenhouses in Pana, and at its peak in the 1950s, the town's rose industry had six major wholesalers producing nearly nineteen million roses annually. Fully aware it was borrowing a nickname from Pasadena, California, and not seeming to care, the town newspaper began referring to Pana as "The City of Roses." The name stuck.

The Amlings were one of the most prominent families in Pana. In addition to his successful flower business, Martin helped found St. Paul Lutheran Church and he was a longtime member of the Pana Township board of education. Martin and his wife Matilda, whom everyone affectionately called "Tillie," raised five sons including a future attorney and Mayor of Pana, a longtime educator, a bank president, a cartographer for the U.S. Air Force, and one who would eventually take over the family business and become a renowned horticulturist, specializing in cultivation of new rose hybrids.

Before any of that, however, the Amling boys explored Pana from one end to the other from their home base, a brick two-story home at the corner of Vine and Third streets. They participated in such childhood escapades as exploring the town's "Hobo Jungle" at the railroad yard while most summers were spent either working the hothouses for their father or swimming in the cool pond waters at the Northwest Ohio family farm on which their mother grew up.

Despite the Great Depression, during which one of every four workers in the United States was unemployed, the rose business was remarkably resilient and gave each of the Amling boys the opportunity to go to college. The oldest, William Henry, decided to stay close to home and attended the University of Illinois, later enrolling in law school, while second-born Martin Charles became interested in the family business and wished to study horticulture. His father had a network of contacts across the Midwest, including those in the Agriculture Department at Ohio State, facilitating young Martin's enrollment. Once he got to Columbus, he joined the football team and became a member of the 1942 Buckeyes that won the school's first national championship.

A year later, Warren arrived on campus, not particularly because he wanted to follow in his brother's footsteps. "I would have just as soon stayed closer to home," he said, "but I wanted to be a veterinarian, and in those days there were no colleges in Illinois that had veterinary schools. In fact, the only three veterinarian schools in the Midwest were at Iowa State, Michigan State, and Ohio State. They were all about four hundred miles or so away from home, but Ohio State had something the other two didn't. My brother was already there, so I decided Ohio State was the place for me."

Martin returned to the football team in the fall of 1943 and encouraged his brother to join him although Warren balked at the suggestion at first.

"I played fullback and was a team captain in high school, but I wasn't very big, and to tell the truth, I didn't think I was that good," Warren said. "I didn't win any state awards or anything, so I didn't receive any invitations from any colleges to play football. But it had always been a fun thing to do, and since my brother was on the team, I just decided to go out for football. I just thought it was like you did in high school. If you wanted to be on the team, you just went out, and if you were good enough, they'd give you a uniform."

His first few practice sessions provided something of a rude awakening as he was pounded on and tossed about by fellow freshmen who had been named to all-state or All-America high school teams. But after about a week, he found his footing and got that uniform. His first year was spent mostly on the scout team, mimicking opposing teams' plays in practice against the varsity. It also provided him a chance to go against his brother with one Amling on the offensive line and the other lining up on defense.

Unfortunately, the escalation of World War II forced the Buckeyes to field a depleted roster, and the team followed its national championship season with six losses in nine games. The war also made the Columbus reunion of the Amling brothers a short-lived one. Martin enlisted in the U.S. Army where he served with a field artillery unit in Europe, specifically in France and Germany following the D-Day invasion. Warren also enlisted in the Army and served stateside for about a year until a shortage of military veterinarians led to his being allowed to return to Ohio State and resume his studies in the spring of 1944 while he was still in the service, but with the stipulation that he couldn't play sports. A few months later, however, he received his discharge and was free to play.

It was a fortunate turn of events for Amling even though the Buckeyes had changed coaches by the time he returned. Paul Brown, who guided the team from 1941 through 1943, had enlisted in the U.S. Navy, and top assistant Carroll C. Widdoes had taken over as head coach. That year, the team went undefeated in nine games, won the Big Ten championship, and were named Civilian National Champions.

Although he didn't start that season, Amling said he played as much as anyone on the team. "I was, more or less in 1944, a utility lineman that played both guard and tackle positions offensively and defensively," he recalled. "When anybody got hurt or needed rest or something, I would be there to fill in."

To be named Civilian National Champions was a great honor to the program, but something remained in Warren's mind as Ohio State finished second in the official national polls behind an Army team featuring future Heisman Trophy winners Glenn Davis and Felix "Doc" Blanchard in the same backfield. Many experts look at the 1944 Army squad as one of the best college teams of all time, but Amling hinted the Buckeyes could have played the Cadets on an even scale.

"They called us the 'Baby Bucks' because we were so young, but I think that group of (Heisman Trophy winner) Les Horvath, Bill Willis, Bill Hackett, Ollie Cline, Bob Brugge, and Dick Flanagan could have played with anyone," he said. "When you look back, you always have to have a little confidence in yourself, and I think if we had been able to play them, we could have won."

One of the highlights of the season was when the Buckeyes hosted a team from the Great Lakes Naval Base in late October and stung the sixth-ranked team with a 26-6 defeat. The victory was made even sweeter since the Great Lakes team was coached by former OSU head coach Paul Brown. "It was comparable to the Michigan game," Warren recalled. "But it was a different kind of hype. It was the kind of thing that you wanted to show the old coach that we still had some pretty good boys here, too."

As the war continued to wage in Europe and the Pacific, most of the "Baby Bucks" from the 1944 team grew old enough to be drafted and broke up what could have been an Ohio State dynasty for the next three years. As a result, the 1945 team didn't experience the kind of success it might have. The Buckeyes still managed to win seven of nine games, and Warren received his first postseason award, earning a consensus nomination to the All-America first team as a guard. He was elected team captain the following year, and earned consensus first-team All-America honors again, this time after switching to a tackle position. But the team struggled through another coaching change, and slipped to a disappointing 4-3-2 finish.

The mild-mannered Widdoes had tired of the pressure-cooker atmosphere that accompanied being a head coach at Ohio State, and resigned following the 1945 season despite a sterling two-year record that featured sixteen wins against only two defeats. In his place, assistant Paul Bixler was elevated to the head coaching job, and Amling said he might have put too much pressure on himself to be the team leader during the coaching change.

"Maybe it was that I wasn't able to do the job of captain like I should have," he said. "I should have molded things together better. It was just one of those years where we were up and down and really couldn't put anything together. We opened with and tied Missouri, a team we were supposed to whomp pretty badly. Then the following week,

USC was supposed to whomp us out there, and we beat them, 21–0. We thought we were coming along pretty well at times, but it wasn't the case. We just couldn't ever keep up our momentum."

The team was still in the Big Ten race in November, but finished with a narrow 17–6 loss at Illinois and a 58–6 blowout loss to Michigan. It was the most lopsided game in the rivalry series since the Wolverines rolled to an 86–0 win against a fledgling Ohio State program in 1902.

"I hate to even mention that game because we got beaten so badly at home by them," Warren said, "but it was one of those games where everything went right for the opponent and nothing went right for us. They passed us to death. They had very good, tall ends who ate us up in the secondary. They had a fine team."

In addition to his football career at Ohio State, Amling was also a two-year starter on the men's basketball team with the highlight of his career coming in the 1945–46 season. The Buckeyes won the Big Ten championship in the 24th and final season with Harold Olsen as head coach, and advanced to the Final Four held in Madison Square Garden. They lost their national semifinal match in overtime to North Carolina, but defeated the University of California in the consolation game to take home third place in the NCAA Tournament. On the hardwood, Amling played what he termed the "back guard" position, explaining, "My job was to make sure nobody got by me to score an easy basket."

After graduation, Amling was contacted about potential opportunities with several pro teams, including the New York Giants of the National Football League, and the Baltimore Colts and Cleveland Browns of the All-America Football Conference. The Giants were from the more established league, but the Browns were dominating the AAFC and joining them would have given Amling his chance to play for Paul Brown. But he decided to remain on the career path he had set prior to his playing days.

"I went to school for veterinary medicine, and at that time, the war was over and the economy was picking up, so I thought I should get into practice," Warren said. "That was going to be my life's work, not football, so I never pursued any of the other situations."

He initially returned to his Illinois hometown to start a veterinary practice, but returned to Ohio within two years to join fellow former Ohio State All-America lineman William Hackett in a joint practice located in London, Ohio, about thirty miles west of Columbus. He also spent more than a quarter-century as staff veterinarian for the J. Sawyer Company in London, and for a time was adjunct associate professor at The Ohio State College of Veterinary Medicine.

His athletic career continued to follow him throughout his professional life. He was elected to the Ohio State Varsity "O" Hall of Fame in 1981, an honor followed three years later by his induction into the College Football Hall of Fame.

Amling went into what he called semi-retirement in the mid-1990s, but stayed busy with such activities as volunteering with his wife Barbara for Meals on Wheels, delivering food to the elderly. The couple was also a regular staple at Ohio State home football games, and enjoyed spending time with their children and grandchildren. "We say we don't do much," Warren said, "but we always seem to stay so busy. But that's the way we like it."

And that was the way it stayed until his death on November 1, 2001, at the age of seventy-six.

Once asked what he would like for his epitaph to read, Warren thought for a moment before responding, "Oh, I don't know. You talk about the athletic honors when we were at Ohio State, or some of the things we might have accomplished in veterinary medicine. But if I'm to be remembered for anything, I would like it to be as a good husband and a good father. I'd settle for that."

JOHN BORTON

OSU QUARTERBACK, LINEBACKER 1951–1954

HOMETOWN: Alliance, Ohio

HEIGHT: 6 ft 0 in **WEIGHT**: 200 lb

NFL DRAFT: 1955, Cleveland Browns

20

The numbers stick out like the proverbial sore thumb.

A single-season yardage record that stood for nearly a quarter-century. A single-game mark for touchdown passes that was not eclipsed for more than 60 years.

During the modern era of spread formations and point-per-minute offenses, it has become standard for college quarterbacks to amass tremendous numbers in terms of yardage and touchdowns passes. Ohio State redshirt freshman C.J. Stroud threw for 300 or more yards nine times during the 2021 season, and totaled five or more touchdown passes in five of those games.

But this is now. Way back when, those kinds of numbers were unheard of—especially in Columbus.

Seven decades ago, Woody Hayes was beginning the second season in what would become a run of twenty-eight years as head coach of the Buckeyes. It was a tenure marked by a run-first mentality on offense that produced a string of All-America fullbacks as well as history's only two-time Heisman Trophy.

In 1952, however, Hayes had not yet settled upon the three-yards-and-a-cloud-of-dust approach that would ultimately lead to five national championships and thirteen Big Ten titles. Ohio State football was in a period of unrest in 1952. Hayes was the program's fifth head coach in a decade and the Buckeyes had just one conference title to show for its previous seven seasons—a shared crown with Michigan in 1949—and an 0-6-1 record against the archrival Wolverines during that stretch.

Hayes, coming off a nondescript first season during which his 1951 team finished with a 4–3–2 overall record and 2–2–2 in the conference that was good enough only for fifth place in the league standings, was looking for a new approach and stumbled upon what he was looking for during the offseason.

Longtime University of Missouri head coach Don Faurot had written a book titled *Football: Secrets of the Split-T Formation*, outlining and explaining the future College Football Hall of Famer's innovative offensive alignment. As described by its name, the offensive line in the Split-T was spread over almost twice as much ground as the basic T-formation, prompting the defensive front to widen as well and create gaps for the offense to exploit.

Hayes devoured Faurot's book and then traveled to the University of Oklahoma during the summer to receive a crash course on how to implement the offense. While in Norman, Hayes met with Sooners offensive line coach Gomer Jones, who had been an All-America lineman at Ohio State in the 1930s. Jones showed Hayes the kind of philosophy and technique needed to utilize the Split-T, and the coach returned to Columbus with a new philosophy with regard to his offense.

"Gomer Jones was extremely helpful to me along with the rest of the Oklahoma staff," Hayes said. "I came back to our spring practice and put in the Split-T exactly the way it had been explained to me. Going out to Oklahoma in the spring of 1952 (was) where I really learned the basis of our running game."

Well...almost.

The Buckeyes had yet to recruit such future fullback stars as Bob White, Bob Ferguson and Jim Otis, whose combination of power and speed would become the ultimate weapons in Hayes' version of the Split-T. But while the formation created acclaim for running backs, it still relied upon the quarterback and his quick assessment of the defensive alignment for success.

Earning the starting nod at quarterback in 1952 was heady sophomore John Borton, a handsome three-sport star from Alliance, Ohio, whose good-natured personality and easy smile belied something of a difficult early childhood.

Seth Harry Borton, a day laborer who specialized in home construction work, met and courted Alice Hopkins, a pretty young woman two years his junior who lived just three blocks away in Alliance, the northeastern Ohio city so named by the combining of three smaller communities in the 1850s. Seth and Alice began courting, decided to get married in January 1932, and just before Christmas, welcomed baby boy John Robert on December 14. A daughter, Sara Kathryn, joined the family two years later, and another girl, Ellen Lou, was born in 1937.

Unfortunately, a growing family and continuing financial problems as the Great Depression continued into its second decade put a tremendous strain on John's parents and the couple ultimately split in 1939 with Seth moving to Florida—ultimately remarrying in 1941—and Alice taking the children and moving back with her parents.

The divorce took its toll on young John, who felt it was his duty to look after his mother as head of the household. There were childhood skirmishes whenever someone dared bring up his parents' split, but by the time he reached his teenage years, John had grown into a self-confident young man, confident in his own skin. It also didn't hurt that his athletic six-foot, 200-pound frame dissuaded any loudmouth looking for a fight.

Borton's biography in his high school yearbook took up nearly a quarter of a page and boasted such honors as membership in the Spanish Club, writer for the school newspaper, Student Council President, Class President as a sophomore, junior and senior, and serving as a delegate to Buckeye Boys' State, where he was elected governor. Somehow, John also found time to star in baseball, basketball and football, and he earned All-Ohio honors during his senior season of football with the Aviators. After spending time on the freshman squad at Ohio State, John was able to beat out several teammates for the starting job in the fall of '52, including two-year starter Tony Curcillo, who was moved to defense for his senior season.

Borton didn't seem like a perfect fit for the Split-T formation. After all, he was a drop-back passer who had also played linebacker during his freshman season in 1951 with the Buckeyes. But Hayes became convinced Borton had the athleticism and intelligence necessary to run his new offense. That would become more and more evident as Borton went on to rewrite the program's record book for passing.

The Split-T formation—the one that would become more and more familiar to Ohio State fans in the coming years—worked well during the 1952 season opener. Freshman sensation Howard "Hopalong" Cassady rushed for a pair of touchdowns and caught a 27-yard TD pass from halfback "Fearless" Fred Bruney as the Buckeyes rolled to a 33–13 victory against Indiana.

No one could foretell the kind of season Borton would have, however. He was a modest 6 for 13 passing for 87 yards against the Hoosiers, a performance that included a 15-yard scoring toss to Bruney early in the first quarter.

The euphoria of the opening-day win lasted only a week before the mistake-ridden Buckeyes dropped a 21–14 decision to Purdue. The eventual winning score came following a Borton interception in the third quarter, one of three OSU turnovers in the game.

Borton made amends the following week, however, directing the offense on drives of 88, 64 and 55 yards to lead the Buckeyes to a 23–14 upset victory against top-ranked Wisconsin. The week after that, however, served as the quarterback's coming-out party.

With Washington State selling out its defense to stop the Ohio State running attack, Borton completed 15 of 17 passes for a school-record 312 yards and five touchdowns during a 35–7 romp over the Cougars. The 88.2 completion percentage remains the fourth-highest for a single game in OSU history and the yardage figure remained the highest for nearly three decades until Art Schlichter threw for 458 yards against Florida State in 1981.

Five touchdown passes in a single game was a record not equaled by an Ohio State quarterback until Bobby Hoying did it against Purdue in 1994, and the mark was not broken until Kenny Guiton threw for six TDs against Florida A&M in 2013—more than 60 years after Borton established the record.

Four of Borton's scoring passes against Washington State went to senior end Bob Grimes, who finished with 12 receptions for 187 yards. No OSU receiver had more catches and yardage in a single game until Gary Williams totaled 13 receptions for 220 yards against Florida State in 1981, and although three players have equaled Grimes' four touchdowns in a game, no one in an Ohio State uniform has ever exceeded that total.

Borton's single-game pass efficiency mark of 339.4 is a number that has never been surpassed by an OSU quarterback.

"Maybe the strangest part of that game was the fact that Washington State was supposed to have the stronger passing game," longtime OSU football historian Jack Park said. The previous season, Cougars quarterback Bob Burkhart had set a new Pacific Coast Conference record with 15 touchdown passes, while receiver Ed Barker had established a new NCAA record with 847 yards receiving.

"Looking back at that game, and knowing what would come after it and in subsequent seasons under Coach Hayes, what John Borton was able to accomplish that afternoon was truly remarkable," Park said.

Three weeks later, Borton was at it again.

Despite a 21–14 loss to Pittsburgh, he threw an amazing forty-four times, completing twenty-five of those attempts for 282 yards and two touchdowns. No Woody Hayes quarterback had ever attempted that many passes in a single game, and no one ever came close to that number of attempts again during Hayes' tenure.

The Buckeyes closed out the 1952 season with a 27–7 win at Illinois and a satisfying 27–7 victory against No. 12 Michigan, their first win in the series since 1944. Borton put an exclamation point on his season by accounting for all four touchdowns against the Wolverines—three scoring passes and a 4-yard run.

Ohio State finished with a 6–3 record in 1952 and in third place in the Big Ten standings. But what made the season so remarkable were the passing stats piled up by Borton. He obliterated most of the program's record book with 115 completions in 196 attempts (58.7 percent) for 1,555 yards and 15 touchdowns against only six interceptions.

Only six times in Hayes' twenty-eight seasons in Columbus did he have a quarterback who threw for 1,000 or more yards in a single season, but no one ever approached the 1,555 yards Borton amassed in 1952. Schlichter came closest when he threw for 1,250 as a freshman in 1978, Hayes' final year as head coach.

Likewise, no Hayes quarterback ever had more completions, attempts or touchdown passes in a single season than Borton totaled in 1952.

The following season, Borton was poised to repeat his exploits and the Buckeyes broke from the gate with easy wins against Indiana and California. But during a 41–20 loss to Illinois in week three, Borton suffered an injury to one of his fingers on his passing hand. It was likely ligament or tendon damage—injury reports were sketchy at best in those days—but the injury plagued him the rest of the season. He finished with only 552 passing yards as a junior and eventually lost his starting job to Dave Leggett, a more run-oriented quarterback.

Borton returned for his senior year in 1954 and was named a team co-captain. But he could not unseat Leggett and mostly watched from the bench as Ohio State enjoyed an undefeated season that led to a national championship. The Buckeyes cemented their title with a 20–7 win against USC in the Rose Bowl, a game that was well in hand in the fourth quarter when Hayes began to empty his bench.

Normally, Borton would have been called upon to take the final snaps—a fitting climax to the career of the senior co-captain. However, Borton went to Hayes and suggested the coach put third-string quarterback Bill Booth into the game instead. Booth's father, Dick, had played fullback for Pittsburgh in the 1928 Rose Bowl and was watching the 1955 game from the stands.

"At that time, there had never been a father-son combination that had played in the Rose Bowl and Borton somehow knew that," Park said. "Borton told Woody that it would mean a lot more to Dick Booth if he put (Bill) in. Woody complimented

John became OSU's first-ever 1,000-yard passer in 1952, and held the program's single-season record for twenty-seven years.

him on the gesture and sent Booth into the game to run the last three or four plays.

"John may have been Ohio State's only able-bodied player not to play in that game, but because of his generosity, he gave up his spot so another player could play. I've been told many times that's the kind of unselfish person John Borton was."

Borton, who was a first-team Academic All-American in 1952 and a two-time Academic All-Big Ten selection, finished his college career with 2,129 passing yards and 19 touchdowns. Those career marks weren't approached until Don Unverferth broke the yardage figure in 1965 and Rex Kern tied the touchdown total in 1970.

John was selected in the 1955 NFL draft by the Cleveland Browns, but was obligated for service in the U.S. Naval Reserve. Before his military service began, however, John married Barbara Ann Surbeck, a native of Asbury Park, New Jersey. The couple had met while they were students at Ohio State, and went on to enjoy a family that included two daughters, two sons and three grandchildren.

John completed his military service, played one season with the Browns and then took a job at Youngstown, Ohio-based Republic Steel, remaining there for the next twenty-seven years before retiring in 1985 as a vice president of the company.

Borton's later life was plagued by a bipolar disorder, a condition that sometimes robbed him of his trademark smile. But when he died in 2002 at the age of 69, he was praised as a selfless friend who possessed the intangibles to become practically anything he would have wanted.

"He remained one of my best friends until he died," said former Ohio State teammate Dick Brubaker, who played three pro seasons for the Chicago Cardinals and Buffalo Bills before beginning a long and successful law career in northeast Ohio. "He was really smart and what he wanted to do was go to law school. I think he would have made a helluva lawyer. I think he would have made a helluva football player. What he became, though, was a helluva family man. He was just a great guy and I miss him."

HUBERT BOBO

OSU FULLBACK, LINEBACKER 1954, 1956

42

NICKNAME: Hubie

HOMETOWN: Chauncey, Ohio

HEIGHT: 6 ft 1 in **WEIGHT**: 220 lb

NFL DRAFT: 1957, Philadelphia Eagles

There are as many candidates for the most underrated player in Ohio State football history as there are candidates for the best player in program history, but one who should be at the top of the underrated list has been largely forgotten by much of Buckeye Nation.

In the opinion of many college football historians, including Ohio State's own Jack Park, the 1954 team saved Woody Hayes' job. After Hayes had compiled a nondescript record of 16–8–2 during his first three seasons in Columbus, the coach's job security was tenuous at best. OSU was, after all, known as "The Graveyard of Coaches" since only two of Hayes' eighteen predecessors had been able to hold onto the job for more than five seasons.

But while the rumor mill began churning out a list of potential successors, the 1954 team marched to an undefeated season, topped off by a Rose Bowl victory against USC and a national championship.

That team featured a line anchored by All-American guards Jim Parker and Jim Reichenbach with a triple-threat backfield of quarterback Dave Leggett, halfback Bobby Watkins and future Heisman Trophy winner Howard "Hopalong" Cassady. Also on that team were All-America end Dean Dugger, future NFL receiver Dick Brubaker and All-Big Ten tackles Dick Hilinski and Francis "Moose" Machinsky.

But perhaps the most unheralded player in the 1954 starting lineup was fullback/linebacker Hubert Bobo, a good-looking, fun-loving teammate who was all-business on the field and just the opposite away from it.

Hubert Lee Bobo was born July 2, 1934, in Union Furnace, Ohio, an unincorporated dot on the map hidden in the southeast corner of Hocking County. The village was so named for the blast furnace built on the site during the 1850s when coal production and iron production were becoming the backbone of southeastern Ohio industry. Hubert was the youngest of two children raised by Howard and Hazel Bobo, firm-minded, strong-bodied people of mainland European heritage who had grown up with disparate childhoods.

Howard Elsworth Bobo was born in Vinton County and never strayed too far from the family until he met and courted Hazel Williams, three years his elder and the product of a stern coal miner as well as a family that included 11 siblings. At the precocious age of 23, Howard met Hazel, who at 26 had reached an age when many women of the time had long since married and started a family. When Howard asked Hazel's father, Joseph, for his daughter's hand in marriage, the old man bluntly told Howard he would not give his blessing to a simple farmhand with dirt under his fingernails. Only when Howard agreed to become a coal miner did Joseph Williams relent, and the couple ran off —all the way to West Virginia—to get married.

Howard and Hazel set up housekeeping in the small town of Chauncey, a gray-skied village lined with cracker-box dwellings to house the mining community. Into that environment, the couple welcomed daughter Thorabell, and then five years later, son Hubert was born. In sharp contrast to his quiet older sister, Hubert seemed in a hurry to get into mischief. As a youngster, he became a proficient rock-thrower, hurling stones at everything from neighborhood dogs and cats to unsuspecting passers-by. As a result, young Hubert also became proficient at speedy getaways, something that would serve him well as he became a three-sport star at Chauncey-Dover High School.

Although he was one of the best players on both his basketball and baseball teams, where Bobo truly shone was on the gridiron. Earning the nickname "Touchdown King," Hubert established a state scoring record with 123 career touchdowns from 1949 to 1952. That record remained on the Ohio High School Athletic Association books for 65 years until it was broken in 2017 by Daniel Bangura of Canal Winchester Harvest Prep with 133 touchdowns.

All of that scoring naturally, along with 220 pounds packed tightly into a muscular 6-foot-1 frame, made Bobo one of the most sought-after college prospects in the Midwest. He was on his way to West Virginia University to play for Art "Pappy" Lewis, an Athens-area native who was on the verge of leading the Mountaineers to five Southern Conference championships over a six-year period beginning in 1953.

But when Hayes came calling with the opportunity for Hubert to play big-time football in Columbus, it seemed that Ohio State's second-year coach had secured an important part of the championship puzzle he was trying to put together.

Not that Lewis and several other coaches stopped their pursuit of the prized prospect. Hayes became so paranoid that someone would spirit Bobo away that he stashed the youngster in longtime assistant coach Ernie Godfrey's house for the entire month of August until fall quarter classes commenced.

After spending a year on the OSU freshman squad, Bobo was set to be the second-team fullback behind classmate Don Vicic. But the cocksure sophomore, never one to shy away from the spotlight, earned the wrath of the coaching staff after watching newspaper photographers take numerous pictures of Vicic during the team's annual Photo Day.

"Why don't you guys take pictures of the guys who will play?" Bobo cracked. "These guys around here won't be first-string for long."

The quote made it into the local newspapers and Hubert ran an untold number of punishment laps for his indiscretion. But ultimately he was right. Vicic sustained an injury, Bobo took over the starting fullback position and he never looked back. Operating in back of an ultra-talented offensive line, and in front of his equally-as-talented backfield mates, Hubert was a devastating blocker as well as a talented runner. Despite Cassady and Watkins getting most of the carries, Bobo still managed to rush for 382 yards (averaging 6.1 yards per carry) and three touchdowns.

Defensively, he was equally as effective at linebacker. During the famous goal-line stand in the 1954 game against Michigan, it was Bobo who made the crucial fourth-down stop at the six-inch line to prevent the Wolverines from taking a 14–7 lead early in the fourth quarter. The Buckeyes took over and drove 99 yards the other way for a go-ahead touchdown in what would ultimately be a 21–7 victory.

As much as he excelled at the game, Bobo also had a legendary sense of humor. He was the team prankster, something that nearly cost him dearly one August afternoon inside Ohio Stadium. Hayes conducted preseason two-a-day drills with a three-hour practice session held early in the morning and another session, sometimes as long or longer, beginning in the early afternoon. In between, players would eat lunch, work on their conditioning or simply rest.

Parker, the two-time All-America guard who would go on to a Pro Football Hall of Fame career with the Baltimore Colts, typically found a shady spot somewhere in the stadium bleachers and stretched out to take a nap. After a few days, Bobo was discussing with a teammate the old prank about putting the hand of a sleeping person into some warm water to trigger urination, and decided to see if the trick really worked. Bobo drew some warm water into a bowl, sneaked his way to Parker's location and carefully placed the lineman's hand in the bowl. After a few minutes, when Parker stirred from his afternoon nap and realized what had happened, he took one look at his laughing teammate and immediately began chasing Bobo up and down the steps of Ohio Stadium. Only when the 6–3, 275-pound Parker finally ran out of gas was Bobo spared.

"I think if Jim had caught him," Brubaker said, "ol' Hubie would have been a goner. I truly think Jim would've killed him."

Bobo reportedly enjoyed all the perks of being an Ohio State football player, including the Columbus nightlife and being seen on the arm of several pretty young coeds. Unfortunately, that kind of off-campus lifestyle—including a paternity suit filed against him that was later dropped—coupled with a lack of interest in academics and a litany of knee injuries, conspired to put a premature end to Bobo's college career.

Before that happened, though, Bobo got over a prank on Hayes although it was almost certainly unintentional.

Following the 1954 championship season, Woody took his wife, Anne, on a celebratory trip to Italy. But Ohio State football was never very far from the coach's thoughts. Following an afternoon of hiking in the Italian Alps, Woody put in an overseas call to his assistant coaches to check on players' grades after spring quarter exams. Bobo's academic standing was one in which Hayes was especially interested.

Defensive coordinator Lou McCullough was giving him the rundown when Woody cut him off.

"Dammit, McCullough, just tell me how Bobo did."

"I'm sorry, Coach," the assistant replied, "but he flunked out."

"What?!" Woody erupted. "I go away for a week and you SOBs kill me. I should just kill myself! I should just jump off a goddamned Alp!"

Back in Columbus, Hayes' assistants reportedly gathered around the phone and began chanting, "Jump! Jump! Jump!"

Woody bellowed back, "I will! I will! You tell those SOBs I will!"

Then the phone clattered and went dead as they all knew Woody had pulled it off the wall and smashed it on some Italian innkeeper's floor.

Bobo missed all of the 1955 season, serving an academic suspension from the school, and for a time, contemplated a transfer to the University of Tennessee. But that never materialized, and Hubert returned to Ohio State and appeared in all nine games the Buckeyes played in 1956, although he got only four carries for four yards.

The Philadelphia Eagles took Bobo in the 13th round of the 1957 NFL draft, but his chronic knee injuries cost him any kind of pro career. After a couple of seasons with the Hamilton Tiger-Cats of the Canadian Football League, Bobo played three games in 1960 for the San Diego Chargers in the old American Football League before moving to the New York Titans (later the Jets) where he made twenty-six starts at middle linebacker during the 1961 and '62 seasons. But another knee injury effectively ended Bobo's career and he faded into obscurity.

He lived for a time in Iowa before settling in Laguna Beach, California. Some say Bobo never again returned to Ohio while others claim he came back at least once each fall unannounced to attend an Ohio State game. Whichever is true, this much is known. Hubert Bobo died in Las Vegas on September 1, 1999, at the age of sixty-five.

DON SUTHERIN

OSU DEFENSIVE BACK, PLACEKICKER 1955–1957

45

NICKNAME: Suds

HOMETOWN: Empire, Ohio

HEIGHT: 5 ft 10 in **WEIGHT:** 193 lb

NFL DRAFT: 1958, New York Giants

Never before and never again did Woody Hayes have to rely on a kicker to win him a bowl game. Yet there was Don Sutherin, the pride of all 299 residents of tiny Empire, Ohio, trotting out onto the emerald green turf at the Rose Bowl to try and cement Ohio State's claim to the 1957 college football national championship.

The game, played New Year's Day 1958 under a cloudless cerulean umbrella on a Chamber of Commerce afternoon, was supposed to serve as the final coronation of the Buckeyes, the unstoppable juggernaut of the Midwest, who had lost the opening game of the season and then marauded their way through eight opponents to arrive in Pasadena.

Their opponents? The Oregon Ducks (then known as the Webfoots), losers of three games during the season and Rose Bowl representatives of the Pacific Coast Conference only because Oregon State, which had defeated its instate rivals in the regular-season finale, could not play in Pasadena because the Beavers had played in the game the previous year and the PCC had a no-repeat rule.

Ohio State was heavily favored, reportedly by as many as three touchdowns, but when Sutherin went into the game early in the fourth quarter to attempt a field goal from twenty-four yards, Oregon had played the mighty Buckeyes to a 7–7 tie. The legendary Hayes was a lot of things, but insouciant wasn't one of them. He tore his junior kicker away from longtime kicking coach Ernie Godfrey, looked Sutherin squarely in the eye and screamed, "Keep your goddamned head down and eye on the goddamned ball!"

Sutherin never blinked. After all, earlier that season he had returned a punt more than eighty yards for a touchdown to break open what had been a close game against Washington State, booted an important third-quarter field goal during a pivotal game at Wisconsin, and kicked another field goal while successfully converting two extra points to provide the winning margin in a 17–13 victory against fifth-ranked Iowa.

Keeping his head down and his eye on the ball, Sutherin swung his right leg back and through the football, sending it sailing well over the crossbar to give his team a 10–7 lead, an advantage it would protect for the remainder of the game. Years later, when asked about the three-pointer, Sutherin smiled and said, "That thing went at least fifty. You know how it goes with time. Fish get bigger and field goals get longer."

It was the crowning achievement in the college career of Sutherin, one that might have been nondescript had it not been for his kicking prowess. Standing just five-foot-ten and weighing just over 190 pounds, he could never quite break into the starting offensive or defensive lineup for the Buckeyes. But his versatility earned him a brief stint in the NFL after which his professional career flourished north of the border, eventually earning him a spot in the Canadian Football League Hall of Fame.

That was a long way for Don Paul Sutherin, a leap year baby born February 29, 1936, in an Ohio River village

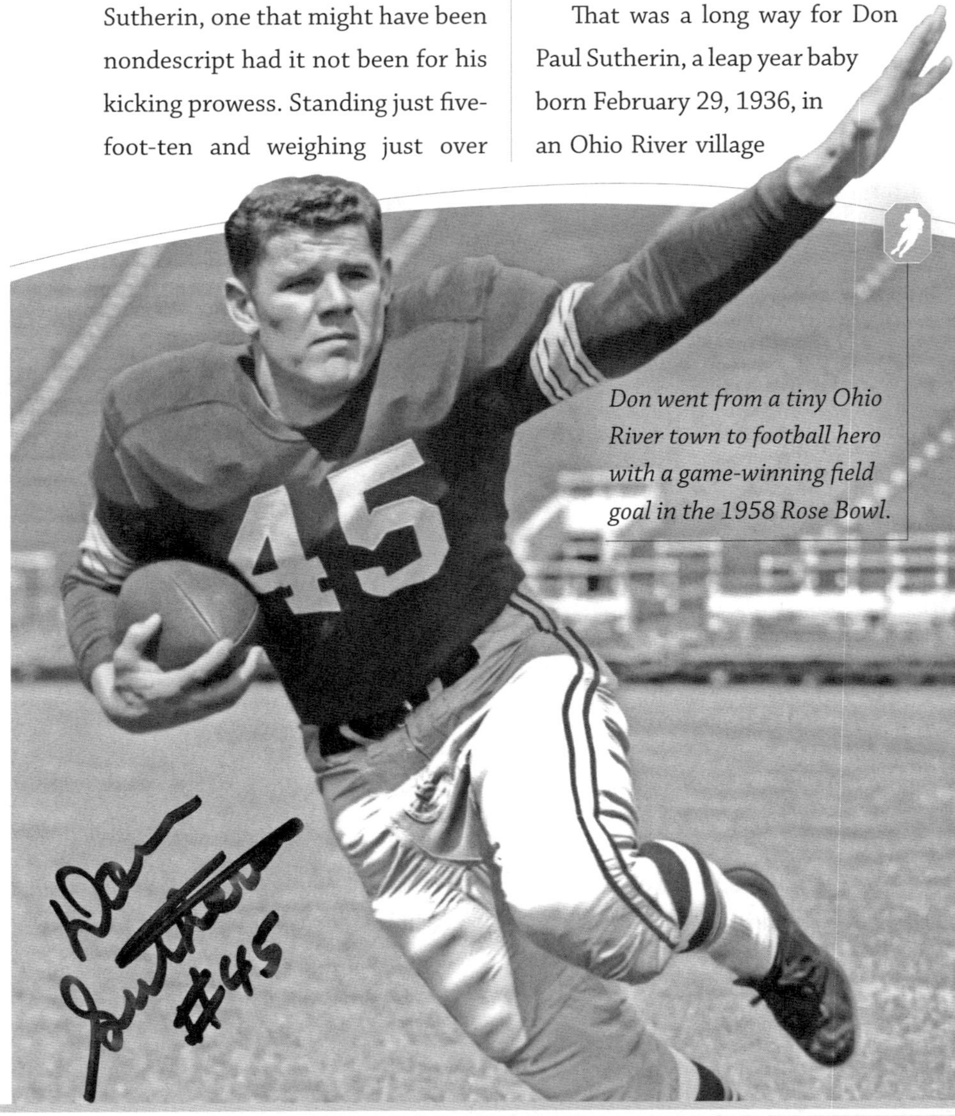

Don went from a tiny Ohio River town to football hero with a game-winning field goal in the 1958 Rose Bowl.

near Steubenville. He was the sixth of seven children born to Albert Sutherin and the former Gladys Loraine Culp, who preferred to be called by her middle name. Albert was a successful laborer who operated baling equipment for local farmers while Loraine cared for the children in the simple cupboard house the couple owned on Main Street in Empire.

Don enjoyed a typical upbringing of most children in the late 1930s and early 1940s as the United States finally dug itself out of the Great Depression before becoming embroiled in World War II. Those were far-off situations that never entered the youngster's life as he played improvised games of baseball and football, and spent countless hot summer days swimming in the Ohio River, located only a few hundred yards from his home.

When it came time to go to high school, he traveled the four miles south to Toronto, a town of 5,000 that must have seemed like a metropolis to young Don. There, he didn't care much for academics, but he excelled in nearly every sport the school had to offer. That was especially true on the gridiron, where he followed in the footsteps of such former Red Knights as John "Hook" Comer, who played professionally for the Canton Bulldogs, and Clarke Hinkle, a future Pro Football Hall of Famer with the Green Bay Packers, to become Toronto High School's next budding star.

As the young quarterback and defensive back began to attract attention from such future College Football Hall of Fame coaches as Charles "Rip" Engle at Penn State and Jim Tatum at Maryland, not to mention Charles "Red" Dawson at the nearby University of Pittsburgh, who was coming off upset victories against eighth-ranked Notre Dame and Ohio State during his first season with the Panthers, Hayes got wind of Sutherin's exploits and made the drive to Toronto on a fall Friday night in 1953 to watch the Red Knights take on Wintersville. Sutherin didn't disappoint, throwing for two touchdowns and running for another, to lead his team past their rivals. He not only won the game that night, he won a scholarship to OSU. But he lost a pumpkin pie.

The customary pumpkin pie that his mother always had waiting for him after games was gone by the time he got home that night. His mom filled him in later that Hayes was impressed not only with Sutherin's performance.

"She told me, 'Woody Hayes was here and ate your pumpkin pie,'" Don said. "And then the next morning, she said, 'Oh, yeah. And you're going to Ohio State.'"

After spending the 1954 season on the Buckeyes' freshman squad, Sutherin was hungry for playing time at the varsity level as a sophomore in 1955. He played throughout the year on both sides of the ball, but got his fill in the season finale against sixth-ranked Michigan in Ann Arbor, playing the entire game as OSU shut out the Wolverines to finish the season as Big Ten champions.

The 17–0 win at Michigan would help senior halfback Howard "Hopalong" Cassady, who was playing in his final game for OSU, secure the Heisman Trophy. Throughout the game, Sutherin regularly moved into Cassady's regular spot at left halfback while Cassady shifted to right halfback. The maneuver wasn't the result of a special plan—Sutherin simply realized that he was better suited to block the Michigan defenders, particularly future College Football Hall of Famer Ron Kramer.

"Hop had trouble blocking those big guys," remembered Don, who outweighed his teammate by at least thirty pounds. "I figured that when a play called for me to carry the ball, I would switch with Hop and block instead. Woody thought that was a good idea and it turned out really well for us."

Cassady ran for 146 yards and a touchdown that afternoon to give him a leg up on the Heisman competition. But it came at a price—at least to Sutherin. Late in the game, a series of scuffles broke out between the teams, and as the final seconds wound down, Sutherin said he was sucker-punched in the face by Kramer.

"My eye went completely closed on me, but it didn't matter," he said. "We won the football game."

Ohio State won six of its first seven games in 1956 but couldn't sustain the success, losing its final two games of the season to seventh-ranked Iowa and ninth-ranked Michigan. But the Buckeyes avenged both of the losses the following season on their way to the Rose Bowl and the program's third national championship.

Don admitted that he and some of his teammates lost some of their focus after the Michigan game, particularly once they arrived in Pasadena. But he had no trouble focusing when he lined up for his game-winning kick against Oregon. As a straight-on kicker, he always did what Hayes had implored and kept his head down—usually well after the kick. But he did allow himself to take an early peek after holder Frank Kremblas exclaimed, "It's good!"

Sutherin looked up just in time to see the ball sailing between the goal posts.

"That was one of the highlights of my football career," he said.

It would be a few years before Sutherin had similar highlights at the professional level. Selected in the eighth round of the 1958 NFL draft by the New York Giants, he didn't play that season for the Giants, who loaned him to the CFL's Hamilton Tiger-Cats so he could gain some more experience.

He returned to the Giants for the 1959 season, but played in just two games before he was released. After finishing that season with the Pittsburgh Steelers, appearing in six games, he returned to the Steelers for the 1960 season and registered his first NFL interception. Unfortunately, he played in just four games for Pittsburgh before he was released.

Understandably discouraged about being cut, Sutherin decided to return to the CFL and re-joined Hamilton for the 1960 season and almost immediately found success. Playing defensive back and handling the kicking duties, he led the Eastern Conference in interceptions and scoring in 1961 and '62, and was an All-CFL selection at defensive back in '62.

The Tiger-Cats reached the championship game in each of Sutherin's first three seasons back in the CFL, only to lose to the Winnipeg Blue Bombers each time. The Tiger-Cats finally got it right in 1963, taking the Grey Cup with a 21–10 win over the B.C. Lions.

"When you win the first one as a player, that's a big thrill," Don said.

"I don't know if it was as big a thrill as the Rose Bowl, (but) certainly it was quite enjoyable."

During his long twelve-year career as a cornerback and placekicker, Sutherin played in eight Grey Cup championship games with his team winning four. A three-time all-league selection on defense, he picked off 58 passes during his career, including 12 in postseason play, and twice led the CFL's Eastern Conference in interceptions.

Somewhere along the way, he picked up the nickname of "Suds." Some say the name came from Don's frequent trips to a neighborhood tavern after summertime softball games, while others claim it emanated from a Columbus laundromat prank gone awry. Nevertheless, the name stuck and even appears in his official bio on the CFL Hall of Fame website.

After his player days, Sutherin became a highly regarded defensive coordinator in the CFL, winning four more Grey Cups in that capacity during a coaching career that spanned more than twenty years and four teams. Early in the 1994 season, he took over as head coach of the Hamilton Tiger-Cats and held that position through the 1997 season before returning to defensive coordinator until he retired following the 2002 season.

He dabbled in coaching at several different levels for the next several years, but spent most of his time with wife Nancy, a former cheerleader at McKinley High School in Canton, and their four daughters and seven grandchildren. The couple eventually settled in the Ohio town of Hartville, just southeast of Akron, where Sutherin died January 11, 2022, at the age of eighty-five.

After his passing, niece Gwen Johnson offered a loving postscript to her uncle's life, calling him "our family's football hero. Uncle Don has always been a bigger-than-life presence in our family. He was always ready to tell us a story or say something funny to make us laugh. We all adored and respected him. He will be missed by all."

AUREALIUS THOMAS

OSU OFFENSIVE GUARD, DEFENSIVE LINEMAN 1955–1957

64

HOMETOWN: Muskogee, Oklahoma

HEIGHT: 6 ft 1 in **WEIGHT**: 204 lb

ALL-AMERICAN: 1957

NFL DRAFT: 1957, Pittsburgh Steelers

COLLEGE FOOTBALL HALL OF FAME: 1989

Aurealius Thomas spent nearly his entire life overcoming adversity of one kind or another. He was born in Dust Bowl-era Oklahoma and attended segregated schools until moving north to pursue his dream of playing college football at Ohio State. After initially being told he was too small to play for the Buckeyes, when Aurealius finally got his chance, he nearly died from heat exhaustion. Later, when a pro career ended before it got started, he reinvented himself and became a successful teacher and coach before embarking upon a third career as an award-winning salesman.

"Adversity is just another word for life," Thomas once said. "Things are presented to us over time, challenges of one form or another, and we have to meet those challenges. In the end, it doesn't matter how many times you face adversity. It's how you respond and whether or not you respond. The old saying is true. It's not how many times you get knocked down that's important. It's how many times you get back up."

Christened with a first name that according to Roman anthology means "the golden one," Aurealius Thomas was born April 6, 1934, in Muskogee, Oklahoma, a windswept town in the eastern part of the state near the Arkansas border. Situated in the middle of territory once ruled by a number of Native American tribes including Cherokee, Muscogee Creek and Choctaw, Muskogee is nearly equidistant from Dallas and Kansas City, but worlds away from those fast-paced metropolitan cities.

Commemorated by the nostalgia of country singer Merle Haggard's 1969 hit "Okie from Muskogee," the town has grown from a village inhabited mostly by fur traders to a city of nearly 40,000 residents featuring a vibrant arts scene, including theaters and a half-dozen museums, and is home to the sprawling Georgia-Pacific plant, a 2.9 million-square-foot manufacturing facility that churns out such paper products as facial and bathroom tissue, paper towels and napkins.

The Muskogee in which a young Aurealius Thomas and his six siblings grew up in the 1930s and 1940s was similar in population to the one of today but light years away in terms of culture. Oklahoma remained a territory until it was granted statehood in 1907, but it had adopted several traits of such neighbors as Texas and Arkansas, former members of the Confederacy that fought against the Union during the Civil War.

"Adversity is just another word for life."

—Aurealius Thomas

School segregation remained very much the law of the land as Aurealius began his academic life. As a youngster, he attended Dunbar and Douglass grade schools—named respectively for noted African-American poet Paul Laurence Dunbar and abolitionist Frederick Douglass—and then graduated to Manual Training High School, where he played football for Walter Cox, an Ohio native and graduate of Oberlin College. Cox knew a budding star when he saw one, and he was the first to suggest Aurealius should move north where he had a better chance at earning a college scholarship.

Luckily, Thomas had two married sisters who lived in Columbus at the time, and he began to spend summers with his siblings, always getting a part-time job to help pay for his room and board. Just before his junior year of high school, Aurealius made the decision to make his move to Columbus permanent, and enrolled in classes at West High School, the huge brick edifice designed by noted Ohio architect Howard Dwight Smith, who also designed Ohio Stadium.

Aurealius made fast friendships at West, where he went by the nickname "Tommy," and joined as many clubs as he could. He was also elected to student council and participated on the track team. But his true calling was football, and after earning all-city and all-state honors while playing for the Cowboys, West head coach Mark Pemberton contacted Woody Hayes for a personal appointment.

"To say the meeting didn't go the way I hoped would be an understatement," Aurealius said years later. "Most of Woody's linemen at that time were about 6-foot-3 and 240 pounds, and I was a 6-foot-1, 195-pound tackle. When Woody saw me, he wasn't convinced Ohio State was the place for me."

Hayes arranged for Thomas to attend the University of Cincinnati, where former Ohio State All-America end Sid Gillman was head coach. But before he was to begin his career as a Bearcat rather than a Buckeye, Aurealius participated in the Ohio North-South All-Star Game in August 1953. Displaying the textbook technique he was taught by his older brother Donald, who had been an All-American at Maryland State College (now Maryland Eastern Shore), the youngster put on a clinic during practice sessions, often outperforming players who were headed to Ohio State in the fall.

"Once Woody found out I could get the job done," Aurealius said, "I was through with Cincinnati. He made me an offer and I was going to Ohio State after all."

Thomas spent his first season on campus as a member of the OSU freshman team, and then entered fall camp in 1954 apprenticing at the right guard position behind All-American and three-year starter Jim Reichenbach. But the week before the season-opening game against Indiana, Reichenbach was injured and couldn't play, and suddenly Aurealius was elevated to first-team status.

Eager to prove he belonged in the starting lineup, the sophomore worked with both the first and second teams during practice sessions. A few days before the opener, the team was holding a scrimmage inside Ohio Stadium under a scorching hot August sun. As the mercury rose above 100 degrees, Thomas worked for about forty-five minutes with the first team, and then took his place with the second team for another forty-five minutes in the sweltering heat. Then after the scrimmage was over, team members did their customary running around the stadium track before heading to the locker room showers.

"I went into the locker room to get some orange juice, and the next thing I know, I'm waking up at University Hospital," Aurealius said. "I had heat exhaustion."

Long before anyone understood the danger of heat exhaustion, the cause of former Ohio State All-American lineman Korey Stringer's death on a Minnesota Vikings practice field in 2001, coaching staffs would routinely limit the amount of liquids their players could consume during practice sessions. That practice very nearly cost Thomas his life.

"I was in the hospital for twenty-eight days," he said. "It was a serious situation, and it took me that long for my body chemistry to adjust. I remember waking up in the hospital, and I moved my fingertips to open my eyelids. They were open but I couldn't see. They had IVs going into both arms to get me the necessary fluids. I don't think at that point anyone knew whether or not I would ever play football again."

The situation led to Ohio State becoming one of the first college football programs to change policies tailored to the well-being of its players. Players were weighed before and after practice, they were given as much water as they could consume, and they were issued newer lightweight jerseys.

Meanwhile, Thomas used a redshirt season to recover and returned in 1955 eager to make up for the time he had lost. He was a backup guard on both offense and defense that season, and then joined the starting lineup in 1956, earning honorable mention on several All-America teams. He was recognized

Aurealius rarely came off the field as he was a valuable two-way player for the 1957 national championship team.

again the following year, this time with first-team All-America honors during the 1957 season as Ohio State lost its season opener and then ran off nine consecutive victories to capture the national championship. Manning the right guard spot on offense and the nose guard position on defense, Aurealius rarely came off the field, averaging 52 minutes per game as a senior.

Despite the accolades, leadership skills and nearly flawless technique, the old bugaboo of size came up again as he prepared for a professional career. Since his fourth year of college eligibility was in 1956, Thomas was selected in the twenty-second round by the Pittsburgh Steelers in the 1957 NFL draft. But because he had missed his sophomore season, he was granted an extra year of college eligibility.

By the time he reached training camp with the Steelers in the summer of 1958, the team was well-stocked with offensive guards and played a defensive alignment that eliminated the nose guard position. In short, there was no room in Pittsburgh for Thomas, and he was released before the 1958 season began.

Returning to Columbus with few prospects for the future, he continued to work out at Ohio State, hoping to receive a tryout call from one of the other NFL teams. But as the days passed, no call came. One day, while sitting on a bench in the OSU locker room, Hayes asked him about his future. Aurealius shrugged off the question, so the old coach sat down beside him and suggested a return to school to work on his Master's degree.

When Thomas said he had no money for postgraduate school, Woody replied, "I'm not talking about money. I'm talking about you getting back here and helping us coach. We'll work out your financial arrangements later."

That began a coaching career that continued for most of the next decade, first at Ohio State and later in the Columbus City School system. He spent three seasons as head coach at Central High School, and then five at East High School, where he was selected coach of the year in Central Ohio in 1964.

Thomas gave up coaching after the 1965 season, but remained a science, health and driver's education teacher until his retirement in 1996. During his summers, he also developed his own successful life insurance brokerage.

After retirement, he stayed extremely active with community involvement, including serving as coordinator of the Columbus Leadership Conference and president of The Columbus Recreation and Parks Department. He was a member of the Alpha Phi Alpha Fraternity and The Ohio State University Alumni Association, a trustee of the university's Student Loan Foundation, an advisor to the Small Business Administration for the southern half of Ohio, and a volunteer for The United Negro College Fund.

Aurealius was also the recipient of numerous awards and honors including enshrinement to the College Football Hall of Fame in 1989 and induction into the Ohio State Athletics Hall of Fame in 1992.

He continued to enjoy a vibrant life, including the joy of three children, seven grandchildren and several great-grandchildren, until his 2021 death at the age of eighty-six.

"I have really had a wonderful life," Aurealius once said. "I have had people sometimes tell me that I am a self-made man, but nothing could be further from the truth. I had loving sisters who took me in to live with them, a brother who taught me the finer points of playing football, and coaches who had nothing but my best interests at heart.

"And I would put Woody Hayes at the top of that list. There were always two sides to Coach Hayes. There was the public side and the side that he shared only with the team. That's kind of sad, too, because I think people nowadays have the perception of him as this crazy, old fool stomping around the sidelines and punching players. Nothing could be further from the truth. Coach Hayes was one of the kindest, most honest, most loyal human beings I have ever met."

DICK LEBEAU

OSU OFFENSIVE, DEFENSIVE HALFBACK 1956–1958

HOMETOWN: London, Ohio

HEIGHT: 6 ft 1 in **WEIGHT**: 185 lb

NFL DRAFT: 1959, Cleveland Browns

PRO FOOTBALL HALL OF FAME: 2010

Dick LeBeau's mother always used to remind him that "age was just a number." Sage wisdom from a woman who lived to be ninety-six. But while LeBeau has spent the vast majority of his eight-plus decades on a football field, it would be improper to say that the life of Bob and Beulah LeBeau's little boy completely revolved around football.

As a way to relax, Dick taught himself to play guitar and would accompany himself in a low baritone voice, singing "mournful" compositions of his own making as chronicled in the 1963 bestselling book *Paper Lion*, the account of author George Plimpton taking part in a professional football training camp.

A few years later, Dick got together with Detroit Lions teammates Joe Schmidt and Bruce Maher to record a 45-rpm whose B-side, a LeBeau song called "The Lonesome One," appeared briefly on the local Detroit pop chart. The unsold copies, which Dick jokingly said numbered in the tens of thousands, collected dust for years in his mother's basement.

During the spring of 1969, film director Robert Aldrich went to the Philippines to make a World War II picture called *Too Late the Hero*. But Aldrich, who had made *The Dirty Dozen* featuring Cleveland Browns star Jim Brown, didn't think normal Hollywood stunt men could handle the grueling requirements of the final scene, repeated takes of a long run across a tropical rice paddy. Aldrich, who obviously liked football and admired football players, enlisted LeBeau as a stand-in for actor Michael Caine, and it is LeBeau and Detroit Lions teammate Pat Studstill at the end of the film running across the open mile with the Japanese gunning at them rather than the movie's co-stars Caine and Cliff Robertson.

Dick loves movies with the 1939 classic *The Wizard of Oz* topping his list. He also favors a 1957 release called *Raintree County*, a film set in Civil War times starring Elizabeth Taylor and Montgomery Clift as lovers brought up on opposite sides of the Mason-Dixon Line. That is perhaps only natural since Dick is also a Civil War buff. "I've read every Civil War book I could get my hands on," he says, "and I've visited all the battlefields and the national parks that do such a wonderful job preserving that history."

Dick also finds time for other sporting endeavors such as pool, poker and golf. Regarding the first two, former Lions teammate Charlie Sanders claims that inside LeBeau's quiet demeanor beats the heart of a killer shark. "You always knew he knew something, but you never knew what it was," Sanders said. "So many guys learned the hard way, including myself, and it always cost us a few bucks."

As for the golf course, hustlers would stay advised to give LeBeau a wide berth there as well. A scratch golfer and owner of two holes-in one, he honed his skills while in college with a pudgy classmate named Nicklaus. "I played with Jack some at Ohio State," Dick said. "One day, we were out on the course and I couldn't decide between my seven- and eight-iron. Jack comes up and says, 'What's the problem? Either hit a full eight or squeeze the ball up a couple of grooves on the seven. You'll get basically the same result.' I knew right then and there that I should stick to football."

Stick to football he did, making discussion regarding the life of Dick LeBeau imperative to include a professional career as player and coach spanning seven decades. LeBeau was active in the National Football League for a remarkable fifty-nine consecutive seasons, the first fourteen as an All-Pro cornerback with the Detroit Lions and forty-five more as a defensive assistant, most notably with the Cincinnati Bengals and Pittsburgh Steelers. He coached in six Super Bowls, helping the Steelers win two, and he received the ultimate honor in 2010 when he was inducted into the Pro Football Hall of Fame.

Before that illustrious pro career, however, LeBeau was the product of a small town in Ohio, wondering if he had what it took to play big-time college football. "I grew up as sort of a big fish in a small pond," he said in a slow drawl and even-metered pace that matches his commitment to consistency. "So when it came time to go to college, I figured I'd follow pretty much the same path. I was thinking I would be going to a smaller school. Then Woody Hayes started talking to my father. That was pretty exciting, but it was something I never thought would happen. I'm a small-town Ohio guy at heart, and I probably never would have left. But there are some things you just have to do."

Named for his paternal grandfather as well as his German great-great grandfather, Charles Richard LeBeau was born September 9, 1937, in London, Ohio, a blue-collar town about twenty-five miles from Columbus with a population of fewer than five thousand. Despite its relative lack of size, London had produced some big-time athletes such as Cincinnati Reds outfielder Bob Bescher, who led the National League in stolen bases for four consecutive years from 1909 to 1912, and Ohio State lineman Warren Amling, a two-time All-American and future member of the College Football Hall of Fame.

Dick grew up almost smack dab in the middle of downtown London,

Before a long NFL career as a player and coach, Dick was a star halfback and cornerback on the Buckeyes' 1957 national championship team.

his boyhood home adjacent to the town post office and within sight of the Madison County Courthouse and its four-sided clock tower serving as the focal point of the town. Dick's father, Robert E. LeBeau Sr., worked as an auditor for Ohio Liquor Board of Control, while his stay-at-home wife, the former Beulah Cleveland, kept house and tried to keep discipline with Dick and his older brother, Bob Jr.

Like most Depression-era small-town families throughout the United States, hardships were plentiful, and the situation didn't improve much during the rationing of such basic materials as food, metal, paper and rubber during the outbreak of World War II. "We were middle class, and that's a nice way of saying kind of poor, but we never knew it because everybody in town was in the same boat," Dick remembered. "They came through the Depression and World War II, and nobody had much of anything. But at Christmas time, you would have thought we were the Rockefellers."

In addition to festive holiday celebrations, the LeBeau home was filled with music. Bob Sr. was a drummer in a local band while Bob Jr. gravitated toward brass instruments, becoming proficient enough with the trombone to eventually become a professional musician. Meanwhile, Dick taught himself how to play acoustic guitar and specialized in classical music, a genre he insisted was easier to play than any other.

It didn't take long for the youngster to gravitate toward sports.

"The day I was big enough to walk, I was playing football," Dick said. "I was born in 1937, so needless to say, that was before video games. It was before video itself. We were outdoors all the time. Bob and I and the neighbor kids played in the post office yard in my little hometown of London, Ohio. We would go and take down the 'Keep Off the Grass' sign because that was our football field. Hell, I kicked my football up on the post office roof all the time."

Dick was never the biggest or fastest player on the athletic field, but his mind was always at work. In the eighth grade, he was captain of his gym class football team. There were five-man tournaments, and it fell upon Dick to draw up the plays. He eagerly welcomed the assignment and spent his study halls sketching offensive formations instead of doing homework. "I always knew," he said, "I wanted to be a coach."

That ambition was only further fueled when he began playing high school football under the tutelage of longtime London head coach Jim Bowlus. "The impact he had on me made me think coaching would be a pretty good way to spend my life," Dick said. " Of course, my vision in those days was probably as a high school coach. Either way, I wanted to become a coach and Coach Bowlus cemented that for me."

Dick first became enamored with London High School football as a seventh-grader in 1949 when his brother Bob, then a sophomore, took over when quarterback Ronnie Kulp broke his leg and led the Red Raiders to six victories. Two years later, Bob capped his senior year by quarterbacking London to the 1951 Mid-Six League championship.

A couple of years later, it was Dick's turn to star for the Raiders as an undersized but determined offensive and defensive back. "I wasn't the biggest by a longshot," he said, "but I didn't exactly shy away from contact. It didn't take opposing players very long to figure out that if they came into my area, they were going to pay for it."

Dick earned all-county honors and even some all-state mentions, but his willowy six-foot, 170-pound frame dictated that if he wanted to continue playing football at the college level, he needed to set his sights on smaller programs. But when Woody Hayes invited him and his father to dine with the coach at the Ohio State Faculty Club, it changed his perspective.

"The whole time we were there, Woody talked to my dad. I don't think he said more than two or three words to me," Dick recalled. "It was pretty surreal. Woody was coming off a national championship in 1954, and I just couldn't for the life of me understand what he wanted me for. But the more he and my dad talked, the more I realized that I was going to Ohio State. Coming from such a small town, that was pretty exciting."

LeBeau first set foot on the OSU campus in the fall of 1955, joining more than a hundred freshmen trying their hardest to stand out. By his sophomore season, Dick played enough to win his first varsity letter, and then he cracked the starting lineup as a junior in 1957. That year, the Buckeyes lost their season-opening game to Texas Christian University, but followed with nine consecutive victories to earn national championship honors from United Press International as well as the Football Writers Association of America.

Dick seemed to reserve his best play for the biggest games that season. During a 17–13 win against fifth-ranked Iowa, he made a crucial interception in the game that clinched the Big Ten championship for the Buckeyes. The following week, he ran for 73 yards and two touchdowns as Ohio State rolled to a 31–14 win against nineteenth-ranked Michigan in Ann Arbor.

The following year, the Buckeyes were near-unanimous choices to successfully defend their national championship, but a three-week midseason slump produced two ties and a shutout loss to Northwestern, ending the team's title aspirations. Ohio State did, however, salvage the season with a 20–14 win against Michigan.

LeBeau was selected by the Cleveland Browns in the fifth round of the 1959 NFL draft, and was eager to get a chance to play for the legendary Paul Brown. But Brown and his team, coming off back-to-back postseason losses, had little use for a smallish defensive back. Meanwhile, the Detroit Lions had just experienced a seven-loss season and needed all the help they could get. They claimed LeBeau off waivers, beginning a fourteen-year relationship that included three Pro Bowl appearances.

By the time he retired following the 1972 season, his sixty-two career interceptions were third all-time behind only Hall of Famers Emlen Tunnell and Dick "Night Train" Lane, and he had set a durability record at the cornerback position of 171 consecutive games played, a record that stood for more than forty years.

LeBeau went straight into coaching after retiring as a player. In his first job, he turned around the Philadelphia Eagles' special teams.

Then he went to work as defensive backs coach for the Green Bay Packers, where his secondary was known as the S.W.A.T. team for its hard-hitting ways. After Green Bay, LeBeau became defensive backs coach for the Cincinnati Bengals. In his second season with the Bengals, the team went to the Super Bowl. He later was promoted to defensive coordinator, and Cincinnati went to another Super Bowl.

A third Super Bowl appearance came after the 1995 season when Dick was defensive coordinator of the Pittsburgh Steelers, and he finally broke through with championships in Super Bowls XL and XLIII during a second stint with the Steelers. In between, he realized another dream by becoming an NFL head coach, spending two and a half seasons piloting the Bengals.

Along the way, LeBeau was credited with inventing the "Fire Zone" defense, also known as the "zone blitz," which employs unpredictable pass rushes as well as disguised pass coverages from various players. Described as an "innovator" and "defensive football genius," LeBeau has on more than one occasion been called the best defensive coach in NFL history. Perhaps longtime *Sports Illustrated* writer Peter King, who first met LeBeau while he was a Bengals beat reporter for the *Cincinnati Enquirer*, summed it up best when he wrote, "Dick LeBeau is a national treasure."

Dick was having none of that.

"I think it's hyperbole," he said with a laugh. "I'm just a guy from a small town who had the good fortune to know what he wanted to do with his life at an early age, and then got to do it. Let's put it this way: I'm a lot closer to being a decent golfer than I am a national treasure."

TOM MATTE

OSU HALFBACK, QUARTERBACK 1958–1960

NICKNAME: Garbage Can

HOMETOWN: East Cleveland, Ohio

HEIGHT: 6 ft 0 in **WEIGHT:** 190 lb

NFL DRAFT: 1961, Baltimore Colts

41

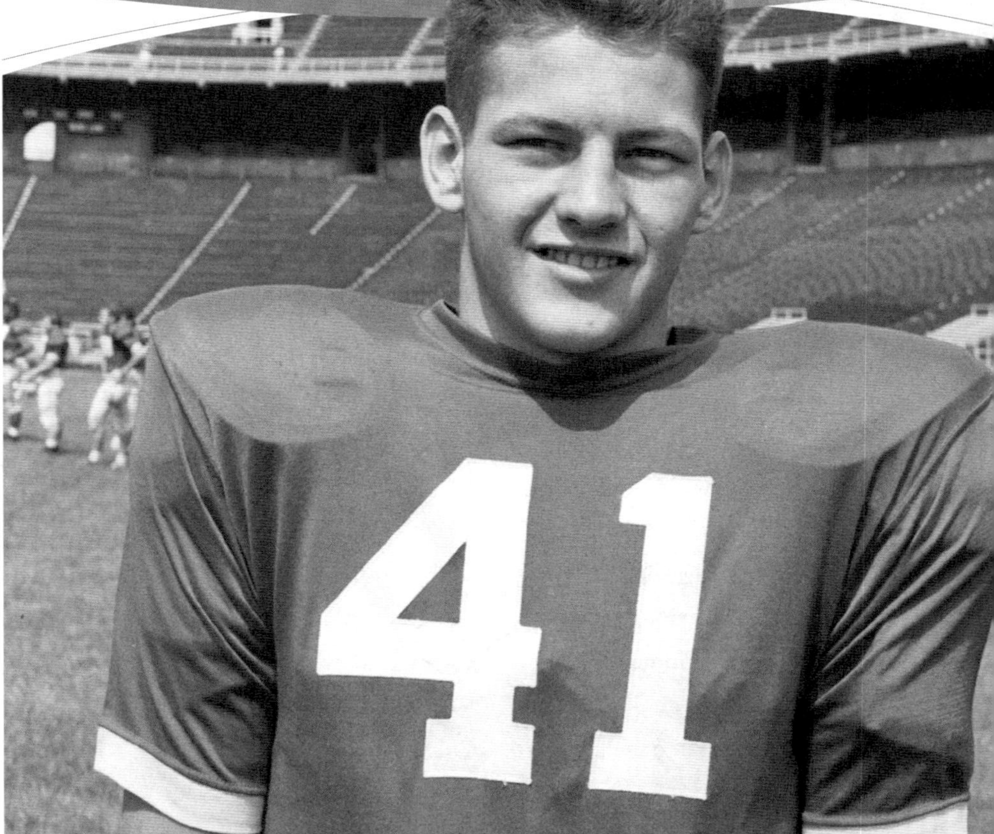

Eagle Scout, quarter-miler, pole vaulter, ice hockey player, All-Pro running back. There didn't seem to be much Tom Matte couldn't do, including excelling at the quarterback position when he was pressed into emergency duty at Ohio State and again in the NFL with the Baltimore Colts.

Add innovator, prankster, broadcaster, mentor, and all-around good guy to that list, too, as Matte left a positive impression upon nearly everyone who ever crossed his path.

"There was no one like Tom Matte," former Ohio State quarterback and Colts defensive back Rex Kern said. "When I was drafted by the Colts, Tom was one of the first guys to welcome me. He just kind of took me under his wing and I can truly say he was like a big brother to me. He was a mentor, a prankster and someone who was a friend to everyone he ever met. I dearly loved Tom Matte."

> "He had to fight his way to school and fight his way home every day. That must have deepened his resolve, I guess, because not much fazed the guy."
>
> —*Roland Matte*

Thomas Roland Matte was born in Pittsburgh on June 14, 1939, into an athletic family that included his maternal grandfather, Thomas Stevens, who was the decathlon champion of Canada, and his father, Joseph Roland Lionel Matte, a native of Ontario, Canada, who played professional hockey for 17 years, including the 1942 and 1943 seasons in the National Hockey League with the Chicago Blackhawks. As a baby, Tom lived with his parents in his grandfather's simple brick house on Pioneer Avenue, one of many lookalike two-story structures on the tree-lined streets of the Brookline neighborhood in the South Hills of Pittsburgh. It was located only about fifteen miles from where Three Rivers Stadium, the home of the six-time Super Bowl champion Pittsburgh

Steelers, would be constructed in 1970, but it might as well have been a million miles away because Joseph and his wife Dorothy bundled young Tom at the age of two and moved to Cleveland Heights, Ohio.

Cleveland Heights was experiencing a population boom at the time, growing from a sleepy town of fewer than 5,000 residents in 1910 to a bare-knuckle populace of nearly 50,000 by the end of the 1930s as construction of streetcar lines brought in thousands of new residents, particularly Jewish families leaving the inner city. It was a rough-and-tumble neighborhood in which Tom grew up, one that apparently helped to shape his inner drive since he was drawn to such contact sports as football and ice hockey.

"He had to fight his way to school and fight his way home every day," said his son Roland. "That must have deepened his resolve, I guess, because not much fazed the guy. As far as his determination, if he said he was going to do something, he followed through."

That was a character trait Matte came by honestly.

"Let me tell you, my dad was one of the toughest," Tom said. "I remember a couple of times where I'd get out of hand, and he'd just come over and pick me up by the shirt and just pick me up off the ground. He had arms on him like a weightlifter. He was a strong guy and a tough, mean guy—played defense on the rink and commanded a lot of respect. If I didn't put up 150 percent, there was a boot in my butt because my dad said, 'You could do better than that.' It was challenging growing up, but I'll tell you what: I count that as a blessing. I knew he loved me and wanted me to be the best I could be."

Although he grew up in Cleveland Heights, Matte went to Shaw High School, located about ten minutes north in East Cleveland, a more affluent suburb that once was the site of the mansion of oil magnate John D. Rockefeller. At Shaw, Tom became a star player in football as well as in track and field, showcasing athletic versatility that belied his rather scrawny six-foot, 190-pound frame.

Little did legendary head coach Woody Hayes know how much he would depend upon the youngster's versatility when he was recruiting Matte to play running back at Ohio State.

"In the opening game of his junior year against Duke, our starting quarterback had not been effective," Hayes once recalled. "Late in the game, we moved Tom from halfback to quarterback. He took the team down the field on roll-out passing, and finally hit end Chuck Bryant for the winning touchdown. On that drive, Tom was so exhausted that he would get down on one knee and tell another back to call the play while he rested, but when the play started, he got up and ran and passed as though he were just entering the game.

"The following year in 1960, he was a great quarterback. In running the option, we have never had a better one. Tom sort of ran flat-footed, but he was able to cut sharply or make the pitch on the option as the situation demanded."

Matte, who also ran track for the Buckeyes—"I had as many offers for track scholarships as I did for football," he once said—and lettered in ice hockey when it was a club sport at Ohio State, said it was his willingness to try just about anything that led to the position switch on the football field.

"I was a jack of all trades and master of none," he said. "I didn't want to play quarterback because my hands were small and it was tough for me to throw a spiral. Woody said, 'That doesn't matter. We're not going to throw the ball that much anyway.' Well, Mr. Three-Years-And-A-Cloud-Of-Dust was right. My main job during the 1960 season was to hand the ball off to our fullback Bob Ferguson. Bob ran for about 900 yards and a whole bunch of touchdowns, so I'd like to think I did a pretty good job."

"I've never met anyone like him. You couldn't be within five feet of Tom Matte and not smile."
—*Bruce Cunningham,* Baltimore sportscaster

Matte barely got the last part of that sentence out before erupting in a hearty laugh, showing the kind of self-effacing humor that endeared him to his teammates and fans. But while he often claimed to be just a complimentary player, he was voted by his teammates as Ohio State's most valuable player in 1960, earned third-team All-America honors, and finished seventh in that season's Heisman Trophy balloting.

"I've never met anyone like him," veteran Baltimore sportscaster Bruce Cunningham said. "You couldn't be within five feet of Tom Matte and not smile. He just bounced through life, and he knew that he lived a charmed life, and he loved the fact that he lived a charmed life. Everywhere he went, there were hundreds of fans in his wake. He was just that guy."

Despite the fact he played the majority of his college snaps at quarterback, Matte was taken by Baltimore with the seventh overall pick in the 1961 NFL draft. "I had no idea what they were thinking," Matte said. "They had John Unitas for Christ's sake. I didn't know what in the hell they wanted with me."

Matte turned out to be one of the most important pieces for the Colts as they developed one of the most potent offenses in the NFL. With Matte teaming with such future Hall of Fame players as Unitas, running back Lenny Moore, receiver Raymond Berry, and tight end John Mackey, Baltimore won five division championships, two league titles, and Super Bowl V following the 1970 season.

Matte spent his entire twelve-year NFL career with the Colts as a gritty running back who earned the nickname "Garbage Can" after Detroit Lions defensive tackle Alex Karras described him as "nothing but a garbage-can runner." That was after a game in 1967 when Matte rushed for 110 yards and two touchdowns during a 41–7 blowout of the Lions.

"I remember he said something like, 'How can a garbage-can halfback like Matte beat us?' We laughed about it," Matte remembered. "Alex and I were really good friends. He gave me that nickname, 'Garbage Can.' And of course, the team loved it. I came into the locker room after the first game I had played (at quarterback), and in my locker, what was there? A garbage can."

Matte is perhaps best remembered in Baltimore for his time at quarterback late in 1965, when the Colts lost Unitas and backup Gary Cuozzo to injuries in successive weeks. Matte, who hadn't taken a snap since college, led Baltimore to a 20–17 upset of the Los Angeles Rams, rushing for 99 yards. Then, in a playoff for the Western Conference championship, he completed 5 of 12 passes for 40 yards and ran for 57 more, but the Packers prevailed in overtime, 13–10.

The Packers went on to win the NFL title while the Colts flew home to Baltimore where it took Matte twenty-five minutes to get through an airport crowd that finally hoisted him on their shoulders and carried him out.

"The fans just about tore the clothes off my back while they passed me down the aisle on top of their shoulders," he said. "But how could I complain?"

While operating at quarterback in 1965, Matte wore a wristband listing plays for him to call. He called it a "cheat sheet," but over the years, it has become a standard piece of equipment for many NFL quarterbacks, including Tom Brady and Peyton Manning.

The actual wristband Matte used in 1965 is on display at the Pro Football Hall of Fame in Canton.

"If I'd have known that wristband was going to be so popular," Matte once said with a laugh, "I'd have patented the damned thing."

Matte was a two-time Pro Bowler, earned first-team All-Pro status in 1969 when he led the league with 11 rushing touchdowns, and finished his career with 4,646 rushing yards, 2,869 receiving yards, and 57 total touchdowns. In addition to his much-decorated playing career, he was also an All-Pro prankster.

"We were in training camp with the Colts one summer, and honeybees kept trying to get into our helmets through the ear holes," Kern said. "Well, Matte gets the idea of walking up behind somebody and making a buzzing sound while sticking a long blade of grass in their ear hole. Of course, the guy would rip off his helmet thinking it was a bee only to find Matte rolling on the ground laughing."

Kern would eventually have the last laugh, however, although it was unintentional.

"We're getting ready to play the Oakland Raiders, and I'm walking off the field after practice thinking about what Kenny Stabler is going to do and whether or not I'm going to be able to cover Fred Biletnikoff," Kern said. "Suddenly, I hear this buzzing sound and feel this thing in my ear. I had been walking with my head down, and as I raised up quickly, I caught Matte flush in the face with the back of my helmet. I looked down and he's bleeding from the mouth with two chipped teeth. I thought, 'Oh, no! I've killed Tom Matte!!'"

Once Kern got to the locker room, some of his veteran teammates gave him a sour look before Hall of Fame defensive end Bubba Smith approached him. As a smile broke over Smith's face, he said, "Finally! Matte finally got what was coming to him."

Kern said he called Matte at home later that evening to apologize. Expecting a firm chewing-out, Matte instead said with a chuckle, "Don't worry about it, Rex. I needed my teeth fixed anyway and now the team is going to have to pay for it."

After retirement from the NFL following the 1972 season, Matte worked briefly as an analyst on CBS coverage of football games, and from 1996 to 2005, he provided color analysis on Baltimore Ravens radio broadcasts. For a time, Matte also provided analysis for college football games involving the University of Maryland. But his most enjoyable pastime was as goodwill ambassador for the city of Baltimore and all of its sports team, something he enjoyed until his death at the age of eighty-two in 2021 following a courageous bout with leukemia.

JIM TYRER

OSU OFFENSIVE TACKLE 1958–1960

NICKNAME: Tyro

HOMETOWN: Newark, Ohio

HEIGHT: 6 ft 5 in **WEIGHT**: 248 lb

NFL DRAFT: 1961, Chicago Bears

AFL DRAFT: 1961, Dallas Texans

77

Early in the morning of September 15, 1980, Jim Tyrer lay awake in his south-side Kansas City home. Insomnia had become just another in the increasingly long line of difficulties visited upon the former football star who had earned honorable mention All-America honors at Ohio State before becoming an All-Pro offensive lineman and Super Bowl champion with the Kansas City Chiefs.

To most of their friends, Jim and Marty Tyrer seemed the perfect couple, married nearly twenty years and living a comfortable suburban life with their four children. Tyrer had played fourteen professional seasons, all but one of them with the Chiefs, and then used what one teammate called "studious entrepreneurism" to make the transition from professional football player to successful businessman.

With a burgeoning family at home, however, Tyrer quickly tired of a job that kept him on the road throughout the week and tried to create financial opportunities for himself. But a string of unfortunate occurrences—poor investments as well as a trio of failed businesses—sent Tyrer into a personal tailspin. After taking a second mortgage on his house and pawning some of his wife's jewelry and furs, Tyrer began selling Amway products as a veil of depression and despair began to shroud his life in darkness.

In the wee hours of that morning more than four decades ago, the forty-one-year-old former football star—known to his many friends and teammates as a gentle giant—fumbled for a loaded .38 caliber revolver he kept in a bedside drawer.

What happened in the subsequent handful of seconds has otherwise canceled what was by all accounts an exemplary life. It has certainly cost Tyrer whatever football legacy he might have earned.

Despite starting at right tackle for Woody Hayes for three seasons from 1958 to 1960, being named team co-captain, and earning first-team All-Big Ten and honorable mention All-America recognition, Tyrer's name is nowhere to be found on the membership list in the Ohio State Athletics Hall of Fame.

"I'm not sure who you would consider a better offensive lineman that ever came out of Ohio State," former OSU halfback/quarterback Tom Matte said. "Maybe Jim Parker. Maybe Orlando Pace. But I'm telling you that Jim Tyrer was right there with those guys. He was one of the best offensive linemen the Buckeyes have ever had."

A third-round selection by the Dallas Texans (who later became the Chiefs) in the 1961 American Football League draft, Tyrer was a nine-time Pro Bowler, six-time All-Pro and three-time AFL champion in Kansas City as well as one of the members of an offensive line that helped neutralize Minnesota's feared "Purple People Eaters" defense in Super Bowl IV resulting in a 23–7 victory for the Chiefs.

But while Tyrer is a member of the Chiefs Hall of Fame, earning induction in 1977, a player with his kind of résumé is conspicuously absent from being enshrined in Canton–especially when Pro Football Hall of Fame bylaws expressly forbid voters to consider anything other than what a player has done on the field.

Kevin Patrick Allen, director of the 2020 documentary *A Good Man —The Jim Tyrer Story*, believes he knows why Tyrer and his career have not been properly recognized. "The only reason Jim Tyrer is forgotten, despite his spectacular life," Allen said, "is the last ten seconds (of that life) were horrible."

James Efflo Tyrer was born February 25, 1939, and grew up in Newark, Ohio, using a 6-foot-4, 225-pound body to star in football and basketball at his high school. He helped the Wildcats win a central Ohio regional championship in basketball and was a two-time all-district performer in football. Those honors helped lead to Tyrer being named the first member of the Newark High School Hall of Fame in 1970.

He grew another inch or two and added another twenty-five pounds during his three years at Ohio State, although his true size is widely debated. Despite being listed at 6-foot-6 and 248 pounds on the official OSU depth chart in 1960, Hayes couldn't resist padding those numbers in his 1973 book *You Win With People!*

"Jim Tyrer stood 6–6 and weighed 260," Hayes wrote. "Jim was a quiet man, a man who led by example and a man who got better in every practice....He is regarded by the Kansas City Chiefs as the best lineman they have ever had."

Before he got to the pros, however, Tyrer became a force on the Ohio State offensive line, starting at left tackle as a sophomore before switching to right tackle for his final two years and paving the way for such halfbacks as Don Clark and Bob Klein as well as fullbacks Bob White and Bob Ferguson.

"Jim was a great guy and a great teammate," former OSU offensive tackle Daryl Sanders said. "He was the right tackle and an established guy when I played my first year of varsity ball as a sophomore in 1960. Bob Vogel and I shared the other tackle spot, and Jim couldn't have been more helpful. It's no wonder why he was voted a team captain."

During Tyrer's senior season at Ohio State in 1960, the eighth-ranked Buckeyes were practicing to play No. 10 Michigan State in East Lansing. The Spartans, led by head coach Duffy Daugherty, were coming off back-to-back shutouts against Notre Dame and Indiana, and presented the OSU offense with its toughest test to date.

Hayes reached back into one of his older playbooks to dust off a play called "41 Quick Trap," which was basically a quick-attack pitch to a halfback who would follow a pulling guard. But success of the play was geared to an offensive tackle—Tyrer in this case—getting off his block to pick off the defender lined up over the pulling guard.

The play was called only twice against the Spartans, but thanks to Tyrer, it worked like a charm. Klein picked up ten yards the first time the play was called, and he turned the second into a 46-yard touchdown as the Buckeyes went on to a 21–10 victory.

"Jim could do anything you asked him to do," Matte said. "Point-of-attack blocking, cut off a guy, make a downfield block, pass protect. He certainly saved my bacon on more than one occasion."

After his college career ended, Tyrer was invited to play in the East-West Shrine Game and Hula Bowl, prestigious honors in their day. But the NFL didn't seem that impressed. Tyrer fell all the way to the fourteenth round of the 1961 draft before the Chicago Bears finally picked him with the 188th overall selection.

The upstart American Football League was more enamored with Tyrer, who was now listed at 6–6 and 280 pounds. The fledgling league, which began play with eight teams in 1960, was more aggressive in its pursuit of young players, especially those who were late-round picks by the NFL. Seeing a chance to play right away, Tyrer spurned a lowball offer from the Bears and signed with the Dallas Texans, who had taken him as the twenty-second player overall in the AFL draft.

Tyrer became an immediate fixture at left tackle for the Texans, who moved to Kansas City in 1963 to become the Chiefs. During his thirteen seasons with the team, Tyrer played in 180 consecutive games—the third-longest streak in franchise history—and became one of professional football's best and most-feared offensive linemen.

"He was the pre-eminent left tackle in all of football," former Houston Oilers defensive lineman Elvin Bethea told reporters upon his 2003 induction into the Pro Football Hall of Fame. "All other blockers I faced in the NFL were mediocre compared to him. He would just swamp me to where I would be lucky to beat him even once in a game. Tyrer was the pioneer of big offensive tackles. He was the best blocker I ever faced."

Hall of Fame head coach Hank Stram, who coached Tyrer during each of the lineman's thirteen seasons with the Chiefs, once said, "If you could pick a prototype (offensive tackle) out of a Sears and Roebuck catalogue, Jim Tyrer would be it."

During Tyrer's era, offensive linemen were prohibited from using their hands to block, so the ability to lead with the head and batter defensive linemen with your helmet was a prized skill. And apparently no one rammed his head into opponents with more authority than Tyrer.

"He was easily the best blocker I ever faced," Hall of Fame defensive end Ben Davidson once said. "He would jam his helmet right up into your sternum where it felt like you were being hit by a truck. He had finesse, too, but power was his game and he knew how to use it."

Photos of Tyrer from his Kansas City days show him wearing a helmet so scarred that the Chiefs logo on either side is almost obliterated. And although the words "chronic traumatic encephalopathy" were decades away from entering the sporting world's lexicon, there seems little doubt now that Tyrer's particular style of controlled brutality in getting his mission accomplished would lead to dire consequences.

"I know Jim wasn't diagnosed with it, but I have to suspect that he was an early victim of CTE," said Sanders, who later played four seasons at offensive tackle for the Detroit Lions. "How else could you explain what happened? Something so completely out of character and so illogical? How do you explain it? The answer is, you can't."

Tyrer had spent the Sunday afternoon of September 14, 1980, at Arrowhead Stadium in Kansas City with the younger of his two sons, ten-year-old Jason. The two watched the Chiefs lose a 17–16 decision to the Seattle Seahawks, a game during which nearby fans recalled Tyrer being oddly transfixed by the action. They said he spent most of the game just staring at the field, paradoxically preoccupied and distant.

When asked if everything was OK, Tyrer reportedly smiled and nodded his head. But everything was most definitely not all right.

During the early hours of the next morning, Tyrer reached for the gun he kept in a bedside table and fired it once. As his startled wife awoke and attempted to get out of bed, Tyrer aimed at her and fired, a fatal bullet striking her in the head. Seconds later, he turned the weapon on himself. It was a murder-suicide that sparked sensational headlines around the country.

"I remember when I heard the news, and I just didn't believe it," said Matte, who played twelve NFL seasons with the Baltimore Colts. "Jim just wasn't that kind of guy. At least, the Jim I knew and played with—he just wasn't that kind of guy. I was really taken aback and it took me a long time to come to grips with it. You just never in your wildest dreams think something like that would ever happen."

During the forty years since the murder-suicide, studies regarding CTE and head trauma have underscored the violent nature of football. In recent years, such former NFL stars as Junior Seau, Dave Duerson and Aaron Hernandez have taken their own lives, and autopsies would seem to confirm in each case that CTE was a contributing cause.

Chris Nowinski, a former Ivy League football player and professional wrestler who is now CEO of the Boston-based Concussion Legacy Foundation, has studied CTE for years and knows the Tyrer story well.

"Having looked at over 200 football players," Nowinski said, "I think it would be nearly impossible that he didn't have CTE."

But since Tyrer played so long ago, and his final act was such a heinous one, his legacy has been forever altered. He was a finalist for the Pro Football Hall of Fame just once, and that was in 1981. Since then, his name is rarely mentioned with the exception of reunions or memorabilia shows featuring Chiefs old-timers.

"Jim Tyrer is a player a lot of people have forgotten about," said Fred Arbanas, an All-Pro tight end who was Tyrer's teammate for nine seasons beginning in 1962. He was also perhaps Tyrer's closest friend.

"Jim was fantastic," Arbanas said. "A helluva pass blocker. And when it came to run blocking, he'd blow the guys right out of there. He was the best that I've ever seen play. He was also a super father and a good friend. What's kept him out of the Hall of Fame was, you know, the way he checked out and did what he did."

In 1982, another of Tyrer's teammates, center Michael Oriard, published a football memoir titled *The End of Autumn*. In the book, Oriard tried to explain what happened while attempting to piece together the radical transformation that had seemingly overtaken Tyrer after his retirement from professional football in 1974. He also believes Tyrer will never be enshrined in Canton no matter how much that honor is deserved.

"If they put him in the Hall of Fame," Oriard said, "the NFL will have to acknowledge how his life ended. And the NFL doesn't want to go there."

PAUL WARFIELD

OSU HALFBACK, KICK RETURNER 1961–1963

42

HOMETOWN: Warren, Ohio

HEIGHT: 6 ft 0 in **WEIGHT**: 182 lb

NFL DRAFT: 1964, Cleveland Browns

PRO FOOTBALL HALL OF FAME: 1983

Growing up practically in the shadow of Municipal Stadium where the Cleveland Browns were dominating professional football, Paul Warfield never really thought he was cut out for the gridiron. In fact, if the youngster's fate had been left up to his father, Paul Warfield would have pursued a career in professional baseball.

Paul Dryden Warfield was born November 28, 1942, in Warren, Ohio, a mid-sized Midwestern municipality located about fifty miles southeast of Cleveland, less than twenty miles from the Ohio-Pennsylvania border, and about a million miles from turn-of-century Guthrie, Tennessee, where his father was born and raised.

Guthrie in the early part of 1900s was a town of about 1,500 split both by race and the Kentucky-Tennessee border. Dryden Warfield was born in 1914 and raised on the Tennessee side. Anticipating a girl, his parents had decided on the name Lena Dryden weeks before his birth and stuck with it, Dryden being the first name of the doctor who delivered his mother.

"I was baseball crazy," Dryden once said. "We played baseball on Christmas if the weather was nice. Baseball. Baseball. I didn't think I could love anything more than baseball." At age twelve or thirteen, Dryden knew he had to have the baseball glove that all but screamed at him from the window of a general store. To a baseball-loving youngster, a glove is a necessity of life. To Dryden's father, trying to support a wife and ten children on a railroad yardman's pay, it might as well have been the Mona Lisa or the Hope Diamond.

"I saw it a little before Christmas," Dryden said. "I think I finally bought it early in April. If you wanted something, well, you put the money back and waited until you got enough. I worked at real little jobs. White people wanted you to do this, that, and the other."

With that glove, Dryden and his buddies occasionally played against white teams. Twice a year at least. So even then, some barriers in sport were stretched, if nowhere close to broken. But never was Dryden at shortstop able to look to his right and see a white third baseman.

"Everything was segregated in those days," Dryden said. "But really and truthfully, where we were from, whites and Blacks got along. There was never diehard segregation like in the Deep South. Everything was amiable as long as you took care of your own affairs. You knew your road and you took that."

Dryden was a fine baseball player, a right-handed-hitting shortstop with power, something on the order of a shorter and slightly more compact Ernie Banks. But in the 1930s, Jackie Robinson was still more than a decade and a half from breaking Major League Baseball's so-called "color line," and Dryden had to make a choice. There was opportunity for young Blacks in pro baseball, and many who saw him play in and around Guthrie pegged Dryden Warfield as a future star in the Negro League.

"But those teams were far away," he said. "And I don't think I would have liked the lifestyle. Eating and sleeping on buses. Up all night and playing the next day, including Sunday. I was comfortable at home. That way of living wouldn't have suited me at all."

Dryden might have been comfortable at home, but steady work was hard to find. An older brother, William, had gone to Warren and gotten a job with Republic Steel. In the summer of 1936, while home on vacation, he told Dryden that Republic was hiring with far better pay than anything available where he was. A couple of months later, just two years out of high school and never having ventured more than twenty miles outside Guthrie, Dryden and his young bride, Omelia, took the train 550 miles and joined William in the Ohio mill town near the Pennsylvania border. Twenty-four years in the future, Dryden's son would face a similar choice regarding his future. Baseball or something else?

"I had just turned fourteen years old and decided I wasn't going to play football in high school," Paul said. "I just thought all the guys on the football team were better than I was. My experience in football up to that point was kind of so-so. I was much better at baseball, and I was pretty good at track and field. My thinking at that point in my life was that I would run track in the spring and then play baseball all summer.

I already had a couple of pro (baseball) scouts keeping track of me, so I never really considered football."

But then Paul attended a mandatory meeting designed to introduce prospective players to the new head coach scheduled to take over the following fall at Warren G. Harding High School. Gene Slaughter, who would later become an assistant coach for Woody Hayes at Ohio State before beginning a quarter-century run as head coach at Capital University in Columbus, was making a pitch for his new program.

"I only went to the meeting because I was ordered to go. I had no intention of playing football," Warfield said. "I had made up my mind that everyone was bigger and better than I was, and if I was to have any success athletically it would be another sport. But after about fifteen minutes of listening to Gene, I got the feeling of watching a promotional film for football. I mean, it was 'the few, the proud, join the Marines' kind of stuff. It really struck a chord. I was scared to death, but I thought I had to go up there and see where I could fit in. It was a life-changing experience for me."

Under Slaughter's tutelage, Warfield excelled as a running back and defensive back for the Panthers, quickly seeing the benefits of his decision. After getting his varsity letter as a sophomore, he tore through

After winning a national championship with the Buckeyes, Paul won NFL titles with the Cleveland Browns and Miami Dolphins.

the competition during his junior year, establishing a new school record by scoring ninety-two points. The following year, he bettered his own mark with ninety-three points, including the only touchdown in a 6–0 upset of state power Massillon Washington. During his senior season alone, he totaled 810 yards rushing and scored fifteen touchdowns, earning not only first-team All-Ohio honors but consensus prep All-America honors as well.

"He's the only one I ever saw putting on moves when he's just walking."
—*George Mira,* Dolphins teammate

It was the kind of performance that led to upward of eighty scholarship offers from nearly every major college program across the country. Offers came from as far away as California, while nearly every Midwestern coach had to unfold a road map so they could find their way to Warren. There were also inquiries from a number of Southern schools, including Ole Miss, which had been awarded the 1960 national championship by the Football Writers Association of America, and Alabama, on its way to the multiple titles under head coach Paul "Bear" Bryant.

"But there was not the ghost of a chance I could consider schools like the University of Alabama," Paul said. "I recall very vividly Governor Wallace standing on the schoolhouse steps, defying a U.S. marshal (to admit Black students). I pretty much restricted myself, at least in terms of big-time college football, to the area of the Big Ten."

So, during the fall of 1959 and the winter of 1960, a who's who of coaches made their way east on Park Street, turned right on Federal and immediately into a double-car driveway to all but beg Paul Warfield to accept their offer of a college scholarship. They might all have saved their breath since Paul and his parents centered on Ohio State and Woody Hayes early in the recruiting process.

It certainly didn't hurt Hayes' cause that he had hired Gene Slaughter as a member of his coaching staff.

Paul began the task of personally informing each of the coaches who had offered him scholarships, as well as lucrative offers from Major League Baseball franchises in Cleveland, Detroit, and Chicago, that he would be heading to Ohio State to major in football with a minor in track and field. After all, he was a state high school champion in the broad jump as well as a state record-holder in the low hurdles.

What followed was a superlative college career as a halfback, flanker, and defensive back for the Buckeyes. He was a vital member of the 1961 team that earned the FWAA version of the national championship, and was looking forward to playing an even bigger role the following season. But the following summer, something happened that made Paul for the first time second-guess his decision to concentrate solely on football.

As a member of the Ohio State track team, he placed second in the long jump at the NCAA Track Championships, hosted in mid-June by the University of Oregon at Hayward Field in Eugene. He was still just a sophomore and seriously considered suspending his football career to make a run at making the 1964 U.S. Olympic team.

"That was a very difficult decision because I seriously thought I could have been a member of the United States Olympic team in 1964 as a long jumper," he said. "I had a world ranking at the time, and had been a member of the U.S. track team the summer before. It would really have been special to represent my country at the Olympic Games in Tokyo. But I had to think of my future, and I knew my future wasn't going to be on the track. It was on the football field."

"Paul is the most graceful athlete we have ever had."

—*Woody Hayes*

Paul returned to the football Buckeyes and won first-team All-Big Ten honors as a junior, topping that performance by being named to the All-America first team during his senior season in 1963.

"Paul is the most graceful athlete we have ever had," Hayes once said. "He certainly was a complete football player for he played both offense and defense, led the team in punt returns for three straight years and kickoff returns his sophomore and junior years. As I look back, if I had played him somewhat less, he would have been even more outstanding."

Warfield was excellent enough that the Cleveland Browns, the team he had grown up cheering for, made him their first-round selection in the 1964 NFL draft. That began a fourteen-year professional career that included six with the Browns, five with the Miami Dolphins, one season with the Memphis Southmen of the upstart World Football League, and two more back in Cleveland. Along the way, he was named to eight Pro Bowls, won back-to-back Super Bowls with the Dolphins, and earned election to the Pro Football Hall of Fame in 1983, his first year of eligibility.

He is a member of the Miami Dolphins Honor Roll, an inaugural inductee into the Browns Ring of Honor, and has a life-sized statue of his likeness outside the stadium at his high school alma mater. Not bad for a guy who had to be coaxed into playing football.

"He got the love of the games from me," his father Dryden once said. "His mother didn't care for sports. And my father had no athletic ability at all. Paul was a natural at almost any sport he tried. But I guess it really was for the best that he chose football over baseball. He never could hit a ball as far as I could."

MATT SNELL

OSU HALFBACK, FULLBACK, DEFENSIVE END 1961–1963

HOMETOWN: Garfield, Georgia

HEIGHT: 6 ft 2 in **WEIGHT**: 214 lb

NFL DRAFT: 1964, New York Giants

AFL DRAFT: 1964, New York Jets

For most of the first part of his life, Matt Snell was a wrecking ball, tearing down opposing defenses with a unique combination of talents that included a slashing athleticism and, when necessary, a run-right-over-the-top-of-you mentality. After football, Snell turned his attention from the destruction of would-be tacklers to the construction of office space as the owner of a construction company in New York.

Despite the fact he played his last down of football a half-century ago, Snell is fondly remembered by two of the most loyal alumni bases in the sport: Ohio State and the New York Jets.

"Oh, I don't know about that," Matt said with a laugh about the way he is remembered. "I was pretty fortunate to play on some pretty good teams with some pretty good players in my time. But that's been a long time ago. I haven't even been around a football since 1972."

That's not exactly accurate. For a couple of years during the early 2000s, Snell provided color commentary for internet broadcasts of Northeast Conference college football games. It was a chance to reconnect with the sport that he enjoyed so much during his youth and was forced to give up when injuries began to take their toll on his body.

Although he is generally regarded as a native New Yorker, Matthews Snell was born August 18, 1941, in Garfield, Georgia, a rural community in the eastern part of the state with a population of about four hundred. Matt's father, Isaac, was a tenant farmer who had quit school after the third grade to concentrate on his chores at home. When he became a teenager, he moved out of the house, courted and married the former Annie B. Ealy, and began a family of his own.

Garfield is located about sixty-five miles due south of Augusta National Golf Club, site of the prestigious Masters Tournament since 1934. But in the Jim Crow South of the early 1940s, Garfield might as well have been on the other side of the planet from Augusta National. Isaac Snell rose before dawn each morning to toil in the often-unforgiving Georgia clay, trying his best to provide for a family that would eventually grow to five children.

Despite his lack of formal education, Isaac was well-schooled enough in the game of life to realize rural Georgia contained no future for his children. He decided to pack up their meager belongings and move closer to relatives in Long Island, New York, where everything from the financial opportunities to the nearby cultural benefits were more conducive to a Black family trying to make its way in post-World War II America.

The Snells landed in Locust Valley, a hamlet on the north shore of the island that served as a summer retreat for the rich and famous including such luminaries as President Roosevelt, Winston Churchill, the Duke of Windsor, and Cole Porter. The move was extremely beneficial for Matt, who attended Carle Place High School, a predominantly white school that featured zero Black administrators or teachers and only two Black students in a graduating class of more than 250.

But if the kid his classmates affectionately referred to as "Mattie" had any trouble fitting in, he either didn't talk about it or it didn't happen. He made a name for himself on the school's track and golf teams, but especially in football where he played halfback and linebacker for the Frogs, who lost only twice during his three years on the varsity squad. During an era when defense ruled the day, Snell tallied forty-eight touchdowns during his high school career while playing for longtime head coach Joe Coady. As a senior in 1959, Matt earned the Tom Thorp Award given annually to the outstanding prep player in Nassau County. Previous winners included such Pro Football Hall of Fame members as John Mackey and Jim Brown.

When it came time to select a college, Matt and his parents were suddenly caught in an avalanche of recruiters with ever-increasing promises of lavish gifts and other enticements. One particular Southwest school, facing the prospect of luring the youngster more than a thousand miles away, assured Matt that his parents would have access to a magic carpet of sorts. A Texas oil millionaire's private jet made weekly business trips to New York and back, and Matt was told it would be no problem for his parents to fly out and watch their son play every Saturday afternoon.

Another offered Isaac and Annie every household appliance that could fit into their shingle-sided house on 13th Street in Locust Valley, including a new refrigerator, stove, dishwasher, washing machine, dryer, freezer, and any other household gadget Annie desired. The Snells, used to paying their own way and doing without until they could, said no.

And then there was Woody Hayes.

"Woody knew the things the recruiters from a lot of other colleges were promising me," Matt said. "He leaned over at me across the desk in his office and said, 'You're not going to get a thing under this table. I'm not going to promise you anything I can't deliver and I'm not going to deliver anything I can't promise you.' Then he shook a finger at me. 'You know darn well that if I'm dishonest with you, I'm going to be dishonest with a lot of other kids, and you probably don't want to play ball for a guy who's going around being dishonest all over the place.' I knew then and there that I wanted to play for that man."

Snell was one of the first high-profile players recruited by Hayes from outside Ohio and its neighboring states. The Buckeyes had won only one Big Ten championship in

Matt was an all-purpose player for Woody Hayes, spending time at halfback, defensive end and fullback during his time with the Buckeyes.

the preceding four seasons, and were coming off a rare losing record in 1959. A whisper campaign had started around Columbus that indicated the seat under Hayes had become increasingly hot, and the legendary coach had begun to expand his recruiting base.

"When I got to Ohio State in 1960, Woody was under a tremendous amount of pressure," Matt remembered. "He had won a national championship a couple of years before that, but then people got to expecting that every year. The year before I got there, they had a losing season and that was just unheard of. So it was very tough playing for Woody in those days because he was really pressing."

After spending the 1960 season on the freshman squad, Snell was ready for his first taste of varsity action. But before that could happen, Hayes had one more task to ask of his highly touted New York prodigy. Knowing he had no ready replacement for quarterback Tom Matte, the legendary coach decided upon an unusual course of action.

"We had finished the season with a 7–0 win against Michigan in a lackluster game," Hayes said. "With Matte graduated, I knew we'd need a new quarterback for 1961, but I also knew that working out a player the following Monday would be a violation of NCAA rules. So, after the Horseshoe emptied, I took two freshmen onto the stadium field. Since both had been outstanding on the freshman team, I was hoping one of them would have the ability to pass. But after a little work, the answer was no in both cases. Their names were Paul Warfield and Matthew Snell."

Woody's loss at quarterback was certainly his gain at other positions. While Warfield went on to enjoy a productive career as a running back and receiver, Snell began varsity play as mostly a battering ram for senior fullback Bob Ferguson, who won first-team All-America honors in 1961 for the second year in a row after rushing for 938 yards and eleven touchdowns. Four of those scores came during a 50–20 blowout victory against archrival Michigan.

The following season, with a lack of able-bodied players on the defensive side of the ball, Snell was asked again to try his hand at a different position. This time, he proved himself to be a natural as a laser-focused defensive end and led the team in tackles for loss. He was also an occasional fill-in on offense at tight end, and caught enough passes to tie Warfield for the second-most receptions for the Buckeyes in 1962.

Switching back to his more natural position for his senior year, Matt enjoyed his most productive season, leading the team in carries, rushing yardage, and touchdowns. Following his college career, he was selected in the fourth round of the 1964 NFL draft by the New York Giants. But another local team also showed interest. The New York Jets of the upstart American Football League took him with their first-round pick.

"I was drafted by the Giants in the fourth round, but they had taken another running back (former Oklahoma All-American Joe Don Looney) in the first round," Matt said. "They also still had Frank Gifford and Alex Webster, and they wanted me to come in, sit behind them, and learn for a year or two. I didn't want to do that. I think you learn by doing, and I saw the Jets as an opportunity to play right away."

Before joining the Jets, however, Snell had a promise to keep. As the first in his family to go to college, he had promised his parents that he would finish his degree work before embarking upon a professional career.

Hayes also played a role in Snell's transition from college to the pros.

"We always had the feeling that Woody wasn't the kind who was through with you when you'd played your last game for him," Matt said. "And for the guys with pro potential, he wouldn't let an agent come near them. He let it be known that all interviews and negotiations would be conducted right in his office by a representative of the pro team. He'd run an agent off campus if he found them in those days.

"Woody would read all the print on the contracts, and he was quick to write in something he thought we should have. At the time I signed with the pros, there was no such thing as an athletic scholarship at Ohio State. We got financial aid based on our need. So if a guy signed a pro contract in the early winter of his senior year at Ohio State, it was evidence that he no longer needed financial aid and he'd have to pay his own tuition for the spring quarter. So, Woody insisted on a clause in my contract that the Jets would pick up my expenses for the last quarter of my senior year. They didn't like it, but they did it, and it was because of Woody."

Snell joined the Jets for the 1964 season and ran away with AFL Rookie of the Year honors after accumulating 1,341 yards and six touchdowns combined rushing and receiving. One year later, the team drafted a brash, young quarterback out of Alabama, and four years after that, Joe Namath would lead the Jets to victory against the Baltimore Colts in Super Bowl III and change the face of professional football forever.

"We really had no fear of Baltimore in that game," said Snell, who rushed thirty times for a game-high 121 yards while scoring the Jets' only touchdown. "Baltimore played a zone defense in the secondary that we knew we could beat. We really thought very early in the week that we were going to win that game."

In fact, Snell remembered that Namath's famous guarantee of victory stemmed from something he'd heard from a teammate earlier in the week. "We'd been watching film for a couple of days," he said with a laugh, "when (tight end) Pete Lammons stood up and told (Jets head coach) Weeb (Eubank), 'Don't show us any more of that. We're going to get overconfident. I guarantee we'll beat these guys.'

"A day later, Joe is out at some function and says the same thing. Of course, he said it in public and that's when it hit the newspapers."

Earning the Super Bowl championship ring along with making the Pro Bowl three times was the pinnacle of Snell's professional career. Unfortunately, it was a career limited to just nine seasons, including

"...but the memories are better than the hardware."
—Matt Snell

the last three that were marked by a litany of injuries. He retired after the 1972 season, and the following year became a partner for new stock issues with DEFCO Securities Inc.

That same year, he was approached by an advertising firm inquiring if he would like to cash in on his football fame. He agreed and became the first television pitchman in a long-running string of television commercials for Miller Lite beer.

Matt remained with DEFCO Securities throughout the 1970s until he got a taste of the construction business by accident. As a member of the board of directors of a construction firm that DEFCO had taken public, Snell took a particular interest in a project repairing antiquated elevators in a Harlem housing program. He enjoyed the project so much that he left DEFCO to form his own commercial construction company, SCI Construction Ltd., headquartered in Jersey City, New Jersey.

It's a long way from the football fields of Columbus and New York, but Snell doesn't waste much time reminiscing. He does, however, allow himself a look back or two on occasion. For example, after Super Bowl III when Namath was handed the MVP trophy, Matt sat on a bench in the winning locker room with a huge smile on his face. When asked about the award, he told reporters, "Joe's our leader. He deserves it."

More than forty years later, he offered only a slightly different answer. "I'm not going to lie and say it wouldn't have been nice to have that trophy sitting on my mantle all these years," Matt said, "but the memories are better than the hardware."

Then he added with a hearty laugh, "Besides, Joe was the man. I mean, he was Broadway Joe. Who else were they going to give it to?"

BILL LONG

OSU QUARTERBACK 1967–1969

24

NICKNAME: Billy

HOMETOWN: Dayton, Ohio

HEIGHT: 6 ft 1 in **WEIGHT**: 180 lb

*A*mid the postgame tumult of the visiting team's Rose Bowl locker room, Woody Hayes waded into the middle of his euphoric, sweat-soaked team and asked for quiet. Ohio State had just achieved a 27–16 victory against the University of Southern California, vanquishing the defending national champion Trojans and their Heisman Trophy-winning running back O.J. Simpson, and Woody was about to begin the time-honored tradition of awarding game balls following such an important win.

First to be recognized was John Muhlbach, the undersized senior center whose leg had been broken during the game. The locker room erupted in cheers as the coach honored Muhlbach for his sacrifice. Next came Jack Tatum, the ferocious sophomore defensive back who had hounded Simpson for much of the game, helping to hold the All-American to just 34 yards rushing in the second half after he had piled up 137 in the opening half. A loud roar erupted as Tatum, who allowed a rare smile to cross his face, lifted the ball over his head.

The ceremony seemed complete—one game ball for offense, another for defense—and players resumed their celebratory whooping and hollering. Then in a surprise move, Woody held up a third ball and called for silence. "Now,"

Bill was starting quarterback for the Buckeyes in 1966 and '67 following a stellar high school career at Dayton Stebbins.

the legendary coach announced, "I would like to give a game ball to Billy Long." The locker room hushed. "Billy was instrumental in preparing our defense to help win this game."

The senior quarterback, who had been a two-year starter before sophomore Rex Kern supplanted him and led the Buckeyes to an undefeated season and the 1968 national title, walked toward his coach in disbelief. Hayes handed Long the ball, shook his hand, and the locker room erupted once more.

As the players showered and headed off to continue the celebration, Long stayed behind for a few minutes to ponder his three seasons as quarterback of the Buckeyes. He stared down at the football in his hands before slowly rising. He then took the ball, and decided it would only be a reminder to him of what was and what could have been. He then stuffed the game ball in his locker and left it there.

William Edward Long made his way into the world June 4, 1947, in West Milton, Ohio, the only male of three children born to Robert Edward Long and his wife, the former Edna Cannell, who went by the nickname "Shorty."

First settled in 1807 and incorporated around 1834, West Milton, apparently named for the English poet John Milton—somewhat strange since Milton never traveled outside Europe during his life which ended more than a century before the United States declared its independence from Great Britain—was a tiny speck of a village with a population of fewer than 2,000, situated less than a half-hour from the center of Dayton, not unlike thousands of other post-war suburban specks dotting the map throughout the country.

What distinguished West Milton from most all of those other tiny towns was its own high school, Union High where Bob Long was an American history teacher as well as head football coach. He was also a house painter during the summer, an amateur poet who would honor his children with some sort of rhyming verse each birthday, and a World War II veteran who seldom if ever talked about his service as an Army sergeant and turret gunner.

After the war, Bob, who was a Columbus native, enrolled in Otterbein College, and while working on his degree, played quarterback for the school's football team. He was also a huge Buckeyes fan and idolized Woody Hayes.

"You could see Ohio Stadium from my grandparents' house in Columbus," Bill remembered. "When we visited, I would sit on their front porch and stare at the Horseshoe for hours, daydreaming about what it must be like to walk through its massive stone gates. But money was scarce during my childhood. I asked my dad many times if we could go to a Buckeyes game, and for years, he and my mother Shorty told me children weren't allowed in Ohio Stadium, a ruse no internet-savvy kid of today would buy for a red-hot second."

That changed when his father announced one day that Ohio State was hosting a special "Children's Day" at the stadium and that he had two tickets for the game. Young Billy Long was seven.

"When we arrived at the stadium, people were yelling and holding up programs for fans to purchase," he said. "Dad bought two and handed me my own, a memento I planned to keep for the rest of my life. As we climbed the endless stairs to C deck, I could hear the fans already cheering inside the stadium. We walked through the tunnel, revealing the deep, green football field far below. From that moment on, the Buckeyes dominated my dreams."

Bill played a variety of sports while growing up, and when he reached high school, played quarterback for his father at Milton-Union. When Bob Long became head coach at Walter E. Stebbins High School in Dayton in the fall of 1964, his son went with him. The youngster played two seasons of football, basketball and baseball for the Indians, and still found time for membership in the Lettermen's Club as well as the Art Club. The 6-foot-1, 173-pounder with the lanky frame, crewcut and bright smile was an easy choice when his senior classmates voted him "Most Athletic."

When it came time to choose a college, Bill and his father were in agreement that Ohio State was the desired destination. But the youngster had developed a desire to see what other opportunities were available, so he planned to entertain whatever major college offers came his way. Bob Long and Woody Hayes had other ideas, however.

During a recruiting trip to Ohio State, Bill and his parents took in a Buckeyes basketball game. At halftime, Woody took Bill to his office on the second floor of St. John Arena, and after several minutes, put on the hard sell. "Bill," the legendary coach said, "why don't we just get this thing over with? Commit now." The teenager mustered all of his willpower, said nothing and just smiled.

After the game, Woody took Bill and his parents to dinner at the Jai Lai restaurant, a white-table establishment on Olentangy River Road where the coach was known to hold court. Longtime *Dayton Daily News* sports editor Ritter Collett just happened to be dining at the Jai Lai at the same time, and Woody said to him, "Ritter, Bill has something to tell you."

"Like an idiot, I said I'd committed to Ohio State," Bill said. "There went the rest of my recruiting trips."

The relationship between coach and player was a tenuous one at best. During his recruiting pitch, Woody said it would be no problem for Long to play baseball as well as football. That was music to the ears of the youngster, who had made the all-state first team as a baseball player but only honorable mention on the gridiron. As many before and after soon discovered, however, the coach's promise held little weight.

> "I was the golden boy, the guy who saved the season and Woody's job. But it turns out I wasn't as golden as I thought."
> —*Bill Long*

Following his sophomore season, when Bill had been the starting quarterback for the Buckeyes, he agreed to participate in spring drills rather than play baseball. But when he returned to Dayton for the summer, he played in a recreational league and tore his right hamstring just one week before fall football practice at OSU was to begin.

When he learned of the injury, Woody refused to even talk to his starting quarterback. Bill threw himself into a furious rehab program to get ready for the 1967 season opener against Arizona. But he was less than full strength and completed only four of eighteen pass attempts while being sacked five times during a 14–7 loss in Ohio Stadium, only the third season-opening loss for Hayes in his seventeen years as head coach to that point.

Long continued to share the quarterback position with backups Gerald Ehrsam and Kevin Rusnak for the next several games, including an embarrassing 41–6 loss to Purdue, the most lopsided defeat in Woody's entire coaching career. The following week, during a particularly ugly 6–2 win on the road at Northwestern, Long was benched altogether.

With the team floundering at two wins against three losses, and the Buckeyes on the brink of extending their Big Ten championship drought to six seasons, Woody's neck was firmly on the chopping block. Aircraft began appearing over the stadium on gameday with banners calling for his firing. *The Columbus Dispatch* published angry letters from irate fans along with stories claiming that Ohio State was prepared to fire Hayes if the team lost one more game.

Knowing his coaching fate was hanging by a thread, Hayes unlocked his doghouse long enough for Long to return to the starting quarterback position and lead the Buckeyes to four consecutive victories to salvage the 1967 season. During those games, which included a 24–14 victory in Ann Arbor against archrival Michigan, Bill had thrown for 343 yards and one touchdown, and rushed for 102 yards and four scores. During the postgame press conference following the Michigan game, Woody credited his junior quarterback with the season's turnaround, telling reporters, "We were not a football team until we got Bill back in the quarterback position."

The era of good feeling wouldn't last long.

Without consulting his coach, Long skipped spring football practice to play baseball for OSU. "What did I have to worry about?" Bill said. "I was the golden boy, the guy who saved the season and Woody's job. But it turns out I wasn't as golden as I thought."

During the spring, sophomore-to-be Rex Kern dazzled the Ohio State coaches with his running, throwing and improvisational abilities, so much so that he was named the 1968 starting quarterback. Long remained Kern's backup early in the season, and even scored a crucial touchdown during a 13–0 upset of top-ranked Purdue in mid-October. But just two weeks later, when Kern was forced out of a close game at Illinois with an injury, Long prepared to enter the game when Hayes suddenly yelled out for sophomore Ron Maciejowski. While Maciejowski led a game-winning touchdown drive in the final minutes to keep the Buckeyes' perfect season intact, Long stared out from the sideline, equal parts frustrated and humiliated.

"You feel like everybody in the stadium is watching you being rejected there—from second to third team," he said. "You feel like everybody's watching, and of course your parents are watching."

Long was further humbled after the game as the team filed out of Memorial Stadium. The Buckeyes traveled on two buses to away

Awarded one of three game balls following the team's 1969 Rose Bowl win, a disgruntled Bill left the ball behind in his locker.

games—one carried the starters and the other was designated as the AYO Bus, short for "All You Others." Even though Long hadn't started that season, he was sort of grandfathered in as a two-year starter and senior and rode on the first bus. But after the game, when it was clear he was now number three on the depth chart, he couldn't bring himself to board the first bus.

"That was the most humiliating thing," he said.

Long was relegated to scout-team status for the remainder of the season, getting only token playing time here and there, including the final three plays of the Rose Bowl which entailed handing off to fellow backups. After the game, he left his game ball in his locker, leaving his Ohio State football career in the past—or so he had hoped.

After earning his degree in fine arts and then attending law school at Capital University—a letter of recommendation from Hayes helped pave the way—Long has been a published author as well as a lobbyist, first with the Ohio Council of Retail Merchants and later championing animal welfare as well as environmental issues and an advocacy of "real food," described as that which comes from local, humane, ecologically sound and fair trade sources.

But he admits the way his college career ended has hounded him for the last half-century-plus.

"As the years passed, I was never brave enough to broach the subject of the '68 season with Woody," Bill said. "He went to the grave before I could question him about my demotion. Was Kern really a better quarterback than me? Was Woody giving Kern some playing time to groom him for a later championship run, a more logical expectation, but the 'Super Sophomores' came through a year early? And why couldn't Woody talk to me about what happened? Didn't he owe it to me? After all, the old man might never have won the national title in '68 if I hadn't helped save his job the year before.

"More than fifty years since that season, I still find myself thinking about Woody. He was in my head then, and he's still there today."

JIM OTIS

OSU FULLBACK 1967–1969

35

NICKNAME: Otey

HOMETOWN: Celina, Ohio

HEIGHT: 6 ft 0 in **WEIGHT:** 214 lb

ALL-AMERICAN: 1969

NFL DRAFT: 1970, New Orleans Saints

It has been said Woody Hayes had the two best college football teams in America in 1969–his starters and his backups. The competition for playing time was fierce at nearly every position, but none more so than at fullback, perhaps the most important spot in Hayes' no-nonsense, up-the-gut, down-the-throat style of offense.

Senior Jim Otis was a two-year incumbent at the position and was coming off the national championship season of 1968 during which he had rushed for 985 yards, more than any Buckeye in any single season in program history, and earned second-team All-America honors. He had been especially effective against archrival Michigan, rushing for 143 yards and tying an OSU single-game record by scoring four touchdowns during a 50–14 routing of the Wolverines.

Behind Otis on the depth chart, but not necessarily in the eyes of the coaching staff, was junior John Brockington, a member of the Super Sophs who had shuffled between the halfback and fullback positions in 1968 and still managed to average better than four yards on each of his forty-five carries despite playing most of the season on a bad ankle.

There was no doubt going into the 1969 season that Hayes favored Otis to be his starting fullback, but there was such a groundswell of support for Brockington among members of his offensive staff that the head coach agreed to put it to a vote. Brockington won in a landslide after which the Ohio State assistants realized once again they were not living in a democracy.

"Well," Hayes said in response to the vote, "you're all wrong."

Hayes was so sure that he ignored both the advice of his assistant coaches and the potential racial implications of starting a white player over a Black one. The lone Black assistant on the OSU staff, running backs coach Rudy Hubbard, briefly wondered if the color of Brockington's skin was hampering his candidacy. But Hubbard quickly concluded that the position battle had nothing to do with race. Hayes had been aggressive about recruiting Black players—signing Hubbard himself to play for the Buckeyes in 1964—and was one of the first coaches in college football to insist upon rooming white and Black players together.

The decision to start Otis over Brockington came down to old-fashioned loyalty, stubbornness, and admiration from the old coach. Otis repaid the loyalty by becoming the Buckeyes' first-ever 1,000-yard rusher and earning team MVP as well as consensus first-team All-America honors in the process.

It was a far cry from just two years earlier when Hayes vowed during halftime of a game that Otis would never play another down at Ohio State.

Hayes was under fire in 1967. His Buckeyes were headed to a sixth straight season without a Big Ten championship, and the program seemed listless. The previous thirteen games had produced only six wins against seven defeats, and the team was headed for another loss, this time trailing 10–0 at home to a mediocre Illinois squad that had entered the game on a three-game losing streak.

Hayes stood at the locker room chalkboard, trying to collect his thoughts as he began to diagram a play. Then he caught a glimpse of Otis, who had fumbled twice in the first half, and the coach couldn't contain himself. He turned suddenly and rammed his way through two rows of huddled players, finally reaching Otis with such force that helmets, chinstraps, water bottles, and cups of Coca-Cola went flying. As the coach pounded away on his sophomore fullback, Hayes screamed that Otis would never play for Ohio State again.

It was a flash of temper the Ohio State players and coaches had seen many times, and normally there was a way to prepare for it if you made him stand on your right side. Hayes was left-handed, so when he stood on your right side, he had to take a step back to throw that left-fisted punch, and you had a chance to get out of the way. But now Otis, wedged into the third row, had nowhere to go, and at that moment, neither did the Buckeyes. Their record was about to fall to 2–3, and there were rumblings that if Hayes lost the season finale at Michigan, he would be fired. Otis thought his career was finished, and in fact he would be benched for the rest of that Illinois game and most of the two after that.

But Otis got off the pine long enough to rush for 149 yards and a touchdown during a win against Iowa in the final home game of the 1967 season, and added another 114 yards in a season-ending victory at Michigan that saved Woody's job and served as a springboard for the Buckeyes and their 1968 national championship run.

"Woody was great friends with my father, so he was very tough on me. Sometimes I thought he was too tough," Jim said. "There wasn't anything phony about him. Woody was my greatest teacher and much of my success is directly because of him. That day against Illinois when he came over three benches to get me... He got me, but just like anything else, the opportunity arose again and I used that situation as a learning moment. There's no doubt in my mind that's why I hardly ever fumbled after that, even in the pros."

If ever there was someone destined to play football for Woody Hayes at Ohio State, it was James Lloyd Otis, born April 29, 1948, in Celina, Ohio, a town with a population of fewer than six thousand people located in Mercer County about a dozen miles from the Indiana border—or as Jim once described it, "about fifteen minutes from the edge of the earth."

His grandfather, Dr. Lloyd Otis, founded Mercer County's first hospital in 1915, and the facility continued operations under the direction of Jim's father until 1977. Medicine was a family business for Dr. James J. Otis and his wife, Betty, the former Elizabeth May Hamel, who was a registered nurse. But athletics had always been a close second for the man everyone called Dr. Jim, who at one time was the oldest practicing physician in Ohio at the age of ninety-three.

Although he received his medical degree from the University of Cincinnati, Dr. Jim did his undergraduate work at Denison University, where he roomed with a strong-willed, barrel-chested kid from the other side of Ohio. His name was Wayne Woodrow Hayes, but everyone called him Woody.

"Woody used to box," Jim said, "and Dad used to announce him and be his cut man in the corner." But the relationship went a lot deeper than that. In addition to being roommates, the two men were also Sigma Chi fraternity brothers. They spent hours and hours in deep conversation, the future physician marveling about the cutting-edge medicine of the day while the future College Football Hall of Fame coach reveled in strategic military history. Despite pursing widely divergent careers after leaving Denison, the men remained close friends. And when Dr. Jim happily announced the birth of his son, he almost immediately began telling Woody what a thrill it would be if the boy could play for his old college roommate someday.

"Almost from the time Jim was born, Dr. Jim kept insisting he was going to be a great football player," Woody said. "As a small youngster, when I saw him run, it was obvious he had great coordination."

When Jim was just seven, he and his father took in a game at Ohio Stadium after which Woody arranged for the youngster to get his picture taken with Howard "Hopalong" Cassady, the Ohio State star who won the Heisman Trophy in 1955. By that time, little Jim had already been playing football for a few years. "I didn't start until I was about four, so I was late there in the community," he said with a laugh. Eventually, his parents groomed their backyard into a football field, even installing goal posts so Jim and his buddies could play realistic pickup games.

At Celina High School, Jim was the classic overachiever. His outgoing personality led to joining the school choir as well as the Thespians Club, and he also found time for membership in other organizations such as American Field Service and Future Teachers of America. But it was in athletics where he really flourished, playing basketball, running track, and earning Western Buckeye League Back of the Year honors on the football field.

During his senior year with the Bulldogs, he rushed for 1,680 yards and scored twenty-four touchdowns in just ten games. He finished his career with 95 yards and his team's only touchdown in a 6–6 tie with Van Wert, the only blemish in a 9–0–1 record for head coach Norm Decker's team.

Once Jim finished high school, he fully intended to follow through

Jim was the leading rusher for the 1968 national champions, and a year later became Ohio State's first member of the 1,000-yard club.

on his long-held ambition to play his college ball at Ohio State. But his future coach wasn't so sure that was a good idea.

"As his college career approached, I became hesitant about his coming to Ohio State because of my close personal relationship with his family," Woody said. "In fairness to him, I told him I thought we were getting another fullback who was bigger and perhaps a little better than he was. His answer to that was, 'We'll find out if he's better.' That attitude typifies Jim, for he was a truly great competitor."

Otis spent the fall of 1966 on the OSU freshman squad and made enough of an impression that he was penciled in as the starter at fullback in 1967. He wound up sharing the position early in the season with classmate Paul Huff, the other fullback Woody had mentioned during the recruiting process. But once Jim broke out with

92 yards and a touchdown during a week two shutout of Oregon, he had the position mostly to himself. That is, until the two fumbles in the first half against Illinois.

Everything came together for the Buckeyes in 1968 when an offense spearheaded by Otis and his new roommate, sophomore quarterback Rex Kern, teamed with a ferocious defense led by Jim Stillwagon and Jack Tatum to lead Ohio State to an undefeated season. Otis was at his best in the biggest games that year. He carried twenty-nine times for 144 yards during a revenge victory against Purdue, punished Michigan for 143 yards and four scores in thirty-five attempts, and then carried thirty more times for 101 yards and a touchdown in the Rose Bowl against the University of Southern California, a 27–16 win that put the finishing touches on that national championship season.

The following year, the Buckeyes seemingly never missed a beat. They ran roughshod over their first eight opponents, outscoring them by the lopsided margin of 371–69, and needed only to vanquish a two-loss Michigan squad to lay claim to a second national title in a row. But under first-year head coach Bo Schembechler, the upstart Wolverines forced the Buckeyes into committing seven turnovers and won a 24–12 decision in one of the biggest upsets in the storied rivalry's history.

"That still bothers me to this day," said Jim, who rushed for 144 yards and a touchdown on twenty-eight flawless carries. "It was Woody Hayes Football 101: You can't turn the ball over. You can't make mental errors. That game was a great illustration of that. We could have all had Superman outfits on and gone up there and there's no way we could have won that game with the mistakes we made. Our problem as seniors was that we never got a chance for redemption. That was our last game, and boy it's left a sour taste ever since."

At barely six feet tall and 220 pounds, Otis was a bit of a mystery to professional teams who didn't quite know how to use him. The New Orleans Saints, still in their infancy and more than fifteen years away from their first winning season, waited until the ninth round of the

1970 NFL draft to select Otis, and then used him only sparingly. The same was true for the Kansas City Chiefs, who traded for the fullback just before the beginning of the 1971 season.

Not until the St. Louis Cardinals picked him up on waivers in September 1973 did his pro career begin to flourish. He rushed for a career-high 664 yards in 1974 and then led the NFC with 1,076 yards in 1975 and earned his only Pro Bowl nomination in the process. He played with the Cardinals through the 1978 season, and finished a nine-year NFL career with 4,350 yards and 19 touchdowns on the ground and another 549 yards and three TDs on 90 pass receptions.

After retiring from the game, Otis put his Ohio State degree in business administration, finance, and marketing to use, and opened his own real estate firm. He remains owner-partner of Otis & Clark Properties, one of the oldest real estate brokerage services in St. Louis. He also got back into football during the mid-1990s serving two years as general manager of the St. Louis Stampede of the Arena Football League.

In addition, he and wife Jan have three daughters and one son, each of whom is either in the medical or real estate/financial fields. That includes Jim Jr., who was a backup quarterback on the 2002 Ohio State national championship team and now works for his father's company.

It's been a rich, rewarding life for Jim Otis with just one regret that has nagged him since 1969.

"And it still lingers," Jim admits. "That loss to Michigan still bothers me. But maybe what bothers me more is listening to those Michigan guys talk about how they really took it to us. Let me tell you something: I'm over 70 and I could still play against them. I could get out there right now and run over their asses."

MIKE SENSIBAUGH

OSU SAFETY, PUNTER 1968–1970

3

NICKNAME: Baugh

HOMETOWN: Cincinnati, Ohio

HEIGHT: 6 ft 0 in **WEIGHT**: 190 lb

ALL-AMERICAN: 1970

NFL DRAFT: 1971, Kansas City Chiefs

From all accounts, Mike Sensibaugh had an idyllic childhood. He was the second of six children born to a minister and his wife, grew up in a small-town suburb with plenty of activities to keep him occupied, and never knew a day when either his stomach or heart wasn't full.

> "Going out in Ohio Stadium in front of 80,000 people? No pressure at all. Sitting in the front row at church? That was killer. That was pressure."
>
> —*Mike Sensibaugh*

It was the kind of loving, nurturing upbringing about which some children can only dream. And yet, young Mike couldn't wait to make his escape.

"Going out in Ohio Stadium in front of 80,000 people? No pressure at all," he once said. "Sitting in the front row at church? That was killer. That was pressure. Going out on the field was easy compared to what I had to live up to as a preacher's kid. Maybe that was more in my head than anything else."

James Michael Sensibaugh was born January 3, 1949, in Lockland, Ohio, a northern suburb of Cincinnati so named because of its proximity to the first set of lock gates on the Miami and Erie Canal, the first water route created between the Ohio River and Lake Erie.

Lockland was a typical small town in the 1950s with its mom-and-pop hardware stores, groceries, bakeries, and auto repair shops each located within walking distance from one another. There was also an abundance of churches, perhaps none more prominent than the Lockland Christian Church, a brick and mortar structure located in the heart of town at the corner of Mill Street and Patterson Avenue. With its arched stained glass windows and classic Corinthian columns greeting worshippers as they enter through gleaming white doors, the church was founded in 1933 with only eight men identified as serving as ministers of the congregation.

One of those was Hugh Sensibaugh, who came to Lockland in 1939 and served as minister of the church for more than forty-five years. Hugh and his wife, Lois Elizabeth Rose Ledbetter, a pretty, fun-loving woman everyone knew as "Betty," moved into the church parsonage and began trying to raise a family. Unfortunately for the couple, their firstborn child, Sandra, died just nine weeks following her birth in 1945. But a year later, Hugh and Betty welcomed daughter Sybil. Three years after that, Mike became the first of four boys, and he was followed by David, Rod (who picked up the childhood nickname of "Socko"), and Dan.

As the eldest of four boys, Mike was the self-professed protector of his younger brothers but picked up the importance of keeping a level head early. He mentioned later in life that "turning the other cheek" was not only a Bible passage but one of the hard-and-fast mottos in the Sensibaugh household.

Somewhat undersized at five-eleven and somewhere south of 180 pounds, Mike nevertheless was a star on his high school basketball and football teams. On the gridiron, he was known for his hard-nosed tackling on defense and his speed and agility on offense. He earned All-Ohio honors as a quarterback, and once scored touchdowns of eighty, forty, and fifty yards in the first quarter of the same game.

Mike had grown up a fan of Ohio State, but when it came time to choose a university, he entertained offers from such faraway places as Florida, Georgia Tech, and Maryland. He even considered Michigan, among several other schools, but always insisted that was no reflection on his feelings toward the Buckeye State's flagship university.

"I don't think I ever was not interested in Ohio State," he said. "I was a preacher's kid, and every place I visited seemed distant. But that was the way I wanted it. I think at the time I was just trying to get as far away as possible."

Only when one of his high school coaches explained that, at 100 miles away, Columbus was "far enough away to be away" did Sensibaugh finally join Ohio State's recruiting class of 1967, one of the most star-studded rosters in program history. But when he arrived on campus, he sized up his competition at the quarterback position. With Rex Kern and Ron Maciejowski also in his class, Mike figured he would be just as happy on the other side of the ball.

"I never came off the field in high school unless I was hurt," he said. "I wasn't that good—we just didn't have that many players, so I had played defense just as much as I had played offense. When I looked at what was there and what was going to be available when we became sophomores, instead of having those guys mess around, I just grabbed (the safety) spot on defense."

Kern would go on to win the starting role at quarterback while Maciejowski played extensively in several games. Meanwhile, Sensibaugh wound up a three-year starter as the last line of defense.

"When we started out as freshmen, Baugh, Mace, and I would take turns taking snaps," Kern said. "Two of us would take the snaps in practice, and on that particular day, the third guy would play defense. Well, one day Baugh went over to play defense and we never saw him again."

Sensibaugh went on to win All-Big Ten honors during his junior and senior seasons, and was named first-team All-America in 1970. He had at least one interception in eighteen of the twenty-nine games in which he played at Ohio State, at one time stringing together seven straight games with at least one pick.

"I'm proud of the (career interception) record," he said in 1993. "To be honest, though, I wasn't sure I was ever going to get much of a chance to play at Ohio State, much less come away with all those interceptions. I was a true safety. They never let me cover anybody because I couldn't cover anybody."

Several years after his career had ended, Sensibaugh admitted he didn't think he would make much of an impact at Ohio State.

The opening game of the 1968 season resulted in a 35–14 victory against Southern Methodist University, a game in which the Mustangs threw the ball 76 times, still a single-game record for an Ohio State opponent. The Buckeyes picked off five of those passes—including Sensibaugh's first career pick on SMU's initial possession—

but the performance evidently didn't win any points with the defensive backs coach at the time.

"There were five defensive backs (in the rotation), and our defensive backs coach, Lou Holtz, used us against each other," Mike remembered. "After our first game, he said he couldn't find me on film, so he benched me. Later in the year, in the Iowa and Michigan games, I wasn't used as a starter, either. I don't think Holtz liked me. So, going into the Rose Bowl, I wasn't sure if I would get to play that much."

Sensibaugh not only started the Rose Bowl against defending national champion USC, he was one of the defensive stars for the Buckeyes. In addition to stopping Heisman Trophy winner O.J. Simpson twice at the goal line in the second quarter, solo tackles that led to the Trojans being forced to settle for an early field goal, Sensibaugh grabbed a fourth-quarter interception and returned it 22 yards. He also punted seven times for 319 yards, and Ohio State clinched the national championship with a convincing 27–16 victory. The 319 punting yards set a program bowl record that stood until Brent Bartholomew broke it with 337 yards in the 1996 Citrus Bowl loss to Tennessee.

Sensibaugh might have underplayed his own talent, but opponents who underestimated him did so at their own peril. From that safety position, he was equally responsible for run support and pass coverage, and seemed to excel at both.

"He was a great play diagnostician and a devastating tackler," Woody Hayes said. "He was particularly adept at studying backfield actions and the movements of the quarterback. Because of that, he was rarely fooled on a run-pass situation."

After his college career, Sensibaugh was an eighth-round selection of the Chiefs in the 1971 NFL draft. He played seven games as a backup during his rookie season, and then moved into the starting lineup in 1972 and led the AFC with eight interceptions. He played five seasons in Kansas City before being traded to St. Louis, where he joined former OSU teammate Jim Otis as a member of the Cardinals. Although he never made a Pro Bowl, Sensibaugh was one of the league's top ballhawks, finishing his career with twenty-seven interceptions (two of which he returned for touchdowns) and twelve fumble recoveries.

In addition to his playing prowess, Sensibaugh had an outgoing personality and a wit to match.

"I just used to laugh at the mere mention of his name," Kern said. "We used to have a locker next to one another, and that son of a gun…he would steal my clothes. Defensive practices would always be over before the offense, and by the time I got back to the locker room, all my clothes were gone. Baugh would take them and hide them. One time, I never did get them back. For all I know, he might have sold them."

Making an extra buck was a common theme for Sensibaugh.

"There was a time when he came to me and asked if I would sign a helmet for some guy," Kern said. "Baugh tells me, 'If you sign it, I think I can get $100 and then I'll split it with you. Well, of course, I don't know what would have happened if we had gotten caught, but anyway, we got the helmet out of the locker room somehow and I signed it.

"Sometime later, a guy comes up to me after a game and says, 'I really appreciate you signing that helmet for me, and I just wanted you to know that I would have paid $350 for it instead of just $250.' I thought, 'Hey, wait a minute. I think I got fleeced.' Of course, when I went back to Baugh about it, he swore the guy was lying. Of course, he had a big smile on his face at the time."

After his football career was over, Sensibaugh settled in the St. Louis area where he owned his own construction business specializing in the installation of swimming pools. In later years, he reportedly battled dementia before suffering a massive heart attack in March 2021. He died at the age of seventy-two, leaving behind a rich legacy of humor and humility.

"Baugh was a guy who would do anything for you—on the field or off the field," Kern said. "I know he had been struggling the last few years, but he never lost his sense of humor. And that's how I'll always remember him. He was a fun-loving guy who was a great teammate, a great friend, and a great family man. I'm sure going to miss him."

RANDY GRADISHAR

OSU LINEBACKER 1971–1973

NICKNAME: Grad

HOMETOWN: Champion, Ohio

HEIGHT: 6 ft 3 in **WEIGHT**: 236 lb

ALL-AMERICAN: 1972, 1973

NFL DRAFT: 1974, Denver Broncos

53

From Ike Kelley, Tom Cousineau, and Pepper Johnson to Marcus Marek, Chris Spielman, and Steve Tovar right through to Andy Katzenmoyer, A.J. Hawk, and James Laurinaitis, Ohio State has produced more than its share of outstanding linebackers, and to single out just one as the greatest the Buckeyes have ever produced at the position would seem an impossible task. That is, unless you never bore witness to the grace, precision, intelligence, and brilliance of Randy Gradishar.

"When I think of Randy Gradishar," former OSU defensive coordinator and longtime NFL coach George Hill once said, "two words come to mind: especially gifted. He had every ingredient needed for greatness—desire, intelligence, quickness, and strength—and he knew how to use all of them. Randy, quite simply, had generational talent. By that I mean his kind comes around only once every generation."

Joe Collier, architect of the Orange Crush Defense for the NFL's Denver Broncos, said he often marveled at how Gradishar was money in the bank during short-yardage situations. "He was unbelievable in short yardage, there's no question about it," said Collier, a professional coach whose career spanned four decades. "We were the best short-yardage goal-line team for all the years that he played, and he was the main reason."

Woody Hayes perhaps put it best: "If there's a linebacker better than Randy Gradishar, I haven't seen him. He's the best linebacker I ever coached."

High praise indeed for the self-described "all-nothing" prospect from a tiny village in northeastern Ohio who overcame a lack of confidence to become a two-time All-American, two-time All-Pro, and the NFL's all-time leader in tackles by the time he retired in 1983.

Randolph Charles Gradishar was born March 3, 1952, the third of three sons to Frank James "Jim" Gradishar and the former Anna Marie Hrusovsky in Warren, the northeastern Ohio town that has produced such divergent personalities as Fox News Channel chairman Roger Ailes, Nirvana drummer and Foo Fighters frontman Dave Grohl, and Daisy Duke herself, actress

Catherine Bach from *The Dukes of Hazzard* television series.

Warren has also been fertile ground for athletes, supplying Ohio State over the years with the likes of Paul Warfield, Van Ness Decree, Aaron Brown, Korey Stringer, and Doug Datish, each of whom were well-decorated Buckeyes during their college careers.

But while Warren claims Gradishar as a native son, Randy actually grew up just six miles to the northwest in the aptly named village of Champion. There, his Colorado-born father of Slavic descent operated a grocery store, the kind of friendly neighborhood gathering place where a freshly cut steak cost less than a dollar a pound and the conversation was free of charge.

Much of that conversation during the late 1960s centered around Jim Gradishar's youngest son, who was tearing up the football fields and basketball courts in and around Champion. Already 6-foot-3 and well north of 200 pounds by the time he was a senior in high school, Randy's athleticism and aggressive sideline-to-sideline and baseline-to-baseline mentality served him well. Despite the fact he hadn't started playing football until he was a high school freshman, and thought basketball was his better sport, Randy was named football team MVP in consecutive years and earned all-county honors as a senior. But because Champion played at a Class AA designation, and often struggled against competition from larger schools, high-profile coaches often stopped at the Warren city limits without venturing the extra fifteen minutes north to Champion.

Since the news of Randy's exploits had made its way to Columbus, whatever the level of competition didn't stop Woody Hayes from finding his way to Champion. The legendary coach got in his car and made the three-hour trip to Randy's high school. Except that Randy wasn't there. He was working at his father's grocery store when the telephone rang. It was the high school principal telling him to come back because Woody Hayes wanted to see him.

"Woody Hayes?" Randy recalled thinking. "To see me? I thought my buddies were playing a major prank on me."

Randy hastily drove the few blocks to the high school where he met the legendary coach, shook his hand, and then sat down to begin what he thought would be a lengthy sales pitch about the Ohio State football program. But after only a couple of minutes, Woody suggested a trip back to the grocery store.

"When we got there, my dad was behind the meat counter, slicing meat," Randy said. "Woody joined him and they stood there for about forty-five minutes behind the meat slicer, talking about World War II. My dad had been in the Army and had fought in the South Pacific. Well, you know Woody was a historian and a war buff, and knew everything about World War II. They hit it off right away. You could say the recruitment of Randy Gradishar was under way."

It wasn't much of a recruitment. Although he politely entertained offers from other schools, Randy never wavered from his affinity for Hayes and his program, and found himself checking into his Ohio State dormitory and reporting for his first practice in August 1970. That's when reality hit.

"I saw all these all-staters and All-Americans, and I was all-nothing," he said. "I thought, 'What in the world am I doing here?' Rex Kern and Jack Tatum were seniors and part of a national championship team, and here I was a freshman going up against them in practice. One time in practice, we called a blitz and I broke free and was just about to tackle Rex when all of a sudden John Brockington came out of nowhere. He hit me so hard I thought he broke my sternum. But I healed, and I figured out I could play with those guys. It was something of a turning point for me."

Manning a defensive back position, Gradishar helped the freshman Buckeyes team to victories against Indiana and Ohio University, and then prepared to join the varsity squad as a sophomore. By the time he was a senior, he had filled out to a muscular 236 pounds and was a defensive terror throughout the Big Ten. Randy earned his third consecutive first-team All-Big Ten honor, was named to the All-America first team for the second year in a row, and finished sixth in the voting for the Heisman Trophy. It was the highest Heisman finish for a true linebacker in more than a decade, and no linebacker would finish higher than sixth in the balloting for another thirteen years.

During Gradishar's three years with the Buckeyes, all as a starter, the team compiled a 25–6–1 record, captured two Big Ten championships, and won the 1974 Rose Bowl to complete a 10–0–1 season that included four shutouts and only 64 points allowed by the defense. In that Rose Bowl, a convincing 42–21 win against a University of Southern California team featuring such All-America players as offensive tackle Booker Brown, running back Anthony Davis, and wide receiver Lynn Swann, Randy was credited with 10 tackles to push his career total to 320, then the most in program history.

After graduating from Ohio State with a degree in education, Randy was selected in the first round of the 1974 NFL draft with the fourteenth overall pick by the Denver Broncos. Playing in defensive coordinator Joe Collier's 3–4 alignment, nicknamed the Orange Crush Defense, Gradishar was one of the NFL's most reliable linebackers over the next decade. He made first-team All-Pro twice and was invited to play in seven Pro Bowls during a ball-hawking career that included 20 interceptions, three of which were returned for touchdowns, and 13 fumble recoveries.

But where he excelled was at the point of attack. There is no way to describe Gradishar other than as a tackling machine with 2,049 stops (including assists) during his ten-year career. He also never missed a game, suiting up for 145 consecutive contests during the regular season—151 if you include the postseason. And when he finally sat down, he was one of only ten linebackers in NFL history with at least 20 interceptions, 10 or more fumble recoveries, and at least seven Pro Bowl appearances.

The other nine are Dick Butkus, Ray Lewis, Joe Schmidt, Jack Lambert, Brian Urlacher, Willie Lanier, Ted Hendricks, Jack Ham, and Chuck Bednarik. Each is in the Pro Football Hall of Fame. Six were first-ballot Hall of Famers, and the three others were named within the first two years of eligibility.

And then there's Randy Gradishar. Since his retirement following the 1984 season, he has been nominated for enshrinement several times, but has made the list of 10 finalists only once. He thought his time had come in 2020 when the Hall of Fame announced it would induct a special Centennial Seniors Class as part of the NFL's 100th birthday celebration. But as Randy and his wife Beth watched as the ten Centennial Class members were announced on national television, Randy's name was not among them.

"To be honest," Gradishar said, "we were both visibly upset. There were tears coming down. Tears from being discouraged and frustrated, just the natural human emotion of being disappointed, from being a modern-day finalist two different times and not hearing your name, from now being a senior candidate..."

Being immortalized with a bronze bust in Canton—just about fifty miles from his hometown—would mean the world to Gradishar. But he keeps busy with a variety of activities. He was president of the Denver Broncos Youth Foundation from 1982–92, and serves as the president of the Phil Long Community Fund, a non-profit organization in the Denver area that works to develop leadership skills and self-esteem in young people through education, sports, and recreation. He is also the longtime director of corporate communications at Phil Long Dealerships in Colorado, and a volunteer at the Mount Carmel Veterans Service Center in Colorado Springs that provides aid to veterans and their families with everything from transitional services to wellness behavioral programs.

It's a full and rewarding life for Gradishar as he passes his milestone seventieth birthday. But he knows there is one chapter left unfinished.

"It's very difficult, very discouraging, and very hard to accept when the Hall of Fame announcement comes and you don't hear your name," Randy said. "But tomorrow's coming. And I believe my day to join the Hall of Fame is also coming. I've passed by the Hall many times in my car, but the only time I've ever been inside is when John Elway was inducted in the summer of 2004. But I believe I will go in some day. It's all in the Lord's timing."

BRIAN BASCHNAGEL

OSU WINGBACK 1972–1975

NICKNAME: Bash

HOMETOWN: Wexford, Pennsylvania

HEIGHT: 6 ft 0 in **WEIGHT**: 192 lb

NFL DRAFT: 1976, Chicago Bears

48

Cornelius Greene arrived on the Ohio State campus in the late summer of 1972 with all the cocksure brashness of an eighteen-year-old who had the world by the tail. Greene came to Columbus from the Washington, D.C., projects intent upon becoming the first Black starting quarterback the Buckeyes had ever had.

"They said Ohio State had never had a Black quarterback or a Black middle linebacker because those positions were supposed to be for the smartest players," Greene said. "But to me, that was just an old stereotype. Plus, I was cocky enough that I wanted to do whatever other people told me I couldn't. I wanted to show them that I could."

When he finally stepped on campus, however, the flamboyant, full-of-brass youngster got a healthy dose of reality shoved down his throat. His roommate was supposed to be fellow freshman Woodrow Roach, another Black player the Buckeyes had recruited out of the D.C. area. But after his first day of summer practice, he returned to his dorm room at Stradley Hall to find Brian Baschnagel, a white kid from the Pittsburgh suburbs, unpacking his bags. Woody Hayes was already testing his freshman quarterback's mettle. If Corny was going to be the first Black starter at his position in program history, he had better learn how to relate to his white teammates.

Somehow, the Black kid from the projects and the white guy who had lived a sort of nomadic childhood hit it off when they discovered they had more in common than they thought.

"I was just worried about making the team and maintaining a starting position, and to me, Corny was in the same boat as I was," said Baschnagel, whose crop top of jet-black hair and quintessentially-Seventies mustache was a sharp contrast to his roommate's towering Afro hairstyle. "There were a lot of athletes out there, Black and white, who were fighting for security on the team, trying to get some playing time on the field. The reality, at least for me personally, was that I was oblivious to the color."

Cornelius agreed, adding, "I'd never been around white people, but Brian and I ended up as best friends.

We did everything as brothers, and he taught me a lot. We covered for each other and shared our backgrounds, and the whole experience made me a better person."

The ability to fit in seamlessly, regardless of the situation, location or people with which he was confronted, and get the job done without fanfare was what made Baschnagel the quintessential "glue guy" that every team needs to realize championship aspirations.

"I showed up at Ohio State as a pretty highly recruited running back, and then I see a kid named Archie Griffin running with the football," Brian said. "Then there's Corny Greene at quarterback and Champ Henson at fullback. It didn't take me very long to realize I wasn't going to get many carries. So, I did what I always did. I improvised."

Brian Dale Baschnagel specialized in improvisation almost from the time he was born January 8, 1954, in Kingston, New York. His father, Arthur C. Baschnagel Jr., was a staff sergeant in the U.S. Air Force when he met pretty Dorothy Cox, nearly two years his senior, while stationed in England. Arthur was transferred back stateside, and Dorothy soon followed, sailing alone across the Atlantic Ocean aboard the Queen Mary to begin a life with Arthur, a life that would eventually include one daughter and three sons.

Brian was the middle of the three boys, but by the time he came along, his father was already a troubleshooter of sorts for the F.W. Woolworth Company, the famous five-and-dime retailer that grew from one family-owned store in upstate New York to nearly six hundred locations nationwide. Arthur's particular expertise within the company was to take over management of a flagging store, return it to profitability and then move on. Over the course of his career, Arthur Baschnagel uprooted his family more than a dozen times, making it especially difficult for his children to maintain any sort of routine in their daily lives.

As a result, Brian threw himself into academics and athletics. "That was my way of fitting in," he said. "All that moving taught me to adapt."

The family stayed put in the Pittsburgh area long enough for Brian to attend high school for three years in the northern suburb of Wexford. Located only about fifteen miles from downtown Pittsburgh, Wexford with its thriving businesses, multitude of churches and mainly upper-middle class population seemed a world away from the smoking, belching foundries and smelting factories of the Steel City.

Brian was barely six feet tall and 180 pounds, but that didn't stop him from becoming a star athlete at North Allegheny Senior High School. Blessed with sprinter's speed, he captained the Tigers track team as well as the football squad, earning all-state honors despite his lack of size. During his senior year, he became the first player in Western Pennsylvania Interscholastic Athletic League history to rush for more than 400 yards in a single game. Dismissed as a fluke against inferior competition, Baschnagel repeated the effort a few weeks later, rushing for 432 yards to establish a single-game league record that would stand for the next seventeen years.

When it came time to decide upon a college, he had already made up his mind.

"I am Catholic and I adored Notre Dame," Brian said. "I was going to go there, but I also wanted to visit some other schools just to be fair to myself."

As the recruiting process neared its final stages, and Brian had narrowed his choices to Notre Dame, Penn State and Ohio State, the Buckeyes were nearly eliminated. Assistant coach Earle Bruce, Bachnagel's primary contact throughout his recruitment, accepted the head coaching position at the University of Tampa.

"Coach Bruce called me, and I was really confused because I thought he was going to try to recruit me to Tampa," Brian remembered. "Instead, he said, 'Look, I don't know where you want to go, but I am stepping out of the recruiting process for obvious reasons. I want you to know this: I can honestly tell you Ohio State is the best place for you.' That really impressed me."

Baschnagel joined an impressive freshman class that not only contained Greene, a future Big Ten MVP, and two-time Heisman Trophy winner Griffin, but included such future All-Americans as safety Tim

Fox and offensive guard Ted Smith. Sizing up his considerable competition, Brian eagerly agreed to move from running back to wingback, a hybrid position in which his talents as a running back and wide receiver would be utilized. But his team-first mentality reached its limits early during his freshman year in 1972.

Following a lackluster season-opening win against Big Ten foe Iowa, the Ohio State running attack was stuck in first gear in a week two matchup versus North Carolina. With his team trailing by an early 7–0 deficit, and desperately searching for any kind of spark, Hayes called for Griffin midway through the first quarter. The freshman from Eastmoor High School on the east side of Columbus exploded for 239 yards and a touchdown, leading the Buckeyes to a 29–14 victory.

It was the beginning of an impressive career for Griffin, one that would include establishing the still-standing program career rushing record, three All-America honors and unprecedented back-to-back Heisman Trophy wins. Less than impressed, however, was Baschnagel. In fact, he was downright angry.

"I didn't know where that left me," he said. "I came to hate Archie over the next few days. Then when he didn't practice that Monday because of all his bumps and bruises, I wondered what kind of character Archie had. For those few days, I was thinking about transferring and I was thinking about quitting."

He might have followed through, too, until Griffin approached him one day, looked him in the eye and said, "Look, you are from Pittsburgh and I am from Columbus. If it were the other way around, they would have asked you to go in the game Saturday and you would have done the same thing."

"I wanted to hug him right there," Brian said. "That taught me a lot. I decided on the spot that I would be proud to play behind Archie Griffin for four years. From that beginning, we grew really close. I wasn't going anywhere. I still get chills every time I think of Archie's words to me."

Over the next four years, the Buckeyes combined one of college football's most lethal offensive attacks with a stingy defense to compile a 40–5–1 record, capture four consecutive Big Ten championships and make a record four straight Rose Bowl appearances. During that time, Baschnagel enjoyed a host of signature moments, including a key catch during his senior year against Michigan.

Trailing 14–7 in the fourth quarter, Ohio State was faced with a third down and ten yards to go on its own twenty-yard line. A perfect season and a chance for the national championship hung in the balance as Greene took a knee in the huddle. But instead of calling a play, the quarterback asked his teammates to hold hands and join him in a short prayer.

Brian was an integral member of teams that won four straight Big Ten titles and made a record four consecutive Rose Bowl trips.

"My first thought," Baschnagel said, "was, 'Corny, you can't ask God to get us a completion here.' But then I realized he wasn't praying for that. The prayer was more about giving us the strength with whatever happened after the play and the game."

He ran a comeback route along the Michigan sideline, and as he turned around, the ball was already on its way. "It was perfectly thrown—close to the sideline where only I could get it," he said. "I caught the ball and then got immediately hit."

Baschnagel held on for a gain of seventeen yards, a first down, and sustained life for the Buckeyes. Eight plays later, they scored the tying touchdown, and when a few minutes later Archie's younger brother Ray intercepted a Michigan pass to set up the game-winning touchdown, Ohio State had a 21–14 victory and only the sixth unblemished regular season record in program history.

The crucial third-down reception was the only catch of the day for Baschnagel, who finished his college career with 56 catches for 794 yards and four touchdowns, 86 carries for 652 yards and six touchdowns, thirty-one punt returns for 167 yards, and 19 kickoff returns for 406 yards. That computes to a tidy 10.5 yards every time he touched the ball as a Buckeye.

"I have never met a finer person and have never coached a more willing athlete," Hayes once said of Baschnagel. "You knew that he was going to produce whenever he got the football in his hands. My only regret is that we didn't get him the football more than we did."

Never recognized by the league for his on-the-field accomplishments, Baschnagel was twice named to the Academic All-America first team, the first Ohio State player and still one of only four in program history to be so honored. He was also a National Football Foundation and College Football Hall of Fame Scholarship winner, given to only a handful of seniors each year, and served as a team captain in 1975.

The following spring, the Chicago Bears made Brian their third-round selection in the 1976 NFL draft, and he settled into another Swiss Army knife role on a team that featured the legendary Walter Payton at running back. Baschnagel played nine seasons as a wide receiver and kick returner in Chicago, including the team's run to the Super Bowl in 1985. Unfortunately, he missed the entire season on the injured reserve list after injuring a knee during training camp. But true to his anything-to-help nature, Brian continued to travel with the team, assisted the coaching staff from a booth in the press box, and helped in practice after recovering from his injury. For his efforts, his teammates voted him a full share of their Super Bowl bonus money and he received a championship ring to go with it.

Baschnagel officially retired after that 1985 season and settled with his wife Mindy and their three children in the northwestern Chicago suburb of Glenview, where he went into private business with North American Corporation, a commercial distributor and supply company, eventually becoming vice president of corporate sales for the company.

In recent years, Baschnagel battled a mysterious illness that caused dizziness and affected his speech. After more than three years of myriad tests, doctors ruled out Parkinson's disease and amyotrophic lateral sclerosis (ALS), better known as Lou Gehrig's disease. Mentally, he remained sharp, and all MRIs returned negative for deterioration of the brain's cerebellum, so it wasn't chronic traumatic encephalopathy (CTE), either.

An electromyography procedure finally determined that his chronic back pain was contributing to his struggles with balance. He is back to working out an hour a day on a stationary bike and enjoys such mundane house chores as mowing the lawn.

"I keep thinking of Lou Gehrig, and his comment when talking in Yankee Stadium about how he was the luckiest man on earth," Brian said. "I feel that way. I've lived a very good life and consider myself to be very fortunate. The lollipops have always outweighed the negatives."

PETE JOHNSON

OSU FULLBACK 1973–1976

33

NICKNAME: Big Pete

HOMETOWN: Fort Valley, Georgia

HEIGHT: 6 ft 1 in WEIGHT: 246 lb

NFL DRAFT: 1977, Cincinnati Bengals

ROSE BOWL HALL OF FAME: 2007

Unlike the steam-snorting, stampeding bull of a fullback he turned out to be, Pete Johnson tried to avoid most of the obstacles he met during the first part of his life. Born to a thirteen-year-old mother in the Jim Crow South, he was reared by his great-grandparents and changed his name for obscure reasons. He always had a round face and a rounder body, but had to be recruited out of the band to play football. Once on the gridiron, his appearance and ability further underscored his contradictions.

Despite weighing upwards of 250 pounds, he could cover 100 yards in less than ten seconds. He could easily dunk a basketball although he stood only an inch higher than six feet. He ran the football with authority and blocked with explosiveness. He did everything that his coaches asked of him, but no more. An acquaintance once remarked that Johnson's idea of punctuality was to arrive within forty-eight hours of the appointed time. Some thought him crass, others immature, and still others believed he just didn't give a damn.

Nothing could have been further from the truth, however. "You put up a ladder and say, 'No one can climb that ladder,' I'll do it," Pete claims. "You make it a little taller and say no one can do it, I'm going to do it. It's not that I was lazy. I was just doing the best I had to do."

By the time he reached Ohio State, that just-enough-to-get-by attitude had come with him. He seemed the natural choice to step in as a freshman when the starting fullback was injured, but a mixture of homesickness and sulking over his place on the depth chart led to what could only be described as lackluster practice efforts. Woody Hayes determined Pete was loafing, an assessment with which the youngster had gotten painfully accustomed.

"I guess it was like the same thing all my coaches thought of me," he said. "They didn't think I applied myself. I think it took Woody the longest to know that I was just being me."

It took two full seasons before the legendary coach finally realized Pete Johnson just being Pete Johnson was the missing ingredient his team needed. Teaming the battering ram of a fullback with the grace of two-time Heisman Trophy winner Archie Griffin at tailback, the elusiveness of Brian Baschnagel at wingback, and the flamboyant flashiness of Cornelius Greene at quarterback, Ohio State won all eleven regular-season games in 1975, defeating opponents by an average of two touchdowns per game.

While Griffin was slashing and dashing his way to a second Heisman, Johnson was pummeling opponents into submission. He carried seven times in a fourth-quarter scoring drive to seal a 17–9 win against seventh-ranked Penn State in the second game of the season, and tallied a school-record five touchdowns a week later against North Carolina. In early November, he broke the Big Ten single-season record by scoring his twenty-first touchdown, and padded that total in the traditional season finale by scoring each of his team's three touchdowns in a 21–14 victory against archrival Michigan, the nation's fourth-ranked team at the time.

"Their offense is the simplest thing to defend," remarked Minnesota head coach Cal Stoll, "but try to go out there and do it on the field. You've got to stop the buffalo, and then Corny or Archie will make the big play." Stoll's team was steamrolled by the Buckeyes in 1975 with Johnson, Griffin, and Greene combining to rush for 276 yards and four touchdowns in a 38–6 romp.

Pete finished that season with 156 points—a Big Ten scoring record at the time and still tied for third all-time—and joined Griffin as the first two Ohio State players to rush for 1,000 yards or more in a season. Griffin, Baschnagel, and Greene had each exhausted their eligibility after the 1975 season, but Johnson returned in 1976 to finish his career with 58 touchdowns and 348 points, forty-eight more than any non-kicker in program history.

Not bad for a roly-poly manchild so many had written off as a lazy lost cause.

He was born Willie James Hammock on March 2, 1954, in Peach County, Georgia, one of the smallest counties in the state but, as its name suggests, one of the state's biggest in terms of the peach-growing industry. His mother was only thirteen at the time of Willie's birth, and he was sent to grow up on his great-grandparents' farm. He loved farm life, running through the orchards and avoiding chores whenever he could. When he turned six, his great-grandfather walked him to his first day of school. By the time the old man returned to his house, little Willie was sitting on the front steps waiting for him.

"I was listening to my aunts," he recalled, "and they were talking about this one teacher who would get mad at them, stick their heads between her legs, and spank them. Man, that used to give me nightmares. I didn't want any part of that."

His great-grandfather piled him in a truck and drove to the farm where pruning season for the peach trees had begun. Branches were cut and put in a pile, then loaded on a wagon to be hauled away. At the tender age of six, Willie was put to work driving the tractor that pulled that wagon. He drove the tractor up one aisle of trees and down the next, monotonous work that changed his mind about school.

"By the time that school year was over, I was praying to go to school," he said. "I just didn't want that fat lady sticking my head between her legs."

Although a lot of his friends were white, Willie attended segregated schools until the tenth grade. He had begun playing varsity football long before that, though. "I was on my way to band practice," he remembered, "and this guy came up to me and said, 'You look big. You should play football.' It was the high school football coach. He didn't know I was only in the seventh grade."

Initially wanting to play quarterback because it was the position "that got most of the girls," Willie played defensive end and offensive guard before settling in at an offensive tackle spot. By the time he was a sophomore, he earned all-state honors as a middle linebacker and then repeated as a junior and senior. By his senior year, the health of his great-grandparents had begun to fail and Willie moved back in with his mother. That proved to be a turning point when his mother found domestic work in New York City.

While his mother worked several jobs in Manhattan, Willie traveled each day to Long Island to attend Long Beach High School and finish his studies. When he learned that he had used all of his high school football eligibility in Georgia, he simply invented a new identity for himself. His father's first name was Johnson, and he borrowed from the neighborhood Peter Pan ice cream truck to become Pete Johnson. He became a star at Long Beach, winning all-state honors with the Marines, and became one of the most sought-after college prospects on the East Coast.

Pete estimated he received more than 250 scholarship offers to play football and another three dozen-plus to play basketball. He signed a letter of intent to play for Bobby Bowden, then the head coach at West Virginia University, but Woody Hayes convinced him to tear it up.

"Woody told me, 'I want you to know something about these schools that are promising you money—you'll get suspended, you won't be seen on national TV, and TV is what gets you in the pros,'" Pete recalled. "That's what he said. That, and going to West Virginia over Ohio State was 'like choosing a Ford over a Cadillac.'"

Comfortable at first with his decision to attend Ohio State, Johnson almost immediately began having second thoughts. "When I got there," he said, "we're driving in from the airport, and then it was just all woods along the way, just one little building here and there. New York had gotten into me and I thought, 'What the hell am I doing here?'"

Things didn't get any better when two-a-day fall practice sessions began. Figuring he was good enough to play with the regular varsity, Pete instead found himself playing fullback on the scout team during the first morning session. On one play, he knocked All-American linebacker Randy Gradishar unconscious, and on another, did the same to all-conference linebacker Rick Middleton.

"I was on the scout team as a fullback, but I wanted to play linebacker," Johnson said. "I figured those guys were the starting linebackers, and those were the guys I needed to take out. I get them out of the game, then I've got a shot. They put me on the scout team in the morning, but I was on the regular team that evening."

Another problem arose when he began suiting up for his first game in the fall of 1973. Remembering Woody's recruiting pitch of playing before 86,000 screaming fans, Pete sneaked out of the locker room before kickoff to sample his first taste of the Ohio Stadium atmosphere.

"I looked around and there were more people at my high school games," he said. "Everybody should be here by now, I thought. I've been lied to, and that's the one thing you don't do to me. You don't lie to me. I don't forget a lie. Right away, I'm feeling down and I'm ready to leave. I went back in and reluctantly put on my shoulder pads, and when we came back out, I'll never forget when they opened that locker room door. The roar of the crowd hit me like someone took an electric socket and stuck it to me. You look at all those people, and they look like a disturbed ant bed. You ever find an ant bed and just kick it? Well, that's the way it looked."

Pete got only two carries during that 1973 season-opening game against Minnesota, gaining a modest three yards in a 56–7 victory for the Buckeyes. He finished his freshman season with 205 yards and six touchdowns, but he considered it a disappointment because he had been passed over on the depth chart. Starting fullback Harold

Pete finished his Ohio State career with 348 points, nearly fifty more than any non-kicker in program history.

"Champ" Henson blew out a knee in the second game of the season, but rather than putting Johnson in a starting role, Hayes went with converted linebacker Bruce Elia, who wound up scoring a team-leading fourteen touchdowns.

"I was pissed off about it," Pete remembered. "I knew I was ready, and again I thought about leaving. But I realized that I still had a lot to learn about how to deal with people and situations."

The maturation process continued the following season when Henson returned from his injury and Elia went back to defense. For perhaps the only time during his long coaching career, Hayes was indecisive about which fullback he wanted to start. He joked before the 1974 season that he would "run Champ Henson to the left and Pete Johnson to the right" as part of "484 pounds of well-directed, devastation-dedication football power," but by the sixth game that year, the offense was centered around the flash and dash of Griffin and Greene, and the duo of Henson and Johnson had combined for only four carries.

Late in the season, Hayes decided he had made a mistake and re-introduced the fullback into the offensive game plan and named Henson the starter. During an early November game at Michigan State, while Johnson sulked on the bench, Henson was stopped twice late in the fourth quarter—one yard shy of a first down on a third-and-three and then at the goal line as time expired on a 16–13 upset loss to the Spartans.

The following week, the smoke emanating from Johnson's ears became a full-fledged fire. With Henson as the starter, Pete saw almost no action on the practice field. But when the Buckeyes needed a fourth-quarter spark the following Saturday against Iowa, he responded with carries of thirty-two, four, and twelve yards, the last one a game-clinching touchdown.

The week after that, in the annual showdown with Michigan, Pete was back in the starting lineup and never looked back. He netted only 20 yards on 10 carries, but he threw several key blocks to help spring Griffin, who rushed for 111 yards as the Buckeyes nipped their archrivals by a 12–10 final score.

Johnson rushed for 1,059 yards and twenty-five touchdowns as a junior, remarkable numbers considering he shared a backfield with Griffin, who totaled 1,450 yards on the way to his second Heisman Trophy. He added 724 yards (in forty-one fewer carries) and nineteen more touchdowns during his senior season, completing a career that finished with 2,308 yards and 56 rushing touchdowns. The yardage figure was fourth-highest in program history at the time, and the rushing touchdowns remain an Ohio State record.

After the Cincinnati Bengals made him their second-round selection in the 1977 NFL draft, Pete reprised the role he had played in college by punishing opposing tacklers and scoring touchdowns. Over seven seasons in tiger stripes, he gained more than 5,600 yards, tallied seventy-six touchdowns, and helped the Bengals to Super Bowl XVI following the 1981 season. He was also named to his only Pro Bowl that year.

Johnson left the NFL with a somewhat bitter taste in his mouth, partly because he felt he had always been paid less than his worth but also because he felt the league had certain rules designed only to take fun out of the game. He suffered suspensions from time to time, and during one such suspension, he found himself back in his old college coach's office. When asked by Woody if he was staying in shape in the interim, Johnson lied and said he worked out every morning and played racquetball every afternoon.

"What time and where do you work out?" Woody asked. When Pete hastily replied, "Seven at the stadium," the coach immediately said, "Okay, I'll meet you tomorrow at seven." When Johnson arrived at 6:30 to get a little sweat working before the coach arrived, Woody was already there waiting.

"We'd be working out and there was just a glow in his face," Pete remembered. "He's like coaching again. Here's an old man, retired, showing up every morning at seven. He didn't have to do that. That man did that because he cared. He cared about Pete Johnson. What more can you ask?"

TOM KLABAN

OSU KICKER 1974–1975

HOMETOWN: Hrmenin, Czechoslovakia

HEIGHT: 6 ft 1 in **WEIGHT**: 184 lb

6

Only once before in his previous 226 games as head coach at The Ohio State University, and never again in the forty-nine contests that would follow, did Woody Hayes ever rely on a kicker to score every single point during a victory.

During the 1951 season, the legendary coach's first in Columbus, Heisman Trophy winner Vic Janowicz's 26-yard field goal in the fourth quarter provided the only scoring in a sloppy 3–0 win against a Northwestern team on its way to a sixth-place finish in the Big Ten. But when it happened again, this time on a wind-swept November afternoon against third-ranked Michigan in 1974, the man responsible for the 12–10 Ohio State win that propelled his team to the Rose Bowl was a Czechoslovakian refugee who had honed his sidewinding kicking talents using tips from his soccer-playing kid sister.

Tom Klaban made every one of his four field-goal attempts in the '74 version of The Game, three from forty yards or farther, after which ABC, the network broadcasting the game to a nationwide audience, awarded a $1,000 scholarship to Ohio State in Klaban's name, honoring him for being the game's most valuable player. Not to be outdone, Hayes stood in the middle of the postgame locker room celebration, declaring that "this was the greatest kicking game I've ever seen." The coach first awarded Klaban the game ball, and then terming it a "battlefield promotion," announced he was giving his kicker a full scholarship, something no other Ohio State kicker had ever been awarded during the Hayes era.

If there was ever an unlikely candidate to kick the Buckeyes to a victory against their sworn archenemies from the north, it would be Thomas Max Klaban, born July 22, 1954 in Hrmenin, Czechoslovakia. Today, Hrmenin is a small town located in the Czech Republic about forty miles northeast of Prague, the nation's capital. But when Tom was born, the region was under rule of the former Soviet Union, buried behind the Iron Curtain.

Stricken with a heart ailment at the age of two, young Thomas was not expected to live to see his third birthday. But his father, Oldrich, heard of a man in a nearby village who practiced holistic as well as naturopathic medicine. Using what he called an "herb potion," the man visited the Klaban house several times a week, and slowly the youngster recovered.

But while their son regained his health, and was joined three years later by sister Johanka, the situation for the Klaban family in Czechoslovakia under Communist rule was bleak. Oldrich Klaban was just ten years old when the Munich Agreement virtually dissolved the country with large chunks in the north, south, and west, areas known as the Sudetenland, swallowed up by Adolf Hitler's Germany while other territories were annexed to Hungary and Poland.

After World War II, Czechoslovakia was re-established, but under iron-fisted, oppressive rule from the Soviet Union. Like many others during the era, especially after the particularly brutal reign of terror during the first six months of 1956, Oldrich and his German-born wife, Briget, longed for the freedom available in the United States and began to plot their escape. With machine gun towers, trained attack dogs, and vast killing fields of land mines honeycombing the countryside, escape plans that failed far outnumbered successful ones.

Somehow, though, the Klabans managed to navigate their way to West Germany, escaping with little more than the clothes they were wearing at the time. Novelists and screenwriters love to romanticize such daring escapes, but the one involving the Klaban family was a gritty adventure featuring bullets whizzing over their heads on more than one occasion. After living in a German refugee camp for six months, a long and arduous trip across the Atlantic Ocean aboard a

Woody Hayes announced he was giving his kicker a full scholarship, something no other Ohio State kicker had ever been awarded during the Hayes era.

steamship followed, but the family finally made it to the New World, stopping for a time in Canada while waiting for immigration quotas in the United States to ease. That occurred in 1967, the family's three-year escape odyssey finally ending when they settled into the Cincinnati suburb of Loveland.

Thirteen-year-old Tom sharpened his English skills by watching television, and eventually attended Princeton High School, where he joined a number of clubs and went out for the swimming team.

The Princeton football program was on its way to becoming an Ohio powerhouse, but the team lacked one important component. The Vikings didn't have a reliable kicker, so longtime swim coach Bill Renner, knowing Tom's background and figuring the youngster probably played soccer from the time he could walk, asked Tom if he would like to take a stab at kicking an American football. The only problem was that sister Johanka, who now went by the nickname of "Jane," was the soccer player in the family.

Still, with some tips from Jane on how to kick a football with the side of his foot, Tom became Princeton's regular kicker at the beginning of his junior year. He became so proficient, and so enamored by the game itself, that after attending his first Ohio State game with some of his teammates, he became fixated on becoming a Buckeye and playing for Woody Hayes.

That was easier said than done, of course. He and his father drove to Columbus on a spring Saturday morning for an unscheduled meeting with Hayes. They waited for several hours at St. John Arena before the coach appeared and graciously granted them a few minutes. Hayes was fascinated by the family's escape from behind the Iron Curtain, and after talking about that for about an hour, Oldrich finally explained that his son wanted to kick for the Buckeyes.

Hayes said that young Tom was welcome to try out for the team, but that he didn't give scholarships to kickers. Klaban was undaunted, though, and he made the team as a freshman in the fall of 1972. He didn't see the field at all that year, and got to attempt only three point-after touchdown kicks as a sophomore. Suddenly, his dream had turned into a nightmare.

"I was frustrated," Tom said. "I thought I was better than the kicker in front of me, and I threatened to transfer. I went to (offensive line coach) Ralph Staub, who was in charge of the kickers at that time, and told him I was going to transfer to Michigan. He told me to just be patient and my time would come. I knew the guy ahead of me was going to graduate, so I waited."

> "My sister was kind of my coach back then. None of the coaches understood soccer-style kickers because there weren't any. Jane told me I was lining up wrong. So, I changed my lineup and after that I felt like I couldn't miss. I truly believe I could have kicked ten field goals in that game. It was just one of those days that you're just on."
> —*Tom Klaban*

If he was so sure of his ability, why didn't he go to the head coach?

"I wasn't that crazy," Tom said with a laugh. "I just told Coach Staub, but I'm sure he never repeated it to Woody. I would have been off the team."

Klaban's persistence finally paid off when he became Ohio State's regular kicker in 1974, a season that began with eight straight victories as the Buckeyes raced to a number one ranking. The team didn't need many kicking heroics, outscoring those first eight opponents by a 360–75 margin, but in game nine at Michigan State, things got a little tougher. Tom converted field-goal attempts of 39 and 20 yards to provide the Buckeyes with a 6–3 lead going into the fourth quarter.

But he oddly missed a 25-yarder early in the final period, a miss that led to Hayes refusing to go for a tie when Michigan State grabbed a late 16–13 lead. The game ended in controversy when officials determined the Buckeyes' final snap, fumbled by quarterback Cornelius Greene and recovered in the end zone by wingback Brian Baschnagel, had occurred after time had expired. After nearly an hour of consultation between officials and Big Ten commissioner Wayne Duke, the play stood as it was called on the field, and the Spartans had their upset victory. It turned out to be Ohio State's only regular-season loss that year, and Klaban blamed himself.

"I was kind of in shock and a bit dazed for about two weeks," he said.

Klaban came out of his self-induced haze just in time for the Buckeyes to host third-ranked Michigan with a conference championship and Rose Bowl berth on the line. During the week leading up to the game, he began visualizing what he had to do.

"That whole week, it just felt different," he said. "I knew how important that game was and I just wanted to make sure I was ready. I just went through this period where it was almost like I was daydreaming. I must have kicked a football a thousand times in my mind that week. And I couldn't sleep. I was just constantly watching myself kick in my mind."

None of the visions included a miss, but while he was warming up before the game, he shanked a couple of attempts. That's when Jane came to the rescue.

"My sister was kind of my coach back then," Tom said. "None of the coaches understood soccer-style kickers because there weren't any. Jane told me I was lining up wrong. So, I changed my lineup and after that I felt like I couldn't miss. I truly believe I could have kicked ten field goals in that game. It was just one of those days that you're just on."

With a record crowd of 88,243 jamming into Ohio Stadium on a cold, windy November afternoon, Michigan took an early 10–0 lead. But on the first play of the second quarter, with a 20-mph wind at his back, Klaban leaned into a 47-yard field goal to get the Buckeyes on the scoreboard. He added two more three-pointers, including one from 43 yards away with two seconds remaining in the first half, to trim his team's deficit to a single point at 10–9.

Ohio State returned the second-half kickoff to near midfield, but the drive quickly stalled and Klaban was summoned again, this time for a 45-yard attempt. No kicker in program history had ever converted three field goals of 40 or more yards in a single game, and Klaban very nearly didn't get a chance to become the first. The snap to Baschnagel was low, skipping off the Horseshoe's artificial surface while Klaban did a kicker's version of a double take.

"Brian did a tremendous job of recovering the ball and getting it down, but I had to stop mid-step and punch the ball," Tom remembered. "In my mind, it felt like it took a full minute to kick that ball." Despite the bad snap and stutter-step, the ball split the north uprights to give Ohio State a 12–10 lead with 10:09 remaining in the third quarter.

Somehow, the Buckeyes made that slim advantage hold up throughout the remainder of the game until Michigan kicker Mike Lantry had his chance at a winning field goal in the final seconds. Klaban said he couldn't bear to watch, but looked up just in time to see the 38-yard try sail just left of the uprights to trigger a wild celebration.

"The thing about toe-kickers," Tom explained, "what would happen is if you didn't get it exactly right, it would sail on you. Lantry was a straight-on toe kicker, and that must have been what happened."

Not only did Klaban win the game for the Buckeyes, the attention he received paid an additional dividend. His grandmother was still in Czechoslovakia and unable to join her family in the United States, but when reports of Tom's exploits reached his homeland, his grandmother went to government offices armed with newspaper articles. She asked that she be allowed to go to the U.S. and watch her grandson kick in the Rose Bowl.

"And you know what?" Tom said. "She got her visa in two days."

CHRIS WARD

OSU OFFENSIVE TACKLE 1974–1977

70

NICKNAME: C-Dub

HOMETOWN: Cleveland, Ohio

HEIGHT: 6 ft 4 in **WEIGHT:** 272 lb

ALL-AMERICAN: 1976, 1977

NFL DRAFT: 1978, New York Jets

The list of offensive tackles to receive first-team All-America status while representing The Ohio State University is a lengthy one. Robert Karch was technically the first, so honored in 1916 although he was not an offensive specialist. Karch also played defense during an era long before football became a two-platoon sport.

Those tackles to achieve All-America status more than once during their careers as Buckeyes is a much smaller assemblage; the group voted All-Americans by a consensus of the myriad entities bestowing such honors whittles the number even more. Meanwhile, the club of those earning back-to-back consensus election to the All-America first team shaves a few more names off the list.

But when you add Academic All-America status to the criteria for membership, that fraternity roll call is limited to one name. Chris Ward earned one of the highest academic honors a college student-athlete can achieve when he was named to the Academic All-America team as a sophomore in 1975, and followed that by a consensus nomination to the All-America first team for his play on the field in 1976. Ward then finished his collegiate career as a unanimous selection to the All-America first team in 1977.

With all due respect to the likes of Orlando Pace and Korey Stringer, or even Bill Willis and Jim Parker, Ward might have been the best of the lot. During an era when offensive tackles specialized in either run blocking or pass protection, but seldom both, Ward was an archetype. With 272 pounds of muscle packed over a six-foot-four-inch frame, he cut an imposing figure, especially after donning shoulder pads roughly the size of an aircraft carrier and his battle-scarred silver helmet. It was bad enough when he brought that bulk to bear on opposing defensive linemen. Imagine being an undersized cornerback or safety facing Ward in the open field, a tackle with 4.75-second speed in the forty-yard dash. That kind of competition was, in a word, unfair.

"He was just physically overpowering," said Bill Myles, a longtime coach and administrator at Ohio State who had come aboard Woody Hayes' staff just before Ward's senior season in 1977 to coach tackles and tight ends for the Buckeyes. "Chris had very quick feet for his size. The most important step in blocking is the second step, and he would take his second step before the other guy could take his. He'd just knock people off the ball."

The results often were devastating. "I have practice film of him," Myles once said, "where Chris hit a guy so hard, he knocked him right out of his shoe."

Knowing what Ward had to overcome to reach the pinnacle of college football, Myles might have added one more superlative—miraculous.

Christopher Lamar Ward was born December 16, 1955, in Cleveland, Ohio, and abandoned by his parents, left in a dumpster to die. Alerted by an anonymous caller who said he had heard cries coming from an alley waste receptacle, Cleveland City Police officers rescued the newborn and turned him over to the Cuyahoga County Division of Children and Family Services.

An elderly couple was awarded custody and moved Chris to the Dayton area when he was still an infant. He didn't learn he was adopted until he was twelve, and wasn't told about what his birth parents had done to him until he was a teenager. He admitted he didn't know how to handle the news.

"You know the Biblical verse about the truth setting you free?" Chris said. "Well, the truth can also cause a tremendous amount of grief. Abandonment issues are not an easy thing for anyone to overcome, especially a kid who's only twelve years old. But it also gave me compassion for others who felt abandoned or discarded. You feel alone but you're not."

Ward found an outlet for his emotions in sports. Taking to anything that featured running, jumping or throwing, he quickly found he had an aptitude for athletic endeavors. By the time he was old enough to drive, he was already a star football player and track athlete at John H. Patterson Cooperative High School in Dayton. Named after an area native and founder of the National Manufacturing Company (later the NCR Corporation), Patterson High School featured a curriculum that allowed students to work at a job for two weeks and then attend school for two weeks. Students could not only work and earn money but also continue to learn in their specific field.

While Chris worked at a variety of jobs in high school with an eye toward a career in business finance, his main priority was sports. He won a total of nine varsity letters for the Crimson and Gray, starring in basketball, football and track. As a senior, he won a sectional title in the shot put competition and established a new state record as he won the Class AAA discus championship. For the Beavers football team, he was an All-Ohio performer as both an offensive and defensive tackle.

An easy smile and an even easier demeanor masked any emotional scars from his early life, and Chris was among the most popular students at Patterson. He held several class offices, was a member of a handful of clubs and organizations, and was voted the most athletic in his senior class.

When it came time to decide upon a college, Chris owned forty to fifty offers from major football programs and at least that many more from schools wanting him exclusively as a track and field athlete. "There were a lot of things being talked about," he recalled. "Things like money and cars and trips. One coach would tell me about how they were going to help me get to the NFL, another would tell me about how they were going to help me get to the Olympics. It was a lot to process for a kid."

That's when coach Woody Hayes stepped into the picture. Longtime Dayton area coach Ken Amlin, who at the time was head coach at Patterson, invited Hayes to speak at a school pep rally during Chris' senior year. Sitting in the crowd, listening to the legendary Ohio State coach deliver five minutes of unprepared remarks, trumped all of the luxuries and extra benefits others had promised.

"I don't know what it was, but I just knew I wanted to play for that man," Chris said. "I knew it wasn't going to be easy. Everybody knew about his reputation as a taskmaster and being very demanding. But there was just something about him. Once I got there, of course, I found out what everybody else who played for him already knew. He loved his players. He was a father figure to a lot of them. Woody never minded taking in some players who might have had some issues. He took them in, fathered them and gave them opportunities in life. And they loved him for it."

As a backup to All-Big Ten right tackle Scott Dannelley in 1974, Chris appeared in eight of the Buckeyes' twelve games during his freshman year, missing the final three due to an injury. But when he was in the lineup, he impressed the coaching staff enough for them to move him to the all-important left tackle spot vacated by graduated All-American Kurt Schumacher. Assigned to protect quarterback Cornelius Greene's blind side as well as trap block for tailback Archie Griffin and fullback Pete Johnson, Ward won the first of three straight first-team All-Big Ten honors as Ohio State featured one of the most potent offensive attacks in college football.

Griffin rushed for 1,450 yards on his way to an unprecedented second Heisman Trophy, Johnson rumbled for 1,059 yards and twenty-five touchdowns to lead the Big Ten in scoring, and Greene threw for 1,066 yards and added 518 more on the ground, winning the *Chicago Tribune* Silver Football, symbolic of the Big Ten's Most Valuable Player. It was the first time in program history the Buckeyes had ever had a pair of running backs eclipse the 1,000-yard mark in rushing during the same season a quarterback had gained more than 1,000 yards through the air.

"As offensive linemen, we always took a lot of pride in those numbers," Chris said. "When it comes to trophies and awards, there isn't a lot of glamour for us. But we know what we're worth because nothing happens without the offensive line, baby."

With the graduation of Greene and Griffin following the 1975 season, the Buckeyes were not nearly as explosive but Ward was every bit as fearsome as the offensive line anchor at left tackle. He was a consensus first-team All-American as a junior in 1976 and then a unanimous selection the following season. He also played the part of recruiting tool for Hayes.

Ralph Staub, Woody's longtime offensive coordinator and line coach who had produced such All-Americans as Schumacher, John Hicks and Ward, left Ohio State following the 1976 season to take over the program at his alma mater, the University of Cincinnati. For Staub's replacement as line coach, Hayes had centered on Myles, who had been an assistant at the University of Nebraska, first under Bob Devaney and later on Tom Osborne's staff.

"I thought I had a pretty good thing going at Nebraska," Myles recalled. "I mean, we were winning championships and I wasn't sure I wanted to leave. But Coach Hayes convinced me to come to Columbus for a visit with no preconceived notions. Well, once I'm there, he preens Chris Ward past me. He was a fantastic-looking guy. I knew I didn't have anyone who looked like that at Nebraska. So, I packed up my family, came to Ohio State, and wound up staying for thirty years."

The physique that lured Myles to Columbus, along with Ward's unique blend of power and speed, dazzled pro scouts as well, and the New York Jets selected the offensive tackle with the fourth overall pick of the 1978 National Football League draft. He was taken three spots behind future Pro Football Hall of Fame running back Earl Campbell, and well ahead of such other future Hall of Famers as wide receiver James Lofton, tight end Ozzie Newsome and quarterback Warren Moon.

Even though Ward was named as the Jets starting left tackle from day one, it wasn't a simple transition from college to the pros. "I had a great time at Ohio State, but I was looking forward to what the pros would hold for me," he said. "I came into camp and I had some adjustments to make from Ohio State because we didn't throw that many drop-back passes. Woody liked to run the ball, and it's a totally different skill-set necessary to block some of those big, strong defensive ends while backing up. I had to learn how to pass block."

The Jets were dismal during Ward's first few years in the league, bottoming out with a 4–12 record in 1980. But they turned the corner and made the playoffs the following season, and in 1982, played in the AFC Championship Game. Chris played seven seasons in New York, starting each of the eighty-seven games in which he appeared, and then spent 1984 with the New Orleans Saints before chronic injuries forced his retirement at just twenty-nine.

"I loved the game," he said. "I always wanted to go to the Pro Bowl. I never did quite get there, and most of the time it seems that Pro Bowl selections for tackles and interior lineman, they're the guys that are in the playoffs continuously. When you look at Hall of Fame stuff, I had hoped to have a Hall of Fame career. I thought I was good enough. I played as hard as I could."

Without football in his life for the first time since early childhood, Ward returned to the Dayton area but his world slowly began to spiral backward. He turned to alcohol and cocaine, and his marriage began to dissolve. He ran off to New Orleans, seeking solace with his old running buddies and found himself at a crossroads.

Watching television after a night of carousing, Ward was flipping channels when famed televangelist Jimmy Swaggart suddenly appeared on the screen. "He pointed at me," Chris remembered, "and he said, 'You're drunk and you've been boozing and womanizing. You're miserable and you need to give your life to the Lord.' I changed the channel and went to sleep. But when I woke up the next day, Jimmy Swaggart was still on TV and pointing at me. At that point, I broke down. I said, 'I can't run anymore,' and I said a prayer of repentance right then and there."

Clean and sober from that night in New Orleans, Ward would eventually become an ordained preacher and now runs an outreach ministry for inner-city youth in the southwestern Los Angeles suburb of Inglewood, California. But he had to go through his own baptism of fire to get there.

In the early 1990s, after his adoptive parents had passed away, Ward shuttered his small financial services business in Dayton and decided to move to Los Angeles. With no job prospects or friends in the area, he quickly exhausted his savings and wound up living out of his 1976 Cadillac for the next three and a half years. He fasted extensively, once getting his post-football weight down from 350 pounds to 237, and bathed at a recreation center in Inglewood. "I'd work out there in the morning, and then shower and shave," Chris said. "Nobody ever knew. A guy asked me one time where I was living, and I told him I was living out of my car. He thought I was playing with him. I opened my trunk and showed him. His mouth fell open."

Living on the streets can be a life-altering experience, but Chris believes it was all part of a divine plan. "When you play in the NFL and live in New York, you're living like the richest one percent of the word. But until you've been where the hopeless and the broken have been, you can't really feel what those people feel. You need to be humbled before you can be equipped to serve."

Ward rebounded from his life on the streets to run a successful youth ministry. He founded the non-profit Ward International Corporation in 1998, an after-school program to help mentor inner-city youth.

"All the children were there by written permission, so that their parents were fully advised as to what their children were doing," Chris said. "And we've had tremendous response in our twenty-plus years. None of our kids that were involved in the program were ever incarcerated. None of them were ever arrested. None of the girls ever had babies before they were married. And we found that most of the kids that came to our ethic classes, their GPA went up one letter grade."

Now remarried and living in Los Angeles with his wife, Blanche, Ward returned to his financial career and is a successful real estate agent, life insurance agent, mortgage loan officer and financial consultant. He has also spent time as president of the Los Angeles chapter of the NFL Players Association as well as president of Pro Players North America, an organization of professional athletes and entertainers committed to changing the lives of young people in North America.

Just to keep himself grounded, though, he still drives the '76 Cadillac that once served as his living quarters. He says it is a reminder that acclaim is fleeting.

"God showed me how futile it could be to have stuff and not be gratified," Chris said. "I have my life's purpose now and it's so fulfilling."

TOM COUSINEAU

OSU LINEBACKER 1975–1978

36

NICKNAME: Kooz

HOMETOWN: Bloomington, Indiana

HEIGHT: 6 ft 3 in **WEIGHT**: 227 lb

ALL-AMERICAN: 1977, 1978

NFL DRAFT: 1979, Buffalo Bills

*M*ercurially free-spirited or just plain crazy? You be the judge of one Tom Cousineau, a man so supremely confident in himself that he has spent almost as much time during his life as a tempter of fate than he has on the football field.

A two-time All-America linebacker at Ohio State whom Woody Hayes called "the best conditioned athlete I ever coached," and once described as being "built along the lines of a lean Arnold Schwarzenegger," Cousineau at one time or another has tested several Harley-Davidson motorcycles to see how fast they could go, jumped out of a jet boat going seventy miles per hour to find out what it feels like to skip over water, and dived fifty feet from a lighthouse into a frigid Lake Erie in the middle of winter.

He's never been afraid to bet on himself. He once bought a $25,000 sports car and then grew so disgusted with it after an hour's use that he sold it and got his money back plus a '55 Chevy. When he bought a house overlooking Lake Erie in the 1980s, rather than trust the rebuilding of an elaborate driveway to a concrete company he didn't know, Tom did the work himself. And after the Buffalo Bills had made him the overall number one pick in the 1979 National Football League draft—selected ahead of such future Hall of Fame players as Dan Hampton, Kellen Winslow, and Joe Montana—a series of what Cousineau considered personal snubs led him to spurn the Bills' offer and go north to play in the Canadian Football League.

Four years in the Great White North, where football takes a backseat to hockey, soccer, and basketball, made him feel like a "yard dog," so he returned to his native country and played for his hometown Cleveland Browns, who looked at Cousineau as the final piece in their Super Bowl puzzle. He wasn't, but still was named to the all-conference first team twice and led the team in tackles for three straight seasons. He has dabbled in coaching, politics, and bass fishing, and still has a lengthy bucket list he knows is the product of his ever-restless nature.

"People have the capacity to do so much more than they do," Tom says. "The things they dream about never get done. That's sad. I won't do that. Not ever."

The magical, mystery tour began for Thomas Michael Cousineau on May 6, 1957, in Bloomington, Indiana, the heart of the basketball-crazed Hoosier State. Bloomington is home to Indiana University and its five national men's basketball championships, and it was also where Tom's parents met. Carole O'Rear was a pretty junior coed while Thomas Richard Cousineau was a ruggedly handsome sophomore who had gotten a late start on his college education after having served three years in the U.S. Marine Corps.

Tom Sr. was a linebacker for the Indiana football team from 1955 to 1957, a squad that went through two coaches during a period in which the Hoosiers won only seven times against twenty losses. Tom Sr. had a couple of tryouts for professional teams, latching on briefly with the Oakland Raiders. But when a pro career didn't pan out, he uprooted the family from Bloomington to Indianapolis where he became a high school football and wrestling coach. Meanwhile, the former Marine Corps heavyweight wrestler immediately began preparing his son to become a football player.

By the age of ten, young Tom could already bench press 100 pounds ten times, and he was competing in scrimmage matches against varsity athletes. He once squared off against a former Olympic medalist in an impromptu match on the Cousineau's living room floor, the site of many such matches between Tom and his father. Those tussles often devolved into wars with overturned plants, smashed lamps, and demolished furniture infuriating Carole but increasing the bond between father and son.

One time, Tom Jr. suffered a deep gash on his forehead when his head smashed against the fireplace mantel, but despite the fact his son was bleeding profusely, Tom Sr. wouldn't relinquish his grip. Another time, Tom Jr. hit his father with a hold that tore the older Cousineau's shoulder out of its socket, necessitating surgery.

By that time, the family had moved again, this time out of basketball-centric Indiana to football-friendly Northeastern Ohio. Tom Sr. took a job as head football coach at Lakewood High School in the suburban lakefront city just fifteen minutes from downtown Cleveland. There, he ratcheted up the development of his son into a lean, mean football machine.

"My dad was a tough guy and a lot of people thought he was unreasonable," Tom said. "But he was very loving and he challenged me at a very young age because he felt that was the way to get me an advantage among my peers. Sometimes, we bit off a little more than we could chew, or my dad bit off more than I could chew, but in the long run, it helped."

Even though Tom Jr. excelled at wrestling, finishing third as a senior at the state wrestling meet in the heavyweight division, he said he never really liked the sport. Football was his number one passion and the sport for which his father had been grooming him. He set up elaborate weight equipment in the family garage, lectured on linebacker technique, and schooled young Tom in everything from nutrition to the mental aspects of the game. The youngster was like a sponge, always eager to learn any new wrinkle his father brought to him.

"One thing about Tom is that he's always been willing to pay the price," Tom Sr. once said. "In high school, people said he wasn't fast enough, so after his junior year, he spent hours every day sprinting and practicing his starts. That one summer, he brought his forty-yard time down from 5.0 to 4.7 seconds, just from working at it. At the time, it even worried me how dedicated he was."

The work and dedication paid off handsomely. He attended St. Edward High School in Lakewood, the crosstown rival of his father's team, because his mother had flashbacks to her broken living room and refused to allow him to play for Tom Sr. In keeping with his try-anything nature, Tom played several different positions, including center, fullback, and tight end, before settling in at linebacker to become one of the most sought-after players in the country. He was not only a consensus All-Ohio prospect but a consensus prep All-American as well, and received hundreds of scholarship offers. He decided to check in on several opportunities, but there was really only one that held his interest.

"I remember when I got my first letter from Ohio State," Cousineau said. "God, I carried it around because I was so excited. I felt compelled to look at other schools, but my uneducated opinion prior to recruiting was that Ohio State was the place I wanted to go. I liked the proximity to home. My parents could come watch me play, and that was important to me. I also visited Michigan, Notre Dame, and Penn State as well as Indiana because I felt a little bit obligated since my dad had gone there."

His recruiting trip to Indiana was one for the ages. Picked up at the airport by one of his father's old teammates, he looked at the youngster and said, "Tom, you ever drink beer?" Cousineau replied, "Well, yeah, a couple of times." The man reached into the back seat of his car where there were a couple of cases of the frothy stuff on ice. There were a couple of stops along the way to the university, including a tavern where the man said he and Tom's father had waged a legendary barroom brawl, and by the time Tom was delivered to his official destination, he was in no condition to be recruited.

"Lee Corso had every coach from every varsity program lined up, including Bobby Knight, to meet me, and I'm smashed," Cousineau recalled. "I mean *smashed.* I open up the car door and beer cans fall out, rolling down the road. Howard Brown, who had coached my father and was the freshman coach, runs up to me, throws his arms around me and says, "Welcome home, Tom!' I was trying to breathe through my nose. It was embarrassing."

When Cousineau arrived on the Ohio State campus in the autumn of 1975, he was one of five linebackers the Buckeyes had signed in his recruiting class. With that kind of competition, plus veterans such as senior captain Ken Kuhn and Ed Thompson returning, Tom didn't figure he would see much action during his freshman season. That was underscored by his first week of practice when he was introduced to Ohio State football.

"I lined up across from a guy named Ted Smith, who was an All-American guard—huge, fast, explosive," Tom recalled. "I think it was the second day of practice. He cracked my helmet. Whack! He just knocked the shit out of me. I got another one, the same thing happened. Chris Ward, an All-American tackle, comes down on me, breaks my shoulder pads. Now, I've gone through two helmets and a set of shoulder pads in the first week of practice. I'm so sore, I can't move."

By the third week, Cousineau was finally getting his feet under him, adjusting to the speed of the college game. He also began to notice tendencies like when fullback Pete Johnson would move a certain way when an isolation play was coming. So, at the snap of the ball during such an instance, Cousineau shot through a gap, went through Johnson before he could get out of his stance and threw Archie Griffin for a four-yard loss.

An incensed Woody let loose with a string of profanities ending with "Run the goddamned play again." When the result was the same, the legendary head coach blew a gasket. Somewhere among the ripped shirt, smashed wristwatch, and cacophony of curse words that would have made a longshoreman blush, Hayes threw Cousineau off the field. It was the last time he ever performed scout team duty.

Although he had prepared to be mostly a backup during his freshman season, Kuhn went down with an injury in game two against Penn State and Cousineau was quickly pressed into duty. "There's no time to think. When you're in, you're in," Tom said. "I think I put my mouthpiece in backasswards and upside down. It was on my bottom teeth. In fact, I may have swallowed it. I don't know."

He recorded the first three tackles of his OSU career, helping the Buckeyes score a 17–9 victory against the seventh-ranked Nittany Lions, and went on to finish sixth on the team with 70 tackles. That included a 23-tackle performance against his father's alma mater during a 24–14 win over the Hoosiers. It was the first of six career games with twenty or more tackles, easily a program record. No one else has more than two.

Tom won first-team All-Big Ten honors during his sophomore, junior, and senior seasons, and was a consensus selection to the All-America first team in each of his final two seasons. As a senior, he served as a team co-captain, registered a program-record 211 tackles and was voted as the team's Most Valuable Player.

Cousineau finished his career with 569 tackles, a total eclipsed only by Marcus Marek, who had 572. More than forty-five years after he took off the scarlet and gray for the final time, he remains Ohio State's single-season leader in solo tackles with 142.

The following May, Cousineau found himself at the famed Waldorf Astoria Hotel on Park Avenue in New York City, being introduced as the overall number one selection in the 1979 NFL draft. After trading O.J. Simpson to the San Francisco 49ers, the Buffalo Bills held the first pick, and the Bills were ready to rebuild their defense around Cousineau. It was not the proverbial marriage made in heaven.

Cousineau was ready to fly to Buffalo with his agent to discuss a contract, but when they arrived at the airport, the Bills had provided only a ticket for Tom. Then after Cousineau's introductory press conference, a key team executive failed to show up for a dinner meeting. Finally, when Buffalo's contract of-

Tom had six games at OSU during which he registered twenty or more tackles. No one else has more than two.

fer came in beneath expectations at $1.2 million over five years, Tom had had enough. He accepted a three-year deal worth $850,000 from the Montreal Alouettes of the Canadian Football League, a decision he admitted he came to regret.

"As an economic decision, it made sense," Tom said, "but it broke my heart. I wasn't groomed to play in the CFL. That was not what I dreamed about as a child."

Starting at first on the outside and later moving to middle linebacker, Cousineau was named the Alouettes' top rookie and then was selected as the outstanding defensive player in the 1979 Grey Cup. The following year, he was voted the best defensive player in the CFL's Eastern Division. After an injury-riddled third season in Canada, he returned home to play four seasons for the NFL's Cleveland Browns before finishing his career with two seasons playing for the 49ers as a backup.

In retirement, he allowed himself to slow down, but only a little. He coached for a while, including at his high school alma mater St. Edward, and he spent a year as a volunteer assistant on John Cooper's staff at Ohio State. Mostly, though, he enjoys life with his wife, Lisa, who in 2020 gave up a private practice to become director of Obstetrics and Gynecology at Cleveland Clinic Martin Health in Stuart, Florida. The move to the Treasure Coast of the Sunshine State allows the couple to continue their hobbies of boating and fishing as well as entertaining their daughters Kyle and Kacey.

Still, sometimes Tom's mind still wanders as he ponders what's next for him.

"I majored in business marketing and journalism at Ohio State," he said. "I used to write a lot but I don't do it much anymore. In fact, when I was still in school, a journalist from Michigan—a real smartass—was doing a feature story. He asked me what I was studying, and in the same breath added, 'Phys ed?'"

"It was really snide, you know? So I answered, 'Oh no, something much simpler.'

"He looked startled and said, 'What could that be?'

"'Journalism,' I said with a smile before turning my head and adding, 'Asshole.'"

GLEN COBB

OSU LINEBACKER 1979–1982

HOMETOWN: Washington Court House, Ohio

HEIGHT: 6 ft 3 in **WEIGHT**: 212 lb

35

Pepper Johnson enjoyed a much-decorated football career that would ultimately earn him high school and college All-America honors, trips to the National Football League's Pro Bowl with two different teams, two Super Bowl championship rings as a player and three more as a coach. But during the summer of 1982, he was just Thomas Johnson, a prized prep prospect from Mackenzie High School in Detroit eager to make a good first impression as a freshman at Ohio State.

The only thing standing in his way was Glen Cobb, the veteran linebacker referred to by some teammates as half-human, half-horse. As a sort of medieval way of introducing newbies to the rigors of college football, Buckeyes head coach Earle Bruce had devised a rather brutal initiation for prospective linebackers. To prove their endurance and to "help" with their conditioning, players had to complete at least seven laps around the Ohio Stadium track in twelve minutes or less. Quiet and retiring off the field and just the exact opposite on it, Cobb was the undisputed master of the conditioning run.

Johnson had his sights set on becoming a force at linebacker for the Buckeyes. The only way to reach that goal, he figured, was to best Cobb's time in the conditioning run. In other words, to be the man, he had to beat the man.

"I trained all summer for that thing," said Johnson, who acquired his nickname for the penchant of sprinkling pepper on his cornflakes as a youngster. "That's all I thought about. But I misunderstood what we had to do. I thought you just had to finish the seven laps in less than twelve minutes and that would be that. I didn't realize you had to finish running the twelve minutes—no matter what."

Bruce blew his whistle and the linebackers were off with Johnson immediately breaking away from the pack. With a huge smile breaking out over his face, he enjoyed a half-lap lead over Cobb as he sprinted to finish the last of his seven laps.

"I crossed what I thought was the finish line and stopped. That's when everybody started screaming," Johnson recalled. "I was waving, accepting what I thought was their congratulations. I even went over and got a quick drink of water. But they were screaming because I had stopped."

Chief among the screamers was Bruce, the roly-poly coach whose face went from ashen to scarlet to purple as he peppered (pun intended) Pepper with enough superlatives and profanity that the freshman finally began to understand his race was not over.

"About that time, here comes Glen racing right past me," Johnson said. "Have you ever tried to restart running after you've stopped? I took off after him, but I had no chance. Glen completed his eighth lap, Earle blew the whistle and I was still about ten or fifteen yards behind him. I was so disappointed. I bent over, feeling like my lungs were going to explode out of my chest, and then I felt an arm around me and heard someone say, 'Welcome to Ohio State.' It was Glen with a smile on his face. He wasn't even breathing hard."

Three years earlier, Cobb had experienced his own freshman initiation to Ohio State football. "My first year, freshmen came in early prior to two-a-days," he remembered. "We had maybe three practices without pads, and I remember thinking, 'This isn't so bad.' Then came the upperclassmen. We put on the pads and went full contact. Dennis Fryzel was our linebackers coach, and you wouldn't find a more colorful and excitable man."

Excitable might be a bit of an understatement. Fryzel was referred to more than once as "The Madman of the Sidelines," a moniker picked up after losing several teeth during his high school playing days at Garfield High School in Akron. During a coaching career that spanned three different decades, he was noted for his fiery locker room persona, and more than once split his scalp open after excitedly head-butting one of his players following a big play. Fryzel exuded a certain kind of old-school toughness, and demanded the same from his players.

"The very first contact drill he put us through was a tackling drill," Glen recalled. "Nothing fancy—just good, old-fashioned smashmouth football. To make sure that contact would occur, the ball-carrier had to run straight ahead inside of two cones spread a few yards apart. That way, it doesn't allow for much deviation east or west. Both players get to run downhill at each other.

"Well, I had a crack at it both ways. First, I ran the ball and was tackled. No big deal. Then I tackled one of my fellow linebackers. It wasn't pretty, but I got him to the ground somehow. Then we started the second round. This time, I faced Al Washington, who was six-five and weighed about 260 pounds."

Washington might have looked that big to a wide-eyed freshman, but in reality stood just six-foot-three and weighed just over 230 pounds. Still, he was a returning starter who had registered 145 tackles the season before, and listed in the team's official media guide as "one of the fastest and most agile linebackers in the Big Ten."

"I took off with the ball, of course running straight up because I didn't know any better," Glen said. "I had been an offensive tackle and linebacker in high school, so what did I know about running the football? Anyway, I would say that Al put a pasting on me the likes of which I had never seen or felt before. When I got up, my facemask was broken in three places.

"Keep in mind, this was my very first contact drill at Ohio State. It was very entertaining to the upperclassmen, and I think it accomplished exactly the kind of initiation Coach Fryzel wanted. He looked at me, half-smiled and said, 'Welcome to the Big Ten.'"

Baptisms by fire were nothing new for Glen Alan Cobb, born December 21, 1960, in Washington Court House, Ohio, a small crossroads community some fifty miles southwest of Columbus where business and industry has come and gone over the years while agriculture has remained the only constant. He was the youngest of four rambunctious boys born in rapid succession to World War II Army veteran Arthur Benjamin Cobb Jr. and the former Jacquelyn Ann Niles, a pair of native New Englanders who met at a harness horse racetrack in Maine and got married in 1954.

Over the next six years, while the union produced Gardner, Gary, Gregory and Glen, the patriarch of the family pursued his lifelong interest in standardbred horses, the breed best known for its ability in harness racing, where racers compete at either a trot or pace. Arthur Cobb eventually became the manager at Fair Chance Farm, an expansive horse farm located just outside Washington Court House. Fair Chance Farm was world-renowned for its facilities, and served as home for famed pacer Adios Butler, twice voted United States Harness Horse of the Year.

As a youngster, Glen chased behind his brothers, who had the run of the farm, each growing taller and stronger with each passing year. By all accounts, it was an idyllic life until Jacquelyn, a registered surgical nurse, was diagnosed with cancer. She waged a heroic battle against the disease for two years, but eventually succumbed at the age of thirty-nine. Glen was only twelve.

Obviously devastated, the youngster threw himself into as many outdoor activities as he could. Eventually growing to a healthy six-foot-three and about 210 pounds, Glen with his shock of blond hair and disarming smile was a young man on the go when he arrived at Miami Trace High School. In addition to serving as senior class president, he somehow found time to play basketball and compete in wrestling during the winter, and ran track in the springtime. He was an exceptional athlete who excelled at nearly every athletic endeavor he tried, but he was especially gifted on the football field. Blessed with quickness as well as agility, intelligence and an innate ability to always be in the right place at the right time, Glen managed to win all-conference honors on both offense and defense.

On offense, he was a punishing offensive tackle, providing protection for teammate Art Schlichter, a fellow prep All-American whose record-breaking career made him one of the most sought-after high school quarterbacks in the country. Defensively, Glen had no equal as he sought out opposing ball-carriers and delivered teeth-rattling tackles. During his senior season, he racked up an astounding 182 tackles in just ten games.

Schlichter had signed to play for Ohio State, and in 1978 became the first true freshman to start at quarterback for the Buckeyes. But the youngster took a physical beating during that season, a telling reminder for his Miami Trace teammate that the difference between playing football at the high school and college levels was measured in light years.

"The toughest player I ever played with was Art Schlichter. No doubt about that," Glen said. "I saw him time and again take a substantial pounding as a freshman. During our high school days, I saw him get hit with the best of them. And although he might have wavered at times, he always got up."

Still, the physical toll Schlichter absorbed during his first season on the collegiate level gave Cobb more than a little pause about following the quarterback to Ohio State. He briefly toyed with the idea of going to Penn State, the team that had administered one of Schlichter's most severe beatings in 1978. Still, Glen remained intrigued by the prospect of playing for his home-state team, and went on a recruiting trip to Columbus. Invited to watch the Buckeyes practice in preparation for the Gator Bowl, he had a brief but significant sideline conversation with legendary coach Woody Hayes.

"It was a cold, wet December day," Glen recalled. "The practice was being held in the Horseshoe and not many recruits were there that day. I was standing along the sideline when Coach Hayes motioned for me to come over to him. At the time, the team was broken out into individual position groups doing drills. When I reached Coach Hayes, he asked, 'Son, do you see those linebackers over there?' I replied, 'Yeah.'"

Immediately, Glen knew he'd given the wrong answer. Arms folded across a scarlet red windbreaker, the old coach peered over his glasses and said through pursed lips, "You will respond by saying, 'Yes, Sir.'"

The youngster repeated, "Yes Sir," after which the coach continued.

"Son, I want you to watch those linebackers today. You watch them, and if after the end of practice you think you can play alongside them, then I'll give you a scholarship. If you don't, then get right back on I-71 South, go back to the farm and stay there!"

Glen remembered mumbling, "Yes, sir," and then began to contemplate his situation.

"My thoughts turned to farm life," he said. "It's a pretty good life, really. I can do that, I thought. Understand, the mindset I had of Ohio State football was that it was very intimidating. I didn't think I could compete academically or athletically. I remember during that same visit, I watched a tape of the previous season's highlights and said to myself, 'There is no way you can compete at this level.' The whole Ohio State thing was out of my league. However, I really believe that if God wants a person somewhere, He will provide a way."

The rest is Ohio State football history. The best linebacker in program history never to win All-America honors, Cobb played sparingly as a freshman before becoming a fixture in the starting lineup for the following three years. Teamed alongside fellow linebacker Marcus Marek, Glen helped lead one of the most fearsome defenses in college football. During his senior season, he registered 143 tackles to give him 336 for his career. It was the fifth-highest total in school history at the time, and still ranked 10th all-time heading into the 2022 season.

And he was an extremely popular teammate as well, twice earning election as a team captain. That had been an honor bestowed only twice before—to two-time Heisman Trophy winner Archie Griffin in the mid-1970s and Richard T. Ellis in the 1890s when the program was still in its infancy.

Judged by NFL scouts as being undersized, Cobb went undrafted following his college career. He signed a free-agent contract with the Denver Broncos, but was the last linebacker cut by the team just prior to the start of the 1983 season. He received an offer to play in the upstart United States Football League for the Philadelphia Stars, and believes he would have made the team.

"But at that point," he said, "I was just done with football. I just didn't have the passion anymore. It was time to move on in life."

Glen married his high school sweetheart, the former Jan Marie Mossbarger, who in addition to being a cheerleader at Miami Trace when Glen was playing, shared her future husband's lineage regarding harness horse racing. She is the daughter of a veterinarian, breeder of standardbred horses and founder of Midland Acres, the chief rival to Fair Chance Farm for bragging rights in terms of producing championship trotters and pacers.

Meanwhile, Glen decided to use the degree in park and recreation management he earned at Ohio State, parlaying his love for the outdoors to secure a position with the Ohio Department of Natural Resources. He has spent nearly forty years at ODNR, serving in a variety of capacities including as Deputy Director of the department as well as Chief of the Division of Parks and Watercraft.

Together, Glen and Jan, a registered nurse who serves as a consultant and trainer for the Fayette County (Ohio) Board of Developmental Disabilities, raised three athletic daughters, each of whom played college sports. And they were apparently the proverbial chips off the old block.

"What I taught my girls through the years was to make the best of every opportunity," Glen said. "If you want to be excellent—and that should always be the goal of any athlete—one thing that's within your sphere of influence is the ability to work hard and develop skill and a mental toughness. Those were the kinds of valuable lessons I learned at Ohio State. I'm just glad I didn't follow Coach Hayes' advice. I'm glad I didn't go back to the farm and stay there."

A two-time captain with the Buckeyes, Glen was a high school teammate of Ohio State quarterback Art Schlichter.

GARY WILLIAMS

OSU SPLIT END, WIDE RECEIVER 1979—1982

HOMETOWN: Wilmington, Ohio

HEIGHT: 6 ft 2 in **WEIGHT:** 212 lb

NFL DRAFT: 1983, Cincinnati Bengals

44

In the span of just two short years, Gary Williams went from a can't-miss prospect who could do anything in the field of athletic achievement to a bench-warming nobody who couldn't do anything right. And then in a momentary flash of imprudence from an iconic coach, the fortunes of the Ohio State football program changed and Williams' future with it.

Gary Leon Williams was born September 4, 1959, into a family of nine and almost literally hit the ground running. Growing up with so many siblings around naturally leads to a competitive spirit, and while young Gary seemed timid and withdrawn, he was anything but when it came to competition—whether angling with brothers and sisters for that last potato at the dinner table or taking on older, bigger and stronger neighborhood kids in marbles, wrestling, tree-climbing and everything in between.

By the time he reached his teenage years, Gary had become a high school star in football, basketball and track in his hometown of Wilmington, a pastoral small college town straight off the pages of a script from the 1960 television series *Leave It to Beaver* or *My Three Sons*. Located in the middle of the crossroads of county roads, state routes and national highways, the town of which the population has never risen much above 12,000 practically defines the word pastoral with its tree-lined neighborhoods, private college of brick buildings established by Quakers in 1870, and laid-back pace of living that conveys the simplicity and serenity of an earlier time.

About the only time Wilmingtonians get excited is when their high school or college athletic teams are competing, and Gary Williams gave them plenty to cheer about during the mid-1970s. Blessed with a chiseled physique straight out of a bodybuilding magazine even though he reportedly never touched a weight until he arrived on the Ohio State campus, Gary won all-conference and all-district honors in basketball, competed at the state track meet in the grueling 400 meters, and captained his football team while playing quarterback, running back, flanker and defensive back. He also served as the kicking specialist for the Hurryin' Hurricanes, and it was his two field goals against rival Miami Trace High School that provided the winning margin to hand future Ohio State teammate Art Schlichter his only loss during the quarterback's high school career.

But when the sinewy, 6-foot-2, 212-pound Williams with sprinter's speed got to Ohio State, head coach Woody Hayes didn't know exactly what to do with him. Williams was adept at a number of positions, but had gotten by mostly on his athletic abilities and instincts. He had little concept of how receivers ran proper pass routes, downfield blocking techniques or how to decoy opposing defensive backs so that teammates could get open.

Not that he was going to make an immediate college impact anyway. During the annual Ohio North-South All-Star Game played during the summer of 1978, he sustained a knee injury that was exacerbated during his first fall camp with the Buckeyes. He underwent surgery six days after Ohio State's 1978 season opener against Penn State, but rehabbed quickly enough to join the scout team later in the season—albeit as a defensive back.

His speed and range of motion had not yet fully returned, but Williams was eager to prove he was worthy of the scholarship Hayes had given him. The veteran coach, however, was not so sure.

"For some reason, Woody didn't like Gary," Schlichter said. "In fact, he treated him like a dog. During the postseason banquet that followed the regular season, as Woody passed out Gator Bowl watches, he insulted Gary in front of the team, saying, 'You really don't deserve this watch, young man.' If there was anyone happy about the coaching change, it was Gary Williams."

That coaching change was precipitated when Hayes slugged an opposing player on the Ohio State sideline near the end of the Buckeyes' 17–15 loss to Clemson in the 1978 Gator Bowl. The legendary coach was fired shortly thereafter, and the university undertook an exhaustive nationwide search for his successor.

Earle Bruce, who was then head coach at Iowa State and had been an assistant on Hayes' staff from 1966 to 1971, was named to lead the Ohio State program. As part of his new staff, Bruce hired Fred Zechman as his quarterbacks and wide receivers coach. Zechman had been Schlichter's coach in high school, and also knew Williams well enough to know he was being wasted as a defensive back.

"It didn't take a rocket scientist to figure that one out," Zechman said. "I took one look at our roster and could see we had all four starting defensive backs returning. At the same time, I think Doug Donley was about the only receiver we had coming back with any kind of playing experience. Gary was a natural, and I knew that he and Art would have a built-in confidence factor with one another. It was a no-brainer, really."

Donley said one of the first things he did when Bruce named Zechman his quarterbacks and receivers coach was lobby to have Williams move over from defense.

"The first thing that comes to mind when I remember back is Gary's size," Donley said. "His hands were huge, and being six-two or six-three, he was such a big target. He didn't have blazing speed because of his knee injury, but he was certainly plenty fast enough. And anything you threw near him, he was catching the ball."

Williams made the switch to receiver in spring ball and performed well enough throughout fall camp that he was just behind senior Chuck Hunter on the depth chart at split end. But after Donley, who manned the flanker position, banged up his knee late in camp, Bruce decided he needed more speed in his lineup and Williams got his first college start in the 1979 season opener against Syracuse.

"I'd known Art since the eighth grade, and played against him all through high school," Gary said. "I knew and liked his family, so having a chance to work with him at Ohio State was great. Then to start that first game of the season—I knew the hard work I was putting in was paying off."

Williams' first taste of college football was mostly as a decoy. In the 1979 opener, Schlichter's first five passes were short tosses to tailback Calvin Murray before Williams was finally targeted late in the first quarter. The pass was off the mark and too low for the redshirt freshman receiver to catch, and then one play later, Schlichter connected with tight end Ron Barwig for an 11-yard touchdown, the Buckeyes' first score of the season.

Williams finally got his first career reception, good for an 11-yard gain, early in the second quarter. It came on a simple inside hook route with Schlichter delivering a perfect ball this time, and Williams making the catch for a first down.

It was his only catch of the day to begin a modest redshirt freshman season that included 25 catches for 479 yards and two touchdowns. It also began his streak of 48 games in a row with at least one catch, a program record streak that has since been tied but never broken.

The streak nearly ended midway through the 1980 season during a 63–0 rout at Northwestern. Williams had been bothered again by a bad knee, and the Buckeyes didn't figure to need his services much against the hapless Wildcats, who had lost 14 consecutive games and were on their way to an 0–11 record that season. Williams started at his regular split end position, but after Ohio State had jumped out to a 28–0 lead early in the second quarter, he figured to take the rest of the afternoon off. That was when longtime OSU assistant coach Bill Myles whistled another tune in his ear.

"Coach Myles came up to me on the sideline," Williams remembered, "and he said, 'You've got to go back in there.' I just kind of looked at him, and he said, 'Don't you know you've had a catch in every game you've played? You've got to go back in there. We've got to get you a catch.' I'm sure I had some kind of dumb look on my face because I honestly didn't know what he was talking about. That's how much I was paying attention to the streak."

When the Buckeyes got the ball back, Williams gingerly jogged back onto the field, and on the second play of the drive, converted a second-and-seven situation with an eight-yard reception.

"And that was it for me in that game," Williams said. "I didn't really think much about it, but it made Coach Myles happy and that was good enough for me. I would have done anything for that man."

Gary finished his career with 154 catches for 2,792 yards and 16 TDs. At the time, the reception and yardage totals were program records, and his total touchdowns tied Donley for the OSU career record. Since that time, a multitude of players have caught more touchdown passes, but through the 2021 season, Williams' yardage figure remained third in program history and his receptions total was still sixth.

"The thing about Gary—and you could say the same about Art Schlichter and Doug Donley and Cedric Anderson—they got all their yards in an offense that wasn't exactly geared to a great passing game," OSU football historian Jack Park said. "Give Coach Bruce credit for trying to upgrade the offensive mentality in those days, but deep down, Earle was mainly a Woody disciple who thought that the most effective way to win was to control the line of scrimmage with the running game.

"In my opinion, the fact that Art Schlichter and Gary Williams and all of those players who set records during that era, records that lasted for years and years—some of which are still records some thirty and forty years after they played—can be explained only because they were great, great athletes. Had they played in today's sophisticated offenses, there's no telling how many yards and touchdowns they would have been responsible for."

Williams remains one of the most unsung players of his era, but while he didn't possess the brashness of Schlichter, the flashiness of Donley or the hard-nosed, lunch-pail mentality of linebacker Marcus Marek, there is no doubt that Williams brought a tremendous amount of athleticism to the field.

"Gary was one of the most gifted athletes I have ever coached," Bruce once said. "He had great hands, ran like a deer and caught nearly every ball that was thrown to him. And he was tough. Boy, was he ever tough. There were a lot of times when he played hurt, but he never said anything about it. Just went out and got the job done. Any coach would like to have one or two players like Gary Williams on his team every year."

CARLOS SNOW

OSU TAILBACK 1987–1989, 1991

25

NICKNAME: Los

HOMETOWN: Cincinnati, Ohio

HEIGHT: 5 ft 9 in **WEIGHT:** 200 lb

Emmitt Smith and Carlos Snow met in the winter of 1987 at the annual Columbus Touchdown Club awards banquet, and discovered they had much in common. Snow, on hand to pick up the organization's Ohio High School Player of the Year Award, was an inch shorter and seven pounds lighter than Smith, the club's National High School Player of the Year, but both teenagers had the same sort of massive thighs, wiry calves and muscular upper body.

Each player came from solid, working-class families—Snow hailed from Cincinnati while Smith was born and raised in the Florida Panhandle city of Pensacola—and most of the time, their parents and their brothers and sisters attended their games. Whereas Snow had rushed for 104 touchdowns (and three via the pass) at Cincinnati Academy of Physical Education, Smith had 103, plus three more as a receiver when he played at Escambia High School. Snow helped lead the Crusaders to two state championships, and Smith did the same for the Gators.

Smith had a national high school record forty-five career 100-yard rushing games, and Snow had five 200-yard games and a 16.2 yards-per-carry average his senior year. Snow was faster than Smith in the 40-yard dash, but Smith was stronger, able to leg-press 800 pounds.

When it came time to select a college program, each young man decided to stay close to home, Snow packing up his accolades, trophies and speed and heading to Ohio State, and Smith doing the same at the University of Florida.

They were two high school football stars with seemingly endless potential, and they forged a fast friendship during that brief February night among the rich wood paneling and oxblood leather upholstery of the Athletic Club in downtown Columbus. But their lives took decidedly divergent paths after that brief encounter.

Smith became an All-American at Florida, a first-round NFL draft choice and three-time Super Bowl champion while with the Dallas Cowboys, finishing his career as the all-time leading rusher in NFL history. He was elected to the College Football Hall of Fame in 2006 and the Pro Football Hall of Fame in 2010.

Meanwhile, a litany of injuries conspired to prevent Snow from realizing his full potential with the Buckeyes, and he began an alcohol-infused, drug-addled downward spiral that eventually left him homeless and hopeless. Carlos Snow went from the top of the world to a living, breathing example of how life seldom goes according to plan.

Everything seemingly went according to plan during most of the first eighteen years of his life. He was born Carlos Demetrius Snow on October 24, 1968, the eldest of three children to Ralph Snow, a truck driver for the city of Cincinnati, and his wife, the former Mattie Ruth Guines. In between running the St. Elmo Avenue household in the College Hill section north of downtown Cincinnati and serving as a cook at various healthcare facilities in and around the Queen City, Mattie doled out heaping helpings of sage wisdom. One of her favorites was, "If you make a mistake, there's no need to get upset if you learn from that mistake." Another: "In our family, we've always said there are no limits to the heights you can reach."

Her son seemed intent upon seeing how high his athletic talents could take him. Attending high school at Cincinnati Academy for Physical Education prepared him mentally and physically as well as academically for what was to come. Formed in 1977 as a school focused on physical education, CAPE was seen as something of a breeding ground for athletes. But the school had demanding academic standards as well, with tougher eligibility and graduation requirements than many others in the Cincinnati Public School system. It was also home to students with physical disabilities.

While the school focused on athletics, physiology and nutrition, the building lacked even the most primary facilities. For example, the football team practiced on a patch of grass behind the school but was forced to play its home games about five miles away on the campus of Cincinnati State University. It was there that the Crusaders became a powerhouse, winning the Division IV state championship in 1985 and repeating the following year despite moving up in class to Division III.

Carlos was a perfect blend of power and speed, and nearly unstoppable as he sliced, sped and churned his way to 7,856 rushing yards, then an Ohio high school career record. He flourished at CAPE in other ways, too, playing basketball and running track, and getting voted most popular male student in his senior class.

But along a path that had featured nothing but a straight line to glory, there began to appear the odd twist and turn. Carlos was leaning toward attending the University of Georgia to be near his paternal grandmother, who lived just outside Athens. His childhood idol had been Herschel Walker, who won the 1982 Heisman Trophy while playing for the Bulldogs, and Walker was scheduled to guide the youngster around campus when Carlos made his official visit. But when his grandmother died in February, Carlos changed his mind and decided to attend Ohio State.

A few months later, he arrived in Columbus for the state high school track meet, having qualified to defend the 100-meter championship he had won as a junior. He went out drinking the night before the final and showed up for his race hung over. "I finished dead last," Carlos said. "It was embarrassing." Embarrassing enough that he swore off alcohol, a promise admittedly made and broken hundreds of times after that.

When he first set foot on a practice field at Ohio State, Carlos quickly learned that he had gone from elite high school superstar to just another freshman face in the crowd. "All the stuff they were throwing at us, it didn't take long for me to figure out I wasn't in high school anymore," he said. "Football at that level isn't fun anymore. It's a very serious business."

The more serious it became, the less fun it was. Perhaps nothing underscored that more than the second-half kickoff against West Virginia during the opening game of the 1987 season. Ohio State was protecting a 17-0 lead against the Mountaineers, a team on its way to a six-and-six finish and nowhere near the Buckeyes in terms of talent or ability. OSU head coach Earle Bruce figured it was as good a time as any to unveil one of his newest weapons, so it was Snow on the field to open the third quarter, watching and waiting as the kickoff spun through the air. He settled under it, caught it and set sail.

The 88,272 fans on hand at Ohio Stadium roared as the five-nine, 194-pound sprinter broke a tackle and looked for daylight. "I was so excited," Carlos recalled. "I was thinking about taking it back all the way." An instant later, as he was tackled at the 30-yard line, he fumbled. West Virginia recovered, and five plays later kicked a field goal. It was to be the only points scored for the Mountaineers during an eventual 24–3 victory for Ohio State. The fumbled kickoff return was also the only time Snow touched the football during his college debut.

The following week, at the 1:02 mark of the third quarter during another home game, this one against the Oregon Ducks, Snow touched the ball for the second time in his college career, this time on a pitchout from quarterback Tom Tupa. He fumbled again, although this time he was able to fall on the loose football, making his first official college carry a loss of seven yards.

Later on the same possession, Snow got a third chance, a straight handoff from Tupa. He fumbled once more, and this time the ball was recovered by Oregon. That was all Bruce needed to see. After the freshman's third fumble in three tries, he found himself at the far end of the bench.

He persevered and eventually was rewarded with his first collegiate start in an early November game at Wisconsin. Playing in a rainstorm on a slippery, foreign field, Snow led the team with 79 yards on seventeen carries and added four pass receptions for another 38 yards. But he also fumbled again, a second-quarter turnover the Badgers converted into a field goal, and Wisconsin, which had not won a Big Ten game to that point, eventually claimed a 26–24 victory. It was the second of three consecutive losses for Ohio State, which led the university to fire Bruce the week before the annual showdown with Michigan.

Meanwhile, Snow had turned once again to the bottle in hopes of coping with what had been a less-than expected freshman year. He said he blacked out while driving on Indianola Avenue near campus, crashed his car into a telephone pole and took out a gas pump before "a yellow house stopped me." He never lost his driving privileges or even went to court.

"To tell you the truth, I wish something would have happened to me," Carlos said. "In those days, when you were at Ohio State, it was the kind of thing that gets swept up under the rug. But maybe it could have prevented me from what happened later."

He finished his freshman season with a disappointing 381 yards, but still managed to tie for the team lead in rushing touchdowns. The following year, he led the team with 775 yards, and scored his first special teams touchdown, a 100-yard kickoff return during a mid-September game at Pitt. Snow finally had his breakout season as a junior in 1989 when he established career highs with 990 yards and eleven touchdowns, but even that enjoyment was short-lived.

During a routine examination the following spring, a tumor was discovered on his hip. The tumor was benign, but the subsequent surgery and rehabilitation sidelined Carlos for the entire 1990 season. By the time he returned in 1991, the Ohio State program was in a state of constant turmoil after repeated failures against Michigan and in bowl games. Making matters worse, running back Robert Smith, who had taken over the position in Snow's absence, had quit the team just before the season began amid allegations that head coach John Cooper and members of his staff had pressured him to shirk his classroom duties in favor of football.

Somehow, the Buckeyes managed to win eight games in 1991, and Carlos ran for 828 yards, the third time in his career he had led the team in rushing. That was a feat not accomplished since Archie Griffin led Ohio State four straight years from 1972 to 1975. Snow finished with 2,974 yards on the ground, and also caught forty-six passes for 497 yards and four touchdowns. None of those receptions was more significant than a 70-yarder for a touchdown during his freshman year against Michigan that touched off a second-half comeback and allowed the Buckeyes to give Bruce a 23-20 upset win in his final game.

Despite those numbers, Carlos never made an All-Big Ten first team and went undrafted by the NFL. Still chasing the dream of a professional career, he signed with the Denver Broncos as a free agent in 1992. But early in training camp, he suffered a career-ending knee injury. Suddenly, his athletic career was over at the age of twenty-three. "I was one of those guys who put all his eggs in that basket," he said. "It was always going to be the NFL or bust. And it busted."

Snow had left Ohio State without graduating and his prospects were dim. He ran through opportunities, relationships—including two failed marriages that combined to produce three children—and money. He struggled with alcohol dependency while lingering pain from multiple injuries and surgeries during his football days led to self-medication of a different sort, an addiction to prescription drugs. An OVI conviction in 2017 led to more than a week in jail. By 2018, he was reduced to moving around from short stints living with his sister in Cincinnati to homeless shelters to sleeping in his car. Along the way, he admitted to twice attempting to end his life but

Carlos is one of only five Buckeyes ever to lead the team in rushing yardage during three different seasons.

the thought of leaving his three sons fatherless kept him from self-destructing.

Beginning around New Year's Day in 2019, Snow began to slowly turn his life back around when he reconnected with Bernard Master. The retired doctor, who offered his suburban Columbus home as a sort of way station, had met Snow some thirty years prior when he hired the then-Ohio State football player to do odd jobs around the house. With the help of Alcoholics Anonymous, Carlos stopped drinking and using pain-killers. Both of his knees were replaced, and although his right leg still is held together by a metal rod inserted when he had the benign tumor removed back in 1990, he insists he is enjoying a life largely free from pain.

Master also helped Carlos set up a personal online fundraising campaign with the objective to help Carlos return to school and earn a degree. By the time the new millennium began, Snow had returned to Ohio State and was close to obtaining his degree. He had also secured a job at Directions for Youth in Columbus, specifically working with gang members, hoping to help them turn their lives around.

And he has done what he can to repair broken relationships, reconnecting with his three sons as well as a grandson nearly in his teenage years who already has his sights on becoming an Ohio State running back himself someday. "He says he's going to come up here and break Eddie George's records," Carlos said with a laugh. "He just thinks he's going to be the next great thing at Ohio State."

Once billed himself as the next great thing at Ohio State, Carlos Snow has seen how quickly lofty aspirations can turn into depths of despair. And yet he still believes there are successes worth seeking.

"I've been at rock bottom, but this might be the top of something good," he says. "A new Carlos. A new life. A new beginning. My first fifty years, I messed around and did things my way. This next fifty, I want to keep my eye on the prize."

ROBERT SMITH

OSU TAILBACK 1990, 1992

HOMETOWN: Euclid, Ohio

HEIGHT: 6 ft 2 in **WEIGHT**: 195 lb

NFL DRAFT: 1993, Minnesota Vikings

32

It was a twist on an often-told tale.

The saying goes that every story needs a villain because without a villain, the hero is unable to shine. For any hero to be heroic, he must be challenged. There needs to be conflict, and the villain provides that.

But what good is a story that contains only a villain and no hero? Then you have what occurred during the spring and summer of 1991 within the Ohio State football program when star running back Robert Smith abruptly quit the team.

As much or more outspoken than anyone before or since on the pros and cons of being a college student-athlete, Smith accused his coaches of insisting he put too much emphasis on schoolwork and not enough on football. Those accusations were flatly denied, and Smith was systematically vilified as nothing more than a pampered prima donna who was putting his personal interests over that of the team. And as anyone with even a passing knowledge of Ohio State football knows, anything less than possession of a team-first mentality is something one simply does not hold.

Fans were quick to choose sides and Smith didn't come away with many who were willing to accept his version of events. It was a quick, precipitous fall from messiah to pariah for someone who just a few months earlier was seen as the second coming of two-time Heisman Trophy winner Archie Griffin.

The path charted by Robert Scott Smith to Columbus had already been one fraught with obstacles. Born March 4, 1972, onto the sometimes-mean streets in the inner ring Cleveland suburb of Euclid, Ohio, Smith got a quick introduction into just how harsh life can be. His parents divorced before he was born, but continued to live together for part of his youth.

Robert's mother, Emilie, was a bright, nurturing woman who worked as a registered nurse, but sometimes struggled with prescription drugs. His father also had a drug problem but much more pronounced. Emmitt Smith suffered a midlife mental breakdown and could not hold a job. He checked in and out of a number of treatment centers, eventually turning to heroin and cocaine—using as well as selling—and once wound up on the wrong end of a drug deal gone bad, the scar from a bullet entry wound in his chest and an exit wound scar in his back as evidence.

Robert escaped through athletics, and despite his rail-like frame, realized at an early age that he could outrun every classmate by a wide margin. He became an accomplished sprinter, first at a Catholic elementary school and later at Euclid Center Middle School. By the time he enrolled at Euclid High School, he had become a football standout as well as a track star.

During his junior year alone, Smith rushed for more than 1,500 yards and was named Ohio Mr. Football, symbolic of the state's most outstanding player, and won the 100-meter dash championship at the state track meet. He followed that as a senior by rushing for more than 2,300 yards and 34 touchdowns for the Panthers, and became the first two-time Ohio Mr. Football winner. In track, he again qualified for the state meet where he finished runner-up in the 100 meters.

Robert had his pick of scholarship offers—some for football, some for track, some for both—but eventually selected Ohio State over the University of Miami, the University of Southern California, and UCLA. Then he proceeded to rewrite the record books as a Buckeye, setting a single-season rushing record for freshmen when he totaled 1,126 yards and was named Big Ten Freshman of the Year in the process.

Unfortunately, while Smith was gaining a foothold on stardom at the college level, the Ohio State program remained in a transitional period. John Cooper was in his third season as head coach, and to say the team had struggled under Cooper was something of a gross understatement.

The Buckeyes had a decidedly pedestrian 19–14–2 record during Cooper's first three seasons, not exactly what university officials had expected when they hired the veteran coach with the Southern twang and swagger to replace the vanilla blandness of Earle Bruce. Despite the emergence of Smith at running back, the 1990 season was another disappointment, ending with a third consecutive loss to Michigan and an embarrassing 23–11 loss to unranked Air Force in the 1990 Liberty Bowl, a game for which Cooper's team was equal parts ill-prepared and uninterested.

Between the season-ending loss to Michigan and the Liberty Bowl, offensive coordinator Jim Colletto—who had been with Cooper for three years at Arizona State prior to joining him at OSU—was hired as head coach at Purdue. Just three weeks prior to the opening of spring camp in 1991, Cooper made a decision that would impact his program in ways he never imagined. To replace the open-minded Colletto as offensive coordinator, Cooper hired no-nonsense Elliot Uzelac, a twenty-five-year veteran of the coaching wars who brought with him an old-school approach that immediately began to stir an already simmering pot.

There was little indication during spring practice just how much of an impact Uzelac's hiring as offensive coordinator would ultimately have on the Buckeyes. Smith rushed for 100 yards on fifteen carries during the annual spring game and then afterward indicated he was looking forward to working with his new offensive coordinator. "Hopefully by this fall," he said at the time, "we'll have a better understanding of Coach Uzelac's concepts and come out running like a well-oiled machine."

Somewhere between the end of April and the middle of August, that machine not only began to leak oil, it exploded into a million pieces. Fifteen days before the 1991 season opener against Arizona, Smith

Robert had a star-crossed career with the Buckeyes that was interrupted by a well-publicized decision to quit the team in 1991.

quit the team amid allegations that members of the coaching staff—specifically Cooper and Uzelac—cared little about academics and that players were being unnecessarily injured. The sophomore tailback added that he would not consider returning to the team if the two coaches remained in their positions.

Smith later indicated his problem was not really with Cooper, but that Uzelac had told the running back he was at Ohio State to play football and was taking academics too seriously. The allegations produced a firestorm for a head coach and his program already drowning in negative publicity. Smith had separate meetings with OSU director of athletics Jim Jones and Cooper, after which the running back indicated he would consider returning to the team on one condition: Uzelac had to be reassigned or replaced. Cooper continued to talk with Smith, attempting to get him to rejoin the team until just a few days before the season opener, but the stumbling block was always Uzelac. Smith refused to return if the assistant coach remained in charge of the offense, and Cooper insisted that was a deal-breaker.

The Buckeyes had no choice but to move ahead without their No. 1 tailback. Smith sat out the entire 1991 season, briefly considering a transfer and even visiting the campuses at USC and Stanford during the Christmas holiday break. But he wound up staying at Ohio State and the following spring participated on the OSU men's track team. Meanwhile, the stress of the situation took its toll on the 50-year-old Uzelac. Six days after Smith quit the team, and just nine days before the season opener, the OSU assistant underwent an angioplasty procedure at University Hospitals after complaining of chest pains. Uzelac returned to the practice field a few days later and was in the press box for the 1991 season opener, a 38–14 victory against Arizona.

Meanwhile, Smith concentrated on his studies, had his scholarship switched from football to track, and made plans to transfer. However, before leaving Ohio State, he realized he had misread the NCAA rules regarding eligibility for transfer students.

"It was my understanding that you just needed to spend two semesters at another school and then you could play," Smith said. "I went and visited USC again, and I visited Stanford and that's where I met Denny Green (who would wind up drafting Robert as head coach of the NFL's Minnesota Vikings). I went to those places and was going to transfer and play the next year. But as I became aware that I'd have to sit out the next year, I knew I didn't want to do that. I didn't want to take two years off. Coach Cooper had always told me the door was open if I wanted to come back, so I told him I wanted to do that."

Cooper set up a reconciliatory meeting with Smith and Uzelac at which the head coach told them, "You can agree to disagree, just don't be disagreeable. You guys are going to have to be in the same locker room on the same team, and we're going to work this thing out." Fences appeared to be mended until Uzelac asked Cooper if he could have a moment alone with Smith.

"Coach Cooper left the room and Uzelac pulled out a tape recorder," Robert said. "He says, 'Why did you lie to *Sports Illustrated*?' I said, 'Coach, you know I didn't lie to *Sports Illustrated*.' And he repeats the question. I thought, 'This is pointless,' and got up and left the room. Cooper's out there standing in the hall and I said, 'Coach, that guy's got a problem.' Apparently, Uzelac had a lawsuit against *Sports Illustrated* and was asked to withdraw it. But he didn't, and so he was let go. Then the story became that I got him fired."

Smith returned to the Buckeyes but his production slipped to 819 yards as he shared ball-carrying duties with fellow tailback Raymont Harris and fullback Jeff Cothran. Cooper was still under fire after an 8–4–1 season, but at least he managed not to lose to Michigan for the first time in five years. Ohio State erased a 10–3 deficit after three quarters, scoring a field goal and a touchdown in the final period to forge a 13–13 tie with their archrivals.

Meanwhile, Uzelac resurfaced as a consultant on Cleveland Browns head coach Bill Belichick's staff, and then he resumed a coaching career that continues to this day at a high school in Michigan.

Smith left Ohio State for good following the 1992 season, leaving with a year of eligibility remaining to become the Vikings' first-round selection in the 1993 draft. An array of injuries limited his productivity during his first four seasons in the NFL, but beginning in 1997, he was as good as any running back in the league. Over the next four seasons, he averaged nearly 1,250 yards rushing and another 250 yards receiving. He was twice named to the Pro Bowl, including in 2000 when he rushed for a career-high 1,521 yards and seven touchdowns as Minnesota advanced to the NFC Championship Game.

Robert retired after that season, walking away from the game to continue pursuit of a career in medicine. That never materialized, but life was filled with such other pursuits as serving as a football analyst for ESPN and the NFL Network, and dabbling in such diverse fields as writing, acting, and astronomy. He is also founder of an eponymous charitable organization whose goal is provide financial and moral support for Children's hospitals and cancer research.

He has also become more comfortable in his own skin. In 2013, he admitted to fighting alcoholism during his playing career, adding that he sought counseling and achieved sobriety following the birth of his son, Grayson.

And what of his star-crossed career at Ohio State?

Cooper, open and forthcoming on almost any subject, doesn't like talking about the situation that led Smith to quit the Buckeyes and then return a year later. Uzelac has never talked about it. Meanwhile, the player at the center of the controversy seems to finally have achieved some peace. He lives with his wife, Jennifer, and their two children in suburban Houston—with his mother close by—and prefers to live his life through the windshield rather than the rear-view mirror. Still, he knows many Ohio State fans continue to place most of the blame for what happened in 1991 on the spoiled inner-city kid whose over-the-top ego led him to believe he was bigger than the Buckeyes.

But as the saying goes, "The role of the villain is only determined by who's telling the story."

JOEY *GALLOWAY*

OSU SPLIT END 1991, 1993–1994

NICKNAME: Joey G

HOMETOWN: Bellaire, Ohio

HEIGHT: 5 ft 11 in **WEIGHT**: 186 lb

NFL DRAFT: 1985, Seattle Seahawks

7

Joey Galloway is almost too good to be true. The very antithesis of today's coddled athlete, Galloway has always marched to his own drumbeat. Growing up in a small Ohio River village, he usually volunteered for naps, and he hated to miss a day of school even when he was sick. He favored video games and watching sci-fi movies over partying with friends, bought a pair of big-screen TVs with his first professional bonus check and banked the rest, and let his mom decorate his apartment.

His work ethic was also off the charts. Told he was too small to play big-time college football, he got bigger. Informed that speed was not the only facet to a polished receiver, he worked on his quickness and honed his route-running ability. When he missed almost an entire season at Ohio State with a knee injury, he returned the following year to become the first receiver in more than forty years to lead the Buckeyes in scoring.

Then once he entered the National Football League as a first-round selection questioned by critics who thought his tightly muscled five-foot-eleven-inch frame would never hold up against the assault of bigger, meaner linebackers and defensive backs, Galloway enjoyed a sixteen-year pro career as one of the league's most reliable pass-catchers while moonlighting most of those years as a lethal punt return man.

"Joey was such a good kid. Good family, good upbringing. He was like having another son when he played for me," said John Magistro, who was Galloway's high school football coach. "He had natural gifts, of course, but he was always attentive to anything that he thought could make him better. And his work ethic was off the charts. He was a great teammate and just a good kid all the way around. Everybody loves Joey."

Joseph Scott Galloway was born November 20, 1971, the youngest of four sons to James Delois "Deanie" Galloway and the former Carolyn Alberta McDowell, in Bellaire, Ohio, a village on the Ohio River that has dwindled in population from a high of 15,000 in 1920 to a little more than four thousand according to the 2010 census.

"I wouldn't say he was a typical Midwestern child," his mother once said. "For instance, unlike his brothers, he wasn't into cartoons at all. I would ask him, 'Don't you want to watch cartoons?' He'd just shake his head. All he wanted to watch on TV was sports."

Whether it was baseball, basketball and ice hockey games of the week, golf and tennis matches, or even demolition derby, figure skating or cliff diving from Acapulco on ABC's Wide World of Sports, Joey would watch it. But he had a special affinity for football games, especially those of the Pittsburgh Steelers.

"My hometown is only about sixty miles from Pittsburgh, so it was a natural fit," Joey said, cheerfully noting his favorite team was a perennial Super Bowl champion while he was growing up. "I was a Steelers fan through and through. (Terry) Bradshaw, Franco (Harris), (Jack) Lambert, 'Mean' Joe (Greene)...As a kid, I used to wear my black and gold Steelers jersey every Sunday. It was the same as my favorite player. It was a Lynn Swann jersey."

While Joey was either in front of the television watching Swann, or perfecting his own receiving skills in the back yard of the family's Sullivan Street home, his father worked as a technician for the telephone company while his mother was a longtime cashier at the village's Kroger supermarket.

James wasn't just adept at fixing telephone lines, either. When the Galloway residence burned down, he rebuilt it from scratch. "He was amazing," Joey recalled. "He'd grab a book on carpentry, and before you knew it, he'd put in a new room."

Likely from watching his father construct a new home in his spare time or perhaps from the countless times watching him head off to repair telephone lines in every kind of inclement weather, Joey adopted an unyielding work ethic that permeated every aspect of his life.

"He was different," his mother said. "He seemed to be more mature at a younger age. He had priorities."

As a youngster, since he rarely missed school, insisting on attending even when he didn't feel well, his bus driver once saw how ill he was and made him go back home. "He was the only kid I knew who actually wanted to go to school," said his father. "It was like it was his job or something. He never wanted to miss a single day."

Joey later admitted that it wasn't so much that he enjoyed school, but he associated school with playing sports. His love for one made the other absolutely necessary.

He remembered a discussion he had with his parents when he announced he wanted to go to college. "What do you want to major in?" his mother asked. "Football" was Joey's reply. When told he couldn't major in football and would have to choose something else, he thought for a moment and then asked his father, "If I go to college, will you get me a car?" Joey was eight years old at the time.

By the time he reached high school, college was a foregone conclusion even if his major remained undecided. Had Joey set his mind to it, he could have been a major star in any of three sports other than football.

In basketball, he averaged more than twenty points per game at Bellaire High School, led his team to back-to-back conference championships, and won all-state honors. Then there was baseball, where he was a consistent hitter and stole twenty-seven bases in just fifteen games during his junior season. The remainder of his high school springs were spent with the track team, where he used his 4.35 speed in the forty-yard dash to anchor several relay events.

But football was the sport in which Galloway excelled the most. Nicknamed "The Bellaire Bullet," he helped lead the Big Reds to nine victories in ten games and a conference title as a junior. A year later, he grabbed thirty-two receptions for 608 yards and eight touchdowns, and added an average of 15.2 yards per punt return. He earned his third selection to the all-conference and all-area teams as well as a second-team All-Ohio honor in Division III. He finished his high school career with 108 receptions for 2,232 yards and twenty-seven touchdowns, and was considered the top receiver prospect in the Midwest.

His first three seasons at Ohio State showed only flashes of what he would become. Barely 170 pounds when he got to campus, Galloway spent the 1990 season as a redshirt and then got off to a slow start in 1991 due to an ankle injury. He wound up with only fourteen catches for 255 yards and one touchdown in a backup role, but he served notice during the Buckeyes' 24–17 loss to Syracuse in the Hall of Fame Bowl—six catches for 88 yards—that he was going to be ready for a larger role the following season.

Unfortunately, his 1992 campaign was over before it really got started. Galloway electrified the Ohio Stadium crowd with a 50-yard touchdown run on a reverse in the opening game against Louisville, but then tore the ACL in his right knee the following week against Bowling Green. He was out for the rest of the season as well as contact drills for the next spring.

Galloway rehabbed like a demon, however, and returned in 1993 as a chiseled 5–11, 186-pounder who could bench press in the neighborhood of four hundred pounds. In the weight room at Ohio State that spring was a representative cross-section of the program's best and brightest, including future Heisman Trophy winner Eddie George, tight end and future first-round draft pick Rickey Dudley, and Minnesota Vikings running back Robert Smith—all trying to outdo one another in daily feats of strength.

In the middle was Galloway with a body not nearly as imposing as the others. But when the competition got heated, "Joey would smoke them," OSU strength coach Dave Kennedy said. "They absolutely got smoked."

Added former quarterback Kirk Herbstreit, who witnessed the workout sessions from the safety of his Stairmaster, "They're all physical specimens, but what's funny is that Joey set the standard. They all have egos, but when they're alone, they'll always point out that, based on strength and speed, Joey is by far the best athlete they've ever seen."

That new power, coupled with speed regained from the surgically-repaired knee, allowed for a breakout season in 1993. As the Buckeyes compiled a 10-1-1 record, their best finish in fourteen seasons, Galloway led the team with forty-seven receptions for 946 yards and eleven touchdowns. He added two more scores on reverses, allowing him to become the first receiver to lead Ohio State in scoring since Bob Grimes tied for the lead in 1952.

Joey was touted as a preseason Heisman Trophy candidate in 1994 when he took one of the rare false steps in his life. Convinced he was going to leave school early for the NFL, he accepted a small amount of money (reportedly just $200) from a prospective agent. But he changed his mind about leaving school—or more accurately, had it changed.

Carolyn and Deanie Galloway were the ones who convinced Joey to stay at Ohio State and finish college. That was something they never did and neither did any of their three oldest sons. Additionally, Deanie did not want his son's decision to be solely about money.

"As usual they were right," Joey said. "But I didn't stay because I thought I could catch a hundred passes and make more money. I stayed because I wanted to get my marketing degree. Plus, I had another year to hang out with my friends. Why let that get away?"

Although Galloway returned the money, the NCAA suspended him for the first three games of the 1994 season. And although his senior year was limited to ten games, he still managed forty-four receptions for 669 yards and seven touchdowns as well as one more touchdown on the ground and another on a kickoff return of ninety-three yards. He finished his career tied for fourth on Ohio State's all-time list in receptions with 108, fourth in receiving yardage with 1,894 and second in touchdown catches with nineteen.

The Seattle Seahawks made Galloway their first-round selection in the 1995 NFL draft, taking him with the eighth selection overall. He played five seasons in Seattle before moving on to play four years with the Dallas Cowboys, and then six with the Tampa Bay Buccaneers before finishing his career with the New England Patriots and the Washington Redskins.

Over the course of his sixteen seasons in the NFL, Galloway was remarkably consistent, logging nine seasons of fifty or more catches and six seasons of at least one thousand yards. His lifetime statistics for 198 NFL games included 701 receptions, 10,950 yards, and 77 touchdowns. He added five more touchdowns on punt returns.

Upon retirement, Joey figured he would simply return to Ohio and fill his time with family, friends and the occasional round of golf. That's when Herbstreit, a fixture on ESPN since 1996 as a college football game analyst as well as lead analyst of the network's *College GameDay* pregame show, reached out to his former teammate about a possible sports broadcasting gig.

"It was probably more Kirk's plan than mine," Joey said. "My idea was to be prepared if I ever chose that, but he really talked me into it. He put me in touch with the right people, (ESPN) called me, and I thought I'd give it a shot."

Beginning with in-studio analysis of college games in 2011, Galloway has remained with ESPN in a variety of roles including coverage of national rankings and the College Football Playoff. "I enjoy it just because I get to talk about football," he says. "But there's always something new to learn, and I like that aspect of it, too."

In the end, though, Joey Galloway remains what he has always been—the hard-working, determined little kid from Bellaire who never forgets his roots. He has conducted several youth football camps in the area with proceeds going to cancer research, a cause near to his heart. Joey's mom, Carolyn, died in 2011 at the age of sixty-six after a long battle with peritoneal cancer.

When his high school basketball coach Gene Ammirante was inducted into the Ohio Valley Athletic Conference Hall of Fame, Joey awarded him with a brand-new Cadillac. He did the same for Magistro when the football coach retired from Bellaire.

"Giving those guys a car didn't even scratch the surface of what they gave to me over the years," Joey said. "I've been blessed to have so many people in my life, and Coach Magistro and Coach A are near the top of the list. It was just a way for me to say thank you to them with just a token of what they meant to me."

DAN WILKINSON

OSU DEFENSIVE TACKLE 1992–1993

77

NICKNAME: Big Daddy

HOMETOWN: Dayton, Ohio

HEIGHT: 6 ft 5 in **WEIGHT:** 300 lb

ALL-AMERICAN: 1993

NFL DRAFT: 1994, Cincinnati Bengals

Playing a sport typically dominated by large young men, Dan Wilkinson still managed to cut a larger-than-life profile at Ohio State during the early 1990s. From his healthy appetite and oversized personality to even his nickname "Big Daddy," Wilkinson went from pillowy prospect to number one NFL draft pick in a few short years.

Yet deep inside that 6-foot-4, 300-pound mountain of a man beat the heart of a teddy bear. In reality, Big Daddy was just a mama's boy, eager to please his mother and allow her to enjoy some of the finer things life has to offer. In the eyes of her son, Veronda Jean Wilkinson, a hard-working, overachieving widow who managed to raise eleven children and still find time to get a college degree, had earned at least that much.

And when her Daniel's name was the first one called on April 24, 1994, during what the NFL formally called its 59th Annual Player Selection Meeting, Veronda sat quietly in a California living room, counting her blessings. It seemed the good life had finally arrived. Unfortunately, like many good things, it didn't last for long.

Daniel Raymon Wilkinson was born March 13, 1973, in Dayton, Ohio, the second-youngest of eleven children to Oliver Anthony Wilkinson and the former Veronda Jean Locke. The couple had married young—Oliver was eighteen and a high school senior while Veronda had just turned sixteen—after learning a baby was on the way. They welcomed little Koneta Louise in August 1958, the first of five daughters and six sons.

Oliver was a Detroit native who moved to the Dayton area as a youngster and graduated from Dunbar High School, one of nearly a dozen high schools throughout the country named for African-American poet and Dayton native Paul Laurence Dunbar. A big, strong man at six-one and 240 pounds, he found work in various machine shops around the Gem City, settling at the historic Duriron Company, an industrial component manufacturer specializing in such products as control valves, pumps, pipes and fittings for oil refineries. It was an honest but grueling job for the strong-willed, muscular man known in high school as "Doom Daddy," but Oliver worked overtime any day he could to help keep food on the table for his ever-growing family.

As a new boy or girl came along about every year or so, the Wilkinsons settled into a five-bedroom house in West Dayton, a structure that seemed to defy the laws of nature. There would seem to be no way thirteen people could have lived in the house with its sharp angles, compact living space and single-file kitchen. But Veronda said, if you cram a place with bunk beds and love, anything is possible.

"Their friends were always coming over," she recalled, "There always seems to be one house in a neighborhood where everyone always goes, and ours was it. The house, it was always rockin'."

For as many siblings that shared living quarters, brothers and sisters rarely quarreled. The kitchen, described by Veronda "a one-butt kitchen because only one butt could get in it at a time," was about the only site of discord among the Wilkinson children. The fights were always over food, and young Dan was usually involved. His older siblings would buy chicken or pizza with their own money, then try to hide it from him in the back of the refrigerator.

"But Dan would always find it," said Oliver Jr., four years Dan's elder. "We'd come home the next day and it would be gone."

The morning of October 5, 1987, began like any other Monday. After a relaxing Sunday that included attending a service at Mount Pisgah Baptist Church and checking in on the Cincinnati Bengals long enough to watch them lose a 10–9 decision to the San Diego Chargers on a last-second field goal, Oliver rose and ate his breakfast. A nagging pain in his back had caused him to schedule a doctor's appointment for an X-ray, after which he would head across town to his job at Duriron. A few short hours later, he was gone. The victim of a massive heart attack, Oliver Wilkinson was dead at the age of forty-eight.

"I always wondered why the Lord took him and left me," Veronda said. "How was I going to put the kids through school and do what needed to be done? We sat down as a family and talked about it. We had to keep going. I knew if

I stopped, they'd stop—because some already had."

Veronda was particularly worried about Dan. Then fourteen years old and a freshman at Dunbar, he quit the football team the day his father died. Not until his brother pulled him aside did his attitude begin to change. "I said, 'Dan, do you know how big you are? Do you know what you can do in this world?'" Oliver Jr. recalled. "I said, 'Dan, you can be the one to take care of Mama. You can be the one to take care of this family.'"

The Dunbar coaches began picking him up at the house and taking him to practice. He missed two games, but slowly came to the realization that not playing wouldn't bring his father back.

"Dan was quite a player right away," said Albert Powell, one of his first coaches at Stivers Intermediate School. "Dan was only thirteen then, but he was already six-feet tall and 228 pounds. He wanted to be a fullback, but I convinced him that the line was where the real men played. Carl Hairston was in Cleveland at the time, so I told Dan, 'We're going to put you on the defensive line. You're going to be our Big Daddy.' He liked it and the nickname just stuck. He also admitted he didn't miss playing fullback. He told me, 'I like falling on people better.'"

By the time he was a junior in high school, he was listed at six-five and 290 pounds. Somehow, though, Big Daddy wasn't just a hulking hole-plugger on defense. He was light on his feet, explosive at the point of attack and an embarrassing nightmare for offensive linemen with the temerity to take him on.

"I played him at nose guard for a while," said longtime Dunbar head coach Tom Montgomery, "and he was just tremendous. You'd think with his size, he would just bully the center. But no way. He would just swing around them because he's so quick. Would you believe he runs a 4.8 in the 40? Unbelievable when you see him, I know. But it's true."

As he accumulated all-state and prep All-America honors, Wilkinson seemingly had only two obstacles to overcome while college stardom awaited—academics that he had let slide since his father's passing and his love affair with food. He overcame the former, but only after achieving a passing grade on the final college entrance exam of the school year that made him eligible to play football as a freshman. Clearing the latter hurdle was a bit trickier.

When Wilkinson arrived at Ohio State in the fall of 1991 and stepped on the scale, it wheezed and groaned before stopping at 348 pounds. Between his mother's homemade bread, cakes and pies, and late-night runs to the refrigerator for leftover pizza, Dan had gained nearly forty pounds over the summer. Making matters worse, when initial lineups were posted in the Ohio State weight room, he was listed among the offensive linemen. No one his size, he was told, could play defense.

So, head coach John Cooper and Dan reached an understanding. If Big Daddy could shed some of his bigness and get down to 310 pounds, he could play defense for the Buckeyes. Anything above 310, and he would have to line up on the other side of the ball. That was all the incentive he needed. Dan redshirted during the 1991 season, and when camp convened the following summer, he was down to 295 pounds.

It was a good thing, too. During his first college game, the 1992 season opener against Louisville, Wilkinson preserved a one-point Ohio State win by chasing Cardinals quarterback Jeff Brohm to the sideline and forcing him to misfire on a two-point conversion pass with just thirty-three seconds remaining in the game. As the season progressed, opposing offenses were forced to develop blocking schemes to neutralize Wilkinson, but they had little effect. He led the team in sacks, a rarity for a defensive tackle, and was named to the All-Big Ten first team.

The following year, despite playing much of the second half of the season on a severely sprained left ankle, Wilkinson led the Buckeyes with thirteen tackles for loss, repeated as a first-team all-conference performer and added first-team All-America honors to his list of accolades. With little left to prove at the college level, Big Daddy set his sights on the NFL.

Meanwhile, his mother continued work as a computer programmer and analyst at Miami Valley Hospital in Dayton. She earned a degree in business administration and computer information from Central State University in 1986, having attended classes at night for seven years while holding down a job and managing the household.

Once the Bengals took him with the top pick in the 1994 draft, he bought himself a $35,000 Toyota Land Cruiser. Then he leased a Lexus for his mother with the promise of also trading her tiny house on Dayton-Liberty Road for a more spacious one in the affluent suburb of Beavercreek.

"I wanted to get my mother secured. I wanted to give her things she'd never been able to get as soon as I could," Wilkinson recalled.

"The nickname Big Daddy fits him because his is a generous nature," Veronda said. "In that sense, he is a big daddy. I think he thinks he's my daddy sometimes. He tells me what I should and shouldn't do. Daniel told me my job now was to exercise and eat right so I would stay healthy and stay around."

Unfortunately, her son's honeymoon in Cincinnati was short-lived.

Wilkinson spent four seasons in Cincinnati at a time when the Bengals were in the midst of a twelve-year stretch without a winning season. Although he was always among the team leaders in tackles for loss and sacks, as an overall first-round draft choice, fans considered him something of a bust and began booing him. In December 1997, he was quoted as calling Cincinnati "a racist city," adding that its residents were "prejudiced, upright, and stiff."

The remarks caused Bengals owner Mike Brown to trade Wilkinson, despite wearing the team franchise player tag, to the Washington Redskins, saying the defensive lineman "hadn't fulfilled his promise" in Cincinnati despite recording 25 sacks and 177 tackles. "What we found was, when he was of a mind to, he could be a tremendous player on the field. We weren't able to get a consistent performance out of him, and I don't know that we could have with all that developed here. It was best for Dan that he get another crack at it somewhere else."

What no one knew is that Big Daddy's heart had been broken a second time. On February 27, 1996, just two weeks before her son's twenty-third birthday, Veronda Wilkinson's heart of gold gave out.

She was only fifty-three, having gotten to enjoy her new house for less than two years.

His mother's death came at the end of a tumultuous part of Wilkinson's life that began in September 1995 when he was charged with misdemeanor domestic violence for striking his pregnant live-in girlfriend and the birth of his first son, Daniel II, five months later. Before the trial, his girlfriend, Shawnda LaMarr, asked that the case be dropped. Prosecutors declined, and Wilkinson pleaded no contest to a lesser charge of recklessly causing physical harm, paid a fine and entered into counseling at his own initiative. Wilkinson's charitable efforts on behalf of Cincinnati schoolchildren, documented in his court file, were persuasive to the judge in lightening terms of his probation.

Dan and Shawnda were later married and had three more children before divorcing. He has since remarried and has two more children.

Big Daddy played five seasons in Washington and finished his pro career with three seasons in Detroit and one in Miami. He retired following the 2006 season with 390 tackles and 54½ sacks in 195 games, 182 of them starts. Despite those numbers, he never made All-Pro or was voted to the Pro Bowl, and consistently appears on lists of the biggest underachievers in NFL draft history.

If that bothers him, he doesn't seem to show it. Since his playing days, he has dabbled in business, including owning a number of auto repair franchises in Ohio, and indulges in a number of hobbies such as deep-sea fishing.

Most days, however, find him at home with his kids, trying to fill the house with the kind of love and memories befitting of a man known as Big Daddy.

TERRY GLENN

OSU FLANKER 1993–1995

NICKNAME: Grease, T-Glenn

HOMETOWN: Columbus, Ohio

HEIGHT: 5 ft 11 in **WEIGHT**: 185 lb

ALL-AMERICAN: 1995

NFL DRAFT: 1996, New England Patriots

83

It seemed that Terry Glenn spent his entire life running from one thing or another. A traumatic childhood. Relationships. Perceptions. College and professional defensive backs. Trouble. Injuries. Bad influences. Inner demons. Destiny.

Unfortunately, like many other tortured souls before and after him, Glenn realized too late just how impossible it is to run away from oneself. His story, filled with as much against-all-odds triumph as any installment in the *Rocky* film series offset by more tragedy than Shakespeare could have imagined possible, seemed finally on an upward trajectory when it ended suddenly one night by the side of a suburban Dallas highway.

Terrence Tyree Glenn was born July 23, 1974, in Columbus, Ohio, to a teenaged mother and a father he never knew. He never got to know his father, and in later life said he didn't ever want to know him as the young man abandoned his family and was out of the picture throughout Terry's childhood.

His mother, Denetta Dekaye Glenn, just sixteen when Terry was born, never really had a place to call home, and she shuffled her baby boy from place to place within her extended family. But it soon became clear the boy wasn't wanted anywhere he went. His aunts reluctantly looked after him, but they had only daughters and really didn't know what to do with a young boy, passing him from home to home, sometimes as many as four times a year.

As a teenaged, unwed mother, Denetta Glenn tried to balance staying in school and working part-time jobs, but the pay was sporadic at best, and it forced her to rely on welfare checks, and those often didn't cover the bare necessities. "We had nothing," Terry said. "Nothing at all. There were times when we didn't have electricity or gas. Man, you talk about poor. We were there." The financial problems didn't get any better when seven-year-old Terry was joined by sister Dorothy.

His mother continued to drift from odd job to odd job, and unfortunately from one bad relationship to another until October 1987 when she met a man named Kenneth Adams. The brief relationship was always one-sided with Adams apparently feeling more for Denetta than she did for him. Apparently unable to deal with his feelings of unrequited love, Adams abducted Denetta, beat her to death, and left her body in an abandoned building. She was only twenty-nine.

"I was over at my aunt's house when the police called and told us they found a body in a building," Terry said. "They were going to call us back later on after they identified the body to see if it was her, but I had a feeling already. He liked her and she didn't like him. I guess that's why he did it."

Adams was later sentenced to serve thirteen to thirty years in prison, but Denetta's murder forced her young son to make a choice.

"I just started thinking about the consequences of her being gone," recalled Terry, who was only thirteen when his mother died. "What was I going to do? Where was I going to go from there? There didn't seem to be any future for me, so for a while, I didn't want to go on. I didn't care about anything and figured maybe ending things was the way out. But I had a little sister who was also affected. Who was going to take care of her?

"Once I looked at my little sister, who was seven at the time and just so sad, I knew it wasn't just about me. She was the only person I was thinking about once we got the call because how do you explain to a seven-year-old that she wasn't going to see her mother anymore? It was hard. But we just told her right out. And she was strong. She understood."

Dorothy eventually went to live with her natural father in Akron while Terry continued to be shuttled between relatives for the next couple of years. But as he grew older, he began running with the wrong crowd. One of his closest cousins would die from gunshot wounds while other friends and relatives would also become victims of the streets, and his aunts finally threw up their hands in defeat.

"They wanted me to move out," Terry said. "They said they were going to take me to Children's Services, and I guess you couldn't blame them. But then I found someone whose parents were into sports and that's what I always wanted. I asked if they would let me stay over a couple of nights, and those couple of nights turned into eight years."

Charles Lee Henley Jr., whom everyone called "June," was friends with one of Terry's cousins when they met in 1989. The boys were only a year apart, and as their friendship grew closer, June's parents, Charles Sr. and Mary, not only took Terry in, they became his legal guardians.

They went on to become standout athletes at Brookhaven High School, the northeast Columbus alma mater of former Ohio State and NFL defensive back Marlon Kerner as well as five-time Major League Baseball All-Star outfielder Paul O'Neill. While Henley became a highly recruiting running back, eventually playing his college ball at the University of Kansas, Terry initially made his name playing basketball and tennis while running track for the Bearcats. Football wasn't even on his radar until his sophomore year, when football coach Gregg Miller saw him playing hoops and suggested a gridiron tryout.

It turned out that Glenn was a natural. He did a little bit of everything for Brookhaven, playing wide receiver on offense and cornerback on defense, returning kickoffs and punts, and even serving as the team's punter. He helped the Bearcats advance to the state semifinals during his senior season, catching fourteen passes for 416 yards and four touchdowns while earning second-team all-district recognition.

But while those numbers were good, they didn't exactly jump off the page and Terry received only tepid attention from college recruiters. It didn't help that his academic standing was also questionable, leading many coaches to believe he wouldn't be eligible to play even if they did sign him. That didn't seem to deter him, though. His dream was to play football for his hometown Ohio State Buckeyes, doing his best to get close to the school by selling soft drinks at Ohio Stadium on game days.

Without a scholarship offer, he still enrolled in classes at Ohio State during the fall of 1992, maintained his academic eligibility, and walked onto the football team. He played a variety of positions on the scout team and so impressed the coaching staff that he was awarded a scholarship the following spring.

"Terry actually qualified by the end of his senior year in high school," recalled Bill Conley, who at the time was recruiting coordinator on John Cooper's Ohio State coaching staff. "But by the time we knew he was going to be eligible, we no longer had any scholarships available. We knew what kind of an athlete he could become, so we made a commitment to him that he would receive a grant-in-aid the following spring if he would walk on with us. We were sweating it out, hoping no other program would swoop in with a scholarship offer. But Terry always wanted to play for Ohio State and everything worked out."

Still, Glenn's first three seasons with the Buckeyes were quiet ones. After redshirting during his walk-on year, he was locked behind All-Big Ten performer Joey Galloway and speed merchant Chris Sanders on the depth chart at receiver, and caught only fifteen balls for 266 yards and no touchdowns during his freshman and sophomore years.

As a junior in 1995, however, Glenn's stardom took off like a rocket ship. With Sanders and Galloway off to the NFL, the Buckeyes turned to him and he delivered with a big-time flourish. In 12 games, he caught 64 passes for 1,411 yards and seventeen touchdowns, each of which were new single-season program records. During a week-three blowout against the University of Pittsburgh, he grabbed nine receptions for 253 yards and four touchdowns. The touchdown receptions tied a single-game mark that hadn't been equaled since being set in 1952, and the yardage remained an Ohio State record for a quarter-century until Jaxon Smith-Njigba totaled 347 yards during the Buckeyes' 48-45 win against Utah in the 2022 Rose Bowl.

Terry earned consensus acclamation to the All-America first team, becoming the first Ohio State receiver to be so honored since Cris Carter in 1986, and he became the first Buckeye to capture the Fred Biletnikoff Award, given to the nation's top college wide receiver. With nothing left to prove on the collegiate level, he left school with one season of eligibility remaining and made himself available for the NFL draft. But after the New England Patriots made him their first-round pick with the seventh overall selection, Terry found he had to prove his worth all over again.

Patriots head coach Bill Parcells had been outspoken of his desire to draft a defensive player, and was even more outspoken when he was overruled by team management. Then when Glenn suffered a preseason injury and was slow to recover, Parcells made his displeasure known at Glenn's expense, questioning Terry's toughness by referring to the receiver on several occasions as "She." Years later, the Hall of Fame coach expressed regret over the way he handled the situation while Terry remained pragmatic.

"I kind of wish it never would have happened," he said later in his career, "but I look back on it and how far I've come and I can say I'm glad Parcells did that. It kind of pushed me a little bit to get out there and prove to him as well as my teammates that I could play."

Glenn established an NFL rookie record with 90 receptions in 1996, and helped New England advance to Super Bowl XXXI, where the Patriots lost a 35-21 decision to the Green Bay Packers. Terry caught four passes for 62 yards in the game, including a catch of forty-four yards that set up a first-quarter touchdown that gave New England an early 14-10 lead.

It was the first of six turbulent years in New England for Glenn, who endured a litany of injuries and coaching changes but still remained one of the Patriots' most effective offensive weapons. It was during the 2001 season when he caught the first career touchdown pass from a second-year quarterback named Tom Brady.

Glenn was traded during the 2001-02 offseason to Green Bay, and after one season with the Packers, he was dealt again, this time to the Dallas Cowboys where he was reunited with Parcells and his career was reignited. Still bothered by lingering injuries, Glenn remained productive whenever he was on the field, stringing together back-to-back 1,000-yard seasons for the first time in his career and leading the NFL with an average of 18.3 yards per catch in 2005.

Preseason knee surgery cost Glenn the first fifteen games of the 2007 season, but he returned for a token appearance in the final regular-season game that year. He was officially released after the season, and was in talks with the Cowboys on a restructuring of his contract. But with so many injuries behind him, and the prospect of a body breaking down again, he decided to retire at the age of thirty-three. In 137 career games in the NFL, he totaled 593 receptions for 8,823 yards and 44 touchdowns.

He remained in the Dallas Metroplex area after his career and started the 83 Kids Foundation, an organization designed to link donors with non-profits to help provide assistance for foster children and their foster parents.

The foundation took up only so much of his time, however, and it seemed for a time that Terry, saved at a young age by football, was now lost without it. He was arrested twice in 2009, once for public intoxication, and months later after renting a car and failing to return it. Then in early 2011, he was arrested yet again, this time for driving while intoxicated and marijuana possession. Meanwhile, he had an on-again, off-again relationship with one woman before becoming engaged to another woman, all the while trying to be a strong and present father to his seven children.

He finally seemed to be at peace with himself as he reached his 40s, but demons remained that he simply could not outrun. On November 19, 2017, Terry and his fiancée attended a Sunday night game at AT&T Stadium, the billion-dollar home of the Cowboys in the bustling Dallas suburb of Irving. The couple was driving home following a 37-9 loss to the eventual Super Bowl champion Philadelphia Eagles when their car left the highway and struck a concrete barrier. While his fiancée escaped with minor injuries, Glenn was killed. An autopsy showed that his blood-alcohol content was more than twice the legal limit. He was only forty-three years old.

It was the tragic end of the final chapter to the story of a man who managed to overcome great adversity as a child to become one of the most dynamic NFL players of his era. But in the end, there turned out to be only so many demons Terry Glenn could outrun.

LUKE FICKELL

DEFENSIVE TACKLE, ASSISTANT COACH, INTERIM HEAD COACH

99

NICKNAME: Fick

HOMETOWN: Columbus, Ohio

HEIGHT: 6 ft 4 in **WEIGHT:** 270 lb

Throw me to the wolves and I will return leading the pack. —Seneca

Luke Fickell has been thrown to the wolves so many times it might be only natural if he had picked up some lupine ways of approaching crises. When he was in the first grade, his mother dropped him off at wrestling practice to spar against high school freshmen. When he had proved everything he could prove on a college football field, he played his final game with a completely torn pectoral muscle. When Ohio State was desperate for leadership in the wake of the so-called Tattoogate scandal of 2010–11, it was Fickell who stepped into the breach and served as interim head coach, bridging a gap that could have signaled the beginning of the end for a once-proud program.

The Buckeyes suffered through seven losses during the 2011 season, albeit just one of them by more than seven points, and Fickell was passed over for two-time national championship coach Urban Meyer, who had to be coaxed into retaining Fickell, who refused to beg to keep his job. Then, realizing that perhaps the easiest path to further success would have been to stay at Ohio State as an assistant coach for as long as he wished, Fickell chose to branch out and begin a resurrection of the dormant program at the University of Cincinnati, a rebuilding project that almost immediately bore fruit with back-to-back seasons featuring eleven victories for only the second time in a program history that dates to 1885.

When that rebuild was nearly complete, and he had his pick of jobs at higher-profile universities, Luke chose to remain loyal to the Bearcats and continue to build upon the turnaround that began when he left Ohio State. All the while, he maintains a tight-knit family life with his wife, Amy, and their six children, stressing that perhaps his tallest order is trying to keep his priorities of being a father, husband, and football coach in their proper order.

"You try to stay in that order although sometimes it gets out of whack a little bit," Luke says. "I think you know when you get into this business, you know it's exhausting. It's like parenting. It never stops. So, we have eighteen- to twenty-two-years-old, and we have 105 of them. It becomes a part of our life. It becomes a part of your family's life. And that's the only way you can really be successful in this. I don't just mean successful on the field. The only way to be successful as a husband, successful as a father, is if your whole family is all-in and fully engaged in the things you love to do and they're part of it."

Born Luke Joseph Fickell on August 18, 1973, in Columbus, Ohio, he was the first of three children for Patrick Raymond Fickell, who served in the Vietnam War as a member of the U.S. Marine Corps and then worked much of his civilian life in a railroad yard, and the former Sharon Louise Hiles, who made her career as a beautician.

A girl, Leah, followed two years later, and two years after that came second son Michael, who rounded out the family conclave in the white-sided, black-shuttered odd shape of a house on Burns Avenue, a sleepy thoroughfare lined by massive tall trees in the suburb of Westerville. The town was once known as "The Dry Capital of the World" for being home to the Anti-Saloon League, one of the driving forces behind Prohibition during the 1920s.

It was the kind of staid, no-nonsense atmosphere that suited Luke, who even as a youngster possessed an old soul belying his years. Younger brother Mike, who grew up to become an All-America wrestler at Penn University, recalled his older brother as disciplined and earnest as a boy. Mike learned just how earnest when he nearly got caught doing some adolescent mischief in eighth grade. "Luke found out and my parents didn't know," Mike said. "I remember him taking me upstairs and putting a beatdown on me."

When Luke was just seven, his mother began dropping him off at Bishop Watterson High School in Columbus, where his uncle coached, so he could spar with the freshman wrestlers. He didn't always win, but he didn't always lose either, refining his skill until he blossomed into one of the most decorated wrestlers in Ohio high school history.

"His dad was a blue-collar worker; our whole family was middle class," said Wayne Hiles, Luke's uncle, who was head wrestling coach at Bishop Watterson before becoming an assistant at DeSales. "There were no silver spoons. Everyone just worked. That's all he knows."

Just how good was Fickell? Some observers describe him as the best heavyweight high school wrestling champion the state of Ohio has ever produced. Period.

He was a perfect 36–0 as a sophomore at 189 pounds, and as a heavyweight a year later, he won thirty-one times without a loss and recorded twenty-nine of those victories by pinfall. He pinned four of his five opponents at the state meet—in times of ninety-five seconds or quicker—and the only opponent he didn't pin, he scored a 10–0 major decision in the semifinals. As a senior, Fickell was untouchable. With a rock-solid frame of 235 pounds, the six-foot-four senior simply toyed with most of his opponents before pinning them. A handful simply avoided the embarrassment and forfeited their matches. He finished his final three seasons at DeSales with three state championships and victories in 106 consecutive matches without a single defeat.

"What made Fickell so great," wrote longtime wrestling writer Pat Galbincea in 2011, "was he had a heavyweight's strength combined with the quickness of a lightweight. He was the total package. What I'm saying is (Luke) would have easily been an NCAA heavyweight champion and a probable Olympian and gold medal winner. Even the most stupidest of dolts could see Fickell was earmarked for greatness—except for one thing: He had his heart set on football."

That wasn't always the case. "To be honest, as a young kid, I was a wrestling guy," Luke said. "Most of the stuff I was over at Ohio State for was wrestling. Any time I was over there, it was at a wrestling camp or making connections through Chris Ford, the old wrestling coach. Other than that, my only recollection as a little kid about Ohio State football was going to a game because my grandfather was a cop, and they were in charge of the concession stands or something. I just don't have much of a recollection of really, truly being involved in it or even being much of a fan of Ohio State football."

Then one winter day during a snowstorm, there was a knock at the Fickell's front door. When Luke opened the door, there stood a large man who said his car had broken down and wanted to know if he could use the telephone. The large man turned out to be former Ohio State All-America lineman John Hicks.

"What are the odds?" Luke said. "Just by random chance, his car broke down right in front of our house. Dad helped him out, and the next thing you know, next year he's coaching our little league football team, and they were great friends from there on out. John took us kids to an Ohio State-Michigan game when I was about ten, and that's when I started thinking more seriously about football."

Because Luke was a tremendous all-around athlete, he could have pursued a number of avenues after high school. In addition to being unbeatable on the wrestling mat, DeSales baseball coach Phil Callaghan said Luke could have been a major league-caliber fielder around first base because of his great hands and footwork. But although he was completely dedicated to whatever sport in which he was participating at the time, his deepest passion was always reserved for football.

He was a two-time All-Ohio honoree and the state's Division III Lineman of the Year as a senior, the same year he was named a prep All-American by *USA Today* and *Street & Smith's*. He briefly considered a handful of other programs, including Notre Dame as a dutiful Catholic. But the lure of playing for his hometown Buckeyes was just too strong, and Luke entered Ohio State in the fall of 1992 intending to major in sports medicine with a minor in football.

While most incoming college freshmen are works in progress, Fickell was already close to a finished product and he earned appreciable playing time as a backup defensive end in the 1992 season-opening game against Louisville. The game turned out to be a too-close-for-comfort victory of just one point for the Buckeyes, but the freshman recorded his first three career tackles and was eager to use that as a springboard for bigger and better things. During the Monday practice after that game, however, Luke suffered a knee injury while performing a simple tackle drill. The injury, initially diagnosed as only minor, eventually needed surgery. In an instant, his true freshman season was over.

When he returned after an off-season of vigorous rehabilitation, he embarked upon a stellar career that included four consecutive seasons as a defensive line starter and a school-record 50 consecutive starts. Always known as a heady player and master tactician, Fickell was four times named to the Academic All-Big Ten team and twice earned first-team All-Big Ten honors as a defensive end despite playing on the interior of the line as a nose guard. His primary role at that position was as a gap-closer and hole-clogger, but he still managed to finish his OSU career with 212 tackles, including 26 for loss and six sacks.

In his final game in Scarlet and Gray, Luke played the entire 1997 Rose Bowl victory against Arizona State with a torn pectoral muscle, injured during practice the day before the game.

"I told Coach (John) Cooper when it happened, and all I asked for was the opportunity to start," Fickell said. "I told them, 'I'll go in for the first play and I'll tell you if I can't do it, if I can't get the job done. I had no power in my left arm—almost like you're playing with one hand—but it was my last game at Ohio State and I wanted to give it my all. Adrenaline took over, but it was completely torn from my body, so it's not like it was really a stretching pain."

More interested in wrestling, Luke was turned onto football after a chance meeting with OSU All-America offensive tackle John Hicks.

Somehow, he gutted out the entire game as the Buckeyes came from behind in the final minutes to score a 20–17 victory. The following morning, after the team's return flight from Pasadena to Columbus, Fickell underwent surgery to repair the injury.

Major surgeries to bookend his college career, along with the fact that he played a position that most National Football League teams had phased out of their defensive playbooks, caused Fickell to go undrafted in 1997. He signed as a free agent with the New Orleans Saints, but tore an ACL in his knee and wound up on the injured reserve list for the entire season. Afterward, the Saints released him and Luke realized his playing days were over.

"I never had intentions of becoming a coach," he recalled, "but football ended sooner than I wanted it to. I blew my knee out and the opportunities to continue to play were very limited. That's when I started to realize the people that had such an impact on my life, beside just my family, were coaches. And then I remembered (former Ohio State defensive coordinator) Fred Pagac always telling me that he never once felt like he went to work a day in his life. My dad had always told me to find something that you love to do because if you're passionate about something you'll have success in it. Those are the kind of things that stuck in my mind, and that's all of a sudden when I said that this is what I think I want to do."

Fickell got his coaching feet wet as a graduate assistant at his alma mater in 1999 before serving a two-year apprenticeship as a defensive line coach at the University of Akron. By the national championship season of 2002, he was back in Columbus, moving from special teams coach to linebackers coach to co-defensive coordinator before taking over for Tressel in 2011. He admits things came flying at him at the speed of light.

"Holy shit, I could write a book about the mistakes we made or I made," Luke says. "But I think the number one mistake was trying to be somebody I wasn't. I thought I had to be like Jim Tressel, and in reality you can't be like Jim Tressel. Nobody can. But I thought that was what was best to give us an opportunity to be successful and not have a bunch of different changes on people, whether they were the players or the coaches. That was just the conscious decision that I made, and it was probably the one that was detrimental because you can't be consistent being somebody that you're not."

After that season of six wins against seven losses, the first losing campaign in nearly a quarter-century, Ohio State hired Meyer as its permanent head coach. With a cocksure, alpha-dog personality as far removed from Tressel as was possible, Meyer seemed intent upon cleaning house and bringing on an entirely new staff. Tressel reached out to his successor, telling Meyer he owed Fickell at least a conversation out of common courtesy. The new coach reluctantly agreed, figuring Luke would plead his case to be retained. What he got instead was a guy used to being thrown to the wolves.

"You'll be just fine with or without me," Luke told Meyer. "If I'm right for you and what you've got planned for the program, then it's right for me. If it's not right for you, it's not going to be right for me, either. You sure as hell don't need me."

Meyer liked him immediately and hired him for his old position as linebackers coach and co-defensive coordinator. Five years later, Fickell felt he was ready again to lead his own program and took over at Cincinnati. The Queen City quickly adopted him as a favorite son after victory piled on top of victory. And while he and his wife enjoy Cincinnati, looking at the area as one where they can comfortably raise their family, he knows Ohio State fans still appreciate the selfless way he stepped into the head coaching void in 2011 and helped the program avoid disaster.

"Ohio State people have always been nice to me and my family," Luke says. "They are especially so about that 2011 season. They say, 'You did a great job.' Well, I respectfully disagree. We were 6–7 that year. You don't have to bullshit me. That's not a great job and I'm not happy about it.

"Look, I know people are looking for positives when they say, 'You did it with class,' and I appreciate that, too. But to be honest, I'd rather have done it with (less class) and won a little more."

MIKE VRABEL

OSU DEFENSIVE END 1993–1996 **ASSISTANT COACH** 2011–2013

94

NICKNAME: Vrabes

HOMETOWN: Akron, Ohio

HEIGHT: 6 ft 4 in **WEIGHT**: 260 lb

ALL-AMERICAN: 1995, 1996

NFL DRAFT: 1997, Pittsburgh Steelers

Prep All-American. Two-time college All-American. Three-time All-Big Ten first team. Two-time Big Ten Defensive Lineman of the Year. Two-time Academic All-Big Ten. Ohio State all-time career sacks leader. First-team All Pro. Three-time Super Bowl champion. First former Ohio State player to become an NFL head coach.

Mike Vrabel has compiled an exemplary résumé on the football field, a career that continues as head coach of the NFL's Tennessee Titans, a team he has led into the American Football Conference playoffs for three consecutive seasons beginning in 2019. But it is also a career that was nearly derailed before it got started.

During the summer between his sophomore and junior years at Walsh Jesuit High School, a private Catholic school situated on a sprawling 110-acre campus approximately 30 miles south of Cleveland, Mike awoke one morning to a piercing pain in his back. When the pain persisted, the soon-to-be sixteen-year-old was rushed to a family physician who came back with an unusual diagnosis. The youngster had sustained a stress fracture in his back with no prognosis for treatment.

The injury was severe enough to threaten what was rapidly becoming a promising athletic career. In addition to playing basketball as a six-foot-five, 240-pound center, and throwing the shot put and discus in the spring as part of the track team, Mike had already started a number of football games as a sophomore for the Maroon and Gold at Walsh Jesuit, and was already fielding scholarship offers from a number of elite college programs including archrivals Ohio State and Michigan. But in the summer of 1991, all of that was on hold.

"I don't even know how it happened," he said. "There was a point when I didn't know if I was ever going to get to play football again. Obviously, I love the game and certainly didn't want to give it up. But being the son of school teachers, I was already preparing for what was going to come after football."

Michael George Vrabel came into the world on August 14, 1975, in Akron, Ohio, the only child born to Charles Paul Vrabel and his wife, the former Elaine Joyce Petroff, a couple who met when they were each students at the University of Akron. Chuck Vrabel was a longtime school administrator and high school boys basketball coach in the Akron area, including in the late 1970s at Norton High School, while his wife Elaine was also an administrator, most notably serving as principal at Charles F. Brush High School in suburban Cleveland.

Their only child was the ball of fire on their cul-de-sac neighborhood of neatly trimmed hedges and tall fir trees. "What I remember most is Mike and the other kids, always in our backyard, always playing something," Chuck said. "Mike was always involved." They also pushed him as hard in school as you might expect of a kid with both parents working as high school principals.

"Academics was of the highest importance," Mike said, "but as I went along, a lot of other stuff became important, too."

Throughout his youth, Vrabel naturally thought he might like to go into the family business of education. But as he grew into a tall, muscular young man with sharp features and an easy smile, athletics became more and more a possibility. He visited with medical experts at the famed Cleveland Clinic after the stress fracture in his back was discovered, and immediately was impressed enough to think about a future in physical therapy or sports medicine.

While he was at the Cleveland Clinic, Mike was told that his back would heal properly on its own, but in order to return to the football field, he would have to be fitted with a special brace that covered him from his underarms to his hips. He reluctantly agreed to wear the apparatus—something he referred to more as a harness than a brace—and rejoined the Warriors for fall practice. He missed the first three games of his junior season, but eventually returned to the field to record seventy tackles and four sacks as an inside linebacker.

"Once I got the OK from the doctors that I couldn't hurt my back any more, I didn't worry about it," Vrabel said. "But that brace? That thing had to go. There was no way I could have been effective in games while wearing it, so I only wore it in practice to appease the doctors and the coaches."

Mike finished his high school career by earning district player of the year honors as well as being named Ohio Player of the Year by the Columbus Touchdown Club. Longtime Walsh Jesuit fans still remember with reverence the play he made during his senior season, forcing a fumble, picking the loose ball out of midair and then returning it for a touchdown.

"I've never seen a more athletic play than that one," said longtime Walsh Jesuit head coach Gerry Rardin, who coached the Warriors for thirty-five years. "Mike was just so naturally gifted. He played linebacker and tight end for us, and we considered him the cornerstone of our offense as well as the cornerstone of our defense. But in addition to athletic gifts, he was just a natural-born leader. We had kids that were great leaders because of their athletic ability, but Mike would have still been a leader if he had only half of his athletic ability."

Vrabel attended summer camps at the University of Michigan for two years running, but ultimately decided to sign with Ohio State after a recruiting period his parents thought would never end.

"I was concerned about it early on when Mike was getting recruited," Chuck said. "When he started being recruited by Ohio State, well, that can be overwhelming. That's really the big time. But with Mike, those are the kinds of things that don't intimidate him at all. He saw it as a chance to compete against the best of the best."

During his recruiting visit to Columbus, Vrabel's host was fellow defensive lineman Luke Fickell. The two became fast friends, and after Mike enrolled at OSU, he and Luke eventually became roommates, living in an off-campus apartment that Fickell later described as "if it wasn't condemned, it should have been."

Cracking the starting lineup as a defensive end during his sophomore season, Vrabel would go on to appear in 50 games for the Buckeyes between 1993 and 1996, teaming with Fickell and defensive linemate Matt Finkes to help lead the team to a 41-8-1 record, a pair of Big Ten championships, and victories in the 1993 Holiday Bowl and 1997 Rose

Bowl. Vrabel finished his college career with 196 tackles, including a school-record sixty-six of those for losses. He also recorded thirty-six sacks, also a program record still on the books a quarter of a century after he played his final game for the Scarlet and Gray.

Bill Conley, who lettered at tight end for the legendary Woody Hayes in 1970 and 1971, and then went on to serve as an assistant coach and recruiting coordinator at Ohio State under Earle Bruce, John Cooper, and Jim Tressel, terms Vrabel as a once-in-a-lifetime talent.

"Mike Vrabel was the best athlete I encountered during my years as a position coach at Ohio State," Conley said. "I know that's a bold statement considering all the talented individuals I worked with, but the statement just happens to be true. He was big, fast, agile, tough, and intelligent. That's a combination that's pretty hard to beat."

Conley underscored his praise by singling out one particular play during Vrabel's career.

Late in a 1996 game played at South Bend, Indiana, on the famed campus of the University of Notre Dame, the Fighting Irish was facing a 22-7 deficit late in the first half but had driven the ball into Ohio State territory with designs on narrowing the gap before intermission. A touchdown at that juncture of the game, and the fact that Notre Dame was going to receive the opening kickoff of the second half, could have given the Fighting Irish the kind of momentum they needed to mount a comeback.

But on a second-down play, Vrabel literally exploded off the snap of the ball, easily shedding the block of Irish tight end Kevin Carretta, who crumpled face first to the stadium turf. Then, like a wolf stalking its prey, Vrabel zeroed in on Notre Dame quarterback Ron Powlus and threw him for a ten-yard loss. The sack not only ended the rally but wrecked Notre Dame's resolve as well, and the Buckeyes went on to post a 29-16 victory.

"Football is a team game, of course, but winning football games is made up of individual efforts," Conley said. "The play Mike made against Notre Dame was a perfect example of that. Notre Dame had every intention of mounting a comeback in the second half until that play. When they came out for the second half, we could see it in their eyes. We knew the game was over at that point."

Vrabel finished his Ohio State career with numerous all-conference and All-America honors, including twice earning Big Ten Defensive Lineman of the Year honors. About the only accolade not afforded to him was team captain, but his roommate had a simple explanation for that.

"He set high standards for both himself and his teammates, and he had a willingness to be vocal in his attempts to enforce those standards," Fickell said. "Some of the things he did and said...well, let's just say he said things that some people thought shouldn't be said. They helped the team, but they weren't the kind of things that get you elected captain."

Following his days as a Buckeye, Vrabel embarked upon a fourteen-year career in the NFL beginning as a third-round draft choice of the Pittsburgh Steelers. He played four seasons with the Steelers, mostly as a backup, but his career took off when he signed with the New England Patriots as a free agent before the 2001 season.

During his eight seasons with the Patriots, Mike appeared in 148 games as an outside linebacker and

Mike has enjoyed success on nearly every level as a player, assistant coach and now as an NFL head coach.

was credited with 606 tackles, including 412 solo stops and forty-eight sacks. He also forced thirteen fumbles, picked off eleven interceptions, and even lined up to catch eight passes, each of them for touchdowns. Best of all, he helped New England to victories in Super Bowls XXXVI, XXXVIII, and XXXIX.

"I've coached players who were intelligent, brilliant guys, but it never came together for them on the football field," New England head coach Bill Belichick said. "Then there's other guys who, off the field, would have a hard time intellectually, but on the field, they knew instinctively how things were supposed to work together. Mike is an intelligent guy, and at the football level, things come extremely easily to him in that he understands things quickly. Plenty of guys were great players—intelligent football players—but you wouldn't want them doing your taxes. Mike's not one of those."

Mike finished his career playing two seasons with the Kansas City Chiefs, expecting to enjoy retirement with his wife Jennifer and sons Tyler and Carter. But when an old teammate reached out with an unusual job offer, Mike returned to football.

"I never had a Plan B besides playing in the NFL as long as I could," he said. "But when I was with the Patriots, I would drive to work and sometimes talk to Luke on the phone and we'd talk about what we'd do if certain opportunities came up. You love the game and you love competing and trying to get players to become a team and function as a team. It's a great challenge."

Fickell, who had gotten into coaching after a knee injury prematurely ended his NFL career almost before it started, had been thrust into the interim head coaching job at Ohio State just before the 2011 season began. He reached out to his old teammate for help, beginning Vrabel's own second career that included three seasons as an assistant for the Buckeyes under Fickell and Urban Meyer, and four more with the NFL's Houston Texans. Just before the 2018 season began, Mike took over as head coach of the Titans, and through his first four seasons in Tennessee had led the team to a 41-24 record and two AFC South championships.

ANDY KATZENMOYER

OSU LINEBACKER 1996–1998

NICKNAME: The Big Kat

HOMETOWN: Westerville, Ohio

HEIGHT: 6 ft 4 in **WEIGHT**: 255 lb

ALL-AMERICAN: 1997

NFL DRAFT: 1999, New England Patriots

45

When you're the first Dick Butkus Award winner at one of the most prestigious college football programs in the country, a three-time all-conference performer and a consensus All-American, chances are good you don't really care about how the public at large views you. Still, Andy Katzenmoyer was always bothered that people thought of him a poster child of sorts for the proverbial dumb jock.

In 1998, when he was at the height of his college career as a chaos-creating linebacker at Ohio State, Katzenmoyer was the subject of a scathing cover story published by *Sports Illustrated* under the headline "Ohio State is No. 1 if Andy Katzenmoyer Makes the Grade." The beefy linebacker isn't just the subject of the cover; it is emblazoned with his photo in living color, complete with helmet in one hand, a barbed-wire tattoo encircling his right bicep, and the look of total disdain on his face.

Inside, author Austin Murphy paints the picture of a player who is indifferent (at best) about academics, opines that his position coach's overflowing praise of Katzenmoyer's football talents are evidence "he doesn't mean the Big Kat belongs to many book clubs," and even includes a dig at his mother, Dianne, when she told him, "You can get a degree in ballet, in vocal music, sculpture—even in tuba. Maybe you should be able to get a degree in football."

It was a journalistic hit piece that landed squarely on young Andy Katzenmoyer's shoulders like a baby grand piano pushed out of a fifth-story window. It wasn't what he deserved, and it certainly wasn't what he had dreamed about as a child.

> As a young boy, he used to fall asleep listening to *Buckeye Battle Cry*, the team fight song on a windup cotton football that his grandmother Marie had given Andy for Christmas when he was two.

As a young boy, he used to fall asleep listening to *Buckeye Battle Cry*, the team fight song on a windup cotton football that his grandmother Marie had given Andy for Christmas when he was two. Andrew Warren Katzenmoyer was born December 2, 1977, in Kettering, Ohio, but his family moved to Westerville, a suburb northeast of Columbus, when he was six. He spent many days of his youth with his father, Warren, then a state wildlife biologist, hiking nature trails in central Ohio, hunting for rabbit and pheasant, and fishing for bass.

"Dad knew all the good places to go," Andy said.

Warren Katzenmoyer attended Ohio State for two years, and Andy's mother, the former Kathleen Dianne Howard, graduated from there in 1967. An uncle and two aunts also have degrees from the university. Before enrolling at Ohio State, Warren had been a 6-foot-3, 190-pound, all-league standout at Grandview Heights High School, just a stone's throw from Ohio Stadium. He played under the guidance of Robin Priday, a quarterback and defensive back on the 1942 Buckeyes team that won the program's first-ever national championship.

But apparently proximity and a coach who was an OSU alum didn't result in a scholarship offer from Woody Hayes, so Warren accepted a scholarship to play tight end at Iowa State. His stay in Ames was a short one, however. He dropped out after severely injuring his shoulder during his freshman year. One of the seniors on that Cyclones team was a safety/running back named John Cooper. "A pretty good player," Warren recalled of the man who would one day coach his son.

Father and son attended a few home games in Columbus, but mostly the family gathered around the TV set on Saturday afternoons to root for the Buckeyes.

Andy began playing football in the sixth grade, mixing the sport with basketball in the winter and baseball in the spring and summer. By the time he had reached the end of his sophomore year at South High School in Westerville, when he transformed from a chubby 5-foot-10, 250-pounder to a considerably leaner 6–4 and 235 pounds, he had heard enough of his father's football stories and seen enough of Oklahoma linebacker Brian Bosworth to know what he wanted to do.

"A crazy madman on the field," Andy said of The Boz. "Nothing got in his way. I liked the hitting. It comes from wanting to de-cleat somebody. My high school coach used to use that word. That's when you hit a guy so hard that his cleats come out of the ground and he's hanging in midair."

Katzenmoyer quit all sports except football, and the summer before his junior year, he worked out ferociously, pumping iron and running six days a week. That fall, he began his de-cleating of running backs with such abandon that scouts began descending from all over the place.

"He's extremely fast, extremely quick and he gets to the ball well," Westerville South head coach Rocky Pentello said. "He hits like a truck when he gets there, and he's a very unselfish player as far as his role with the team. I truly believe this: With Andy Katzenmoyer, God said, 'I'm gonna make me the best linebacker that's ever been.'"

> "He's a physical freak, and I mean that positively."
> —*John Cooper,* Buckeyes coach

A veritable who's who of coaching made in-person visits to the Katzenmoyer home, a roster that included Joe Paterno of Penn State, Tom Osborne of Nebraska, Lloyd Carr of Michigan and Lou Holtz of Notre Dame, each College Football Hall of Fame members who combined to amass more than 1,000 career victories as well as hoist seven national championship trophies. But no matter what kind of sales pitch was used, they fell upon deaf ears. "Through the whole process," Andy said, "I really had only one college in my mind."

But even as he was wreaking havoc on the football field, his academics were problematic even in high school. Entering his senior year, his grade-point average was borderline for remaining eligible, and keeping that GPA above the minimum for what was required for his college eligibility came down to a final English exam. "It was the most pressure I'd felt in my life," Andy said. But he passed the test and embarked upon an Ohio State career that began by sharing Big Ten Freshman of the Year honors in 1996.

Katzenmoyer exploded mightily onto the scene with a team-leading eight tackles and two sacks in the season opener, a 70–7 blowout of an overmatched Rice team. But his actual coming-out party came a few weeks later when the Buckeyes went to Purdue in mid-October and ran roughshod over the Boilermakers. After spotting the home team an early 14–0 advantage, Ohio State rolled to a 42–14 win during which Katzenmoyer recorded eight solo tackles, including two sacks, a forced fumble and his first interception.

That was the beginning of a four-game streak during which Andy snared an interception, finishing with a 45-yard return for a touchdown during a 45–0 whitewash of Minnesota.

The Buckeyes came within a whisker of winning the national championship in 1996, losing only once in twelve games and finishing runner-up to eventual champion Nebraska. Even during the lone defeat, a 13–9 decision against archrival Michigan, Katzenmoyer did about all he could with eleven tackles, including two for loss. He finished his freshman season with 85 total tackles, including 12 sacks among his 23 stops for loss. That TFL number still ranks second all-time in a single season, eclipsed only by teammate Mike Vrabel, who had 26 in 1995.

During his sophomore season, Katzenmoyer was the constant victim of double-teams from opponents, and despite the fact he upped his tackles total to 97, only thirteen of those went for loss with just two sacks. But that didn't mean he still didn't strike fear into opposing ball-carriers who dared cross his path.

Perhaps the signature moment of his college career came midway through the second quarter of a late September game at Missouri. The upset-minded Tigers were holding a

10–7 lead and dual-threat quarterback Corby Jones had already run for 70 yards and a touchdown. Missouri lined up on third down with ten yards to go, and veteran ABC announcer Brent Musberger picks up the action from there.

"We haven't heard much from young Katzenmoyer so far," Musberger said. As television cameras zoomed in for a close-up of the reflective visor under Katzenmoyer's helmet, Jones went back to pass but was flushed from the pocket. He cut to his left and turned up-field, only to be met by what he must have thought was an onrushing freight train. Katzenmoyer launched his shoulder pads full steam into Jones' chest and nearly ripped the Missouri quarterback's torso from the rest of his body. "There he is!" Musberger exclaimed. "The Big Kat delivers the blow! Hello, Mr. Katzenmoyer." Former NFL quarterback and Musberger's broadcast partner Dan Fouts added, "That's why Katzenmoyer is going to win the Butkus Award as the best linebacker in the country. Nobody in college football hits like that."

It was only the fourth game of the season, but Fouts proved prescient when Katzenmoyer became Ohio State's first-ever recipient of the Dick Butkus Award. He also earned his second straight nomination to the All-Big Ten first team and was a consensus All-American.

Primed for even more accolades, perhaps even a run at the Heisman Trophy, as he prepared for his junior season, Katzenmoyer was rocked by the *Sports Illustrated* story that revealed he had taken summer classes on AIDS awareness and golf, and had a grade in another class changed to stay academically eligible.

"At the time, it bothered me because I knew that I wasn't a dumb person or unintelligent," Andy said. But his public image was set. From that point, Ohio State was seen as nothing but a football factory with Katzenmoyer fitting nearly everyone's perception of a dumb jock.

There seems little doubt the story and its aftermath affected his performance in 1998. Although he still had fourteen tackles for loss and four sacks, his tackles total dropped to a career-low 74 and he failed to grab a single interception. He received a third consecutive first-team All-Big Ten honor, but what few All-America accolades came his way were for the second or third team.

Andy skipped his final year of college eligibility and was a first-round selection (albeit with the third-to-last pick) in the 1999 NFL draft by the New England Patriots. He made the league's all-rookie team after a season that included 79 tackles, including fifteen for loss and three and a half sacks, as well as his first pro interception that he returned 57 yards for a touchdown.

But he also sustained a neck injury that required surgery and forced him to miss the first half of the 2000 season. He appeared in the final eight games, and made three starts, but knew something about his body just wasn't right. He reported for training camp the following summer, but walked out, citing concerns about his neck. It was to be the final time Andy Katzenmoyer would be seen on a competitive football field. Betrayed by a body once lauded for its rare combination of size, speed and physicality, his career was over at the age of twenty-three.

Over the subsequent twenty years, Katzenmoyer got married, divorced, remarried, raised his three children and enjoyed success as a small business owner with a training gym in his hometown. But there was one thing that continued to gnaw at him.

He started and stopped taking classes a couple of times until resuming his education in earnest about ten or twelve years ago, taking exercise science classes at Otterbein University near his Westerville home.

"Then I went through a divorce and everything just kind of got thrown out of whack," he said. "At

"It seemed for a time that God had said, with regards to Katzenmoyer, "I'm gonna make me a sumo wrestler."
—*Sports Illustrated*

that point, I was also running my business (a training gym), so I didn't think I had the time to go back and take classes and do all that."

But after COVID hit, and he decided to close the gym, he decided the time was right. "It was something that I promised myself and my family that I would do back when I was in school," he said. "With the NFL calling and just life circumstances, it took a lot longer."

Some twenty-five years after he first set foot on campus, Andy returned to Ohio State in the fall of 2021. He took some in-person classes, sitting in classrooms beside students who weren't even born when he was playing for the Buckeyes, and finished the rest of his classes virtually. Compounding the changes in curriculum and technology with the ongoing challenges of the COVID pandemic, it wasn't easy. But in his final semester, he achieved a 3.75 grade-point average and graduated with a degree in exercise science and sociology.

What followed was an outpouring of congratulatory texts and tweets, something Andy didn't expect but was gratified to receive. "I had a bunch of people come out of the woodwork," he said. "There's some people that I didn't know had my number who reached out and texted me and said, 'Hey, congratulations. Awesome.' It's been really, really nice to hear from people from my past who say congratulations."

And while admitting that finally receiving praise for his work in the classroom is gratifying, there was really only one person he was trying to please.

"I think you should always try to push yourself to be better, to do great things despite your age," Andy said. "If this helps inspire or propels someone else to go out and achieve something great, that's fantastic. At the same time, I really did this 100 percent for me. I really do feel good about what I've done and that I was able to achieve this."

MICHAEL JENKINS

OSU WIDE RECEIVER 2000–2003

12

NICKNAME: Jenk

HOMETOWN: Tampa, Florida

HEIGHT: 6 ft 5 in **WEIGHT**: 215 lb

NFL DRAFT: 2004, Atlanta Falcons

When it came time for members of The Ohio State University's national championship football team of 2002 to vote for who they thought had made the most significant contributions to the title run, they couldn't decide between Craig Krenzel and Chris Gamble.

Krenzel was the gutty Michigan native who quarterbacked the team to fourteen victories without a loss while Gamble was the gifted Floridian who unselfishly offered to man a cornerback position while continuing to play receiver and return punts and kickoffs. So, when the team Most Valuable Player voting was tabulated, there was a tie for the first time since the award was initiated in 1930.

Krenzel and Gamble were just two of the worthy choices during a most unlikely season that saw the Buckeyes climb from number thirteen in the preseason national rankings to number one after a thrilling double-overtime victory against the University of Miami, defending national champions and owners of a consecutive win streak that had reached thirty-four games.

There was safety Mike Doss, who could have left school for the NFL but returned for his senior season and earned his third berth on the All-America first team, a feat matched by only six other Buckeyes before him. Matt Wilhelm was another defensive stalwart, leading the team with 121 tackles, and both kicking specialists—punter Andy Groom and kicker Mike Nugent—earned first-team All-America honors. Maurice Clarett set a single-season rushing record for freshmen and scored a team-leading eighteen touchdowns, the most of any OSU player in seven years.

But there was another player who seemingly emerged from the shadows every time Ohio State reached crisis mode in 2002, and that was nearly a weekly experience for a team that won seven of its fourteen games by seven points or fewer. His fourth-quarter catch-and-run for forty-five yards against Wisconsin jump-started a sputtering offense and sparked a come-from-behind win. A touchdown catch of fifty yards and two crucial third-down receptions helped the Buckeyes to an overtime win against Illinois. And there was the do-or-die catch during the first overtime against Miami, a heart-stopping sideline reception on a fourth-and-fourteen play that kept Ohio State's hopes alive for a national championship.

That title would not have been possible, however, if not for a catch Michael Jenkins made two months earlier on the wind-swept field at Ross-Ade Stadium, the ancient sub-ground arena on the campus of Purdue University. The last-second, fourth-quarter, fourth-down reception has been forever cemented in Ohio State football lore as "Holy Buckeye!" and with it Jenkins' legacy in the minds of Buckeye fans.

Not bad for a guy who seldom played the receiver position until he got to college and then had to learn on the fly.

Michael Gerard Jenkins was born June 18, 1982, in Tampa, Florida, and he had already seen a large chunk of the world at a young age. His father, also named Michael, had made a career in the U.S. Army, and with more than two decades of service, had been stationed in Germany as well as stateside in Ohio, Kentucky, and Florida. When he retired from service, the family, which included wife Geri, young Michael, and daughter Tiffany, settled into a stucco home on a shaded subdivision corner northwest of downtown Tampa.

Fewer than ten minutes away was A.P. Leto High School, the largest school in Hillsborough County with nearly 1,700 students attending classes on a sprawling campus totaling thirty-seven acres. It was there that Michael first made a name for himself in the winter of 1996 as a slender freshman. His tall, rangy frame allowed him to start on the varsity basketball team as a freshman, and his speed made him a natural for the Falcons' track team.

"I was six-four and 175 pounds. A toothpick basically," he said. "But I was fast and I'd run just about anything they'd let me run. I eventually wound up in the individual 400 meters, the 4 x 100 and 4 x 400 relays, and the triple jump. I won a state title in the triple jump."

When he became a sophomore, Michael decided to go out for the football team and he became an instant star. He lined up at as many as six different positions on the field, at various times playing quarterback, running back, wingback, linebacker, cornerback, and safety while returning punts and kickoffs, sometimes all in the same game. His high school coach believes the ruggedness of his father's military background served Michael well.

"I was always motivated to be one of the best. I didn't just want to be some guy who went to Ohio State. I wanted to be remembered as one of the greats."
—Michael Jenkins

"He developed discipline, and because of that he was very coachable," Leto football coach Andy Martin said. "He took your instruction and criticism, and responded to it. He was always eager to learn new things. And with that discipline came a toughness. Many times he played an entire game for us. Never left the field except when we were in punt formation. That's the only unit he wasn't a part of, so that was the only time he got some rest."

Martin led the Falcons to more than their share of victories, but he favored the Wing T offense, a power alignment that features a running back, fullback, and wingback with two ends playing tight to the offensive line formation. As a result, Jenkins seldom played at the receiver position, at least not in the classic form of a split end lined up well off the line of scrimmage. That led to most college coaches recruiting him as a defensive back.

"In high school, we ran the Wing T, an offense that really doesn't have any receivers," Michael said. "So when I got recruited, it was as a quote-unquote athlete, the kind of player that could play either offense or defense. The problem with that was I didn't want to play defense in college."

Florida, Florida State, and Miami had combined for four national championships and a remarkable eighteen top-three finishes during the 1990s, and typically had their pick of elite high school prospects in the Sunshine State. For some reason, however, neither the Seminoles nor the Hurricanes showed much interest in Michael, and the Gators wanted him exclusively for defense. Meanwhile, the youngster had already begun looking elsewhere.

"I lived in the Cincinnati area for about six years and in Kentucky for a year and a half, and I was thinking I wanted to get back up north where the leaves on the trees change colors," Michael said. "And I kind of wanted to get a little experience living away from home."

Not that his official recruiting trip was the stuff of which dreams are made.

"When I took my recruiting visit, the Buckeyes weren't very good," he recalled. "They went six-and-six in 1999, and at that time, you didn't get to go to a bowl game if you didn't have a winning record. So when I got there for my visit, most all the players were gone. The only ones who were there were guys who had to stay and host recruits. There were only about eight guys there, school was closed, it was cold as balls, and the stadium was being renovated, so I couldn't see the stadium. But I still told my dad when I got home that it was the place I wanted to go. It was just something deep down inside that made me want to be a Buckeye."

The fall of 2001 was a time of transition for both Jenkins and the Ohio State football program. Jim Tressel had taken over for John Cooper as head coach and had replaced Cooper's high-octane offensive attack with one that relied more on power, field position, and special teams. Meanwhile, Michael participated in all twelve games the Buckeyes played that season, but that participation only amounted to twenty minutes of action and he never touched the football on offense.

"I would have liked to have made more of an impact, but it really didn't bother me that much to be honest," he said. "When I got to Ohio State, I really had to learn the receiver position. That took time and that took some learning behind guys like Ken-Yon Rambo and Reggie Germany. It was just a matter of seeing those guys and just grinding, putting in the work day in and day out. I didn't see much of the field at receiver as a freshman, but I played special teams. Then to go in as a sophomore and start, it was just a constant grind. I worked with the receivers coach, the quarterbacks we had at the time, and I just tried to get a little better every day.

"I was always motivated to be one of the best. I didn't just want to be some guy who went to Ohio State. I wanted to be remembered as one of the greats. There were some great receivers like Terry Glenn, David Boston, and Joey Galloway, and that was a great internal motivator for me. I wanted to be mentioned in the same sentence with those guys."

Despite a relative lack of experience at the position, Jenkins became the starting split end for the 2002 Buckeyes and logged his first career reception in the season-opening game against Texas Tech, a first-quarter catch worth seventeen yards during an eventual 45–21 victory. It took almost a month before he grabbed his first touchdown pass, a short four-yard flip from Krenzel during a 45–17 blowout of Indiana in late September.

But that was just the appetizer for the main course that culminated on November 9 at Purdue. Ohio State's offense was stuck in perpetual first gear for much of the game and that seemed especially so in the second half. The team's first four series after halftime consisted of fourteen plays worth just seventeen yards, and the fifth possession was only marginally better, totaling twenty-nine yards before Groom took the field to attempt his eighth punt of the afternoon.

By the time the Buckeyes got the ball back, they were staring at their own mortality with a 6–3 deficit and the clock winding under three minutes. Krenzel took a four-yard sack on first down and then threw incomplete to tight end Ben Hartsock on the next play. Krenzel targeted Hartsock again on third down, this time connecting, but the OSU tight end managed only thirteen of the fourteen yards needed for a first down.

With the clock now ticking under two minutes, Ohio State had a pair of timeouts but didn't use them. Reasoning Purdue would try to overload the line of scrimmage to stop the Buckeyes from running for a first down, Tressel pulled from his sweater vest a play called *King Right 64, Y Shallow Swap,* another tight end pass play. Except nothing went according to plan.

"We were trying to get the ball to Ben coming across underneath," Krenzel explained, "but he got beat up coming across by the blitzing linebacker. Obviously we lost our running backs to pass protection, so at that point I knew I had one play to make."

And that's where veteran ABC play-by-play man Brent Musberger picks up the action.

"It could be up to the offensive line. No, Krenzel's going to throw for it," an excited Musberger shouted into the microphone, his voice rising in octaves as well as decibels. "Gotta get it off. They go for the ballgame!...Touchdown!! Touchdown!! Michael Jenkins!! On fourth and one!! Would you believe it?! Craig Krenzel strikes with a minute and a half left!! Holy Buckeye!!"

The thirty-seven yard touchdown play, scored with just 1:36 remaining, gave Ohio State a 10–6 victory and Jenkins his place in history. "And you want to know the crazy part? I ran the wrong route," Michael said with a sheepish grin. "I just ran a go route, but initially I was supposed to have a post route, and Chris Gamble was supposed to run a dig route. But Chris wound up on the post, so I just ran a go. Just beat the guy. The stars were aligned for me to just run straight."

Jenkins finished that 2002 season with 1,076 yards, becoming only the fourth receiver in Ohio State history at the time with a 1,000-yard season. The following year, he fell just short of a repeat performance, but his 988 yards were good enough to earn him MVP honors from his teammates. He finished his career with a program-record 2,898 receiving yards, a mark that still stands despite the prolific passing game installed by Urban Meyer and perpetuated by Ryan Day.

"I don't know how much longer I can hold it," said Michael, who enjoyed a nine-year NFL career and now balances several successful business ventures in the Atlanta area with raising five children with his wife Tamara. "All these receivers Ohio State has coming in nowadays is crazy, but there's only one ball and only one guy can catch it at a time, so maybe I can hang on to the record just a little bit longer."

MAURICE CLARETT

OSU RUNNING BACK 2002

13

NICKNAME: Reesie, Mo-C

HOMETOWN: Youngstown, Ohio

HEIGHT: 6 ft 0 in **WEIGHT**: 230 lb

To some, the term "mean streets" is a homogenized euphemism for a place of violence, assault, and brutality. But for the people who actually live on those mean streets, there is nothing whatsoever homogenized about them.

The rust-belt northern Ohio city of Youngstown was at one time a proud community of hard-working, salt-of-the-earth miners and steelworkers who served as the backbone of the American Industrial Revolution. Beginning in the early 1800s when iron ore was found lining Yellow Creek and construction of the town's first blast furnace soon followed, Youngstown served as a vital, thriving Appalachian hub for steel production for more than a century and a half.

But when the steel industry in the United States fell into decline beginning in the 1970s, Youngstown fell with it. The labyrinth of smokestacks belching soot and clay into the city skyline was replaced by a different kind of pollution, one marked by shootings, stabbings, home invasions, and rampant drug use. Where steel companies and union bosses once ruled, gangs took over and with them came unspeakable violence that threatened the very existence of Youngstown and its inhabitants.

The city's distress reached its nadir in the mid-1990s, and it was in that setting a teenaged Maurice Clarett found himself. He was only four when his parents divorced. He had yet to reach his twelfth birthday when he stole his first car. Several months later, while watching television one evening, his home was sprayed from front to back with bullets from a drive-by shooting. The sound of breaking glass and projectiles splitting drywall further hardened a young man already filled with a mixture of fear and rage.

"Like any other inner-city community, growing up young and Black in the 1990s, there was an inclusion of gang culture with murder, robbery, domestic violence, and things of that nature," Maurice recalled. "That's when I formed my identity on how I wanted to be viewed toward my peers. Obviously, when you grow up like that, you tend to want to act like you're tough whether you are or not. So, when I'm in the neighborhood, hanging around my older brothers, I'm trying to act tougher than I really am. But that can be a recipe for disaster."

Maurice Edward Clarett was born October 29, 1983, to Youngstown natives Michael "Myke" Clarett and the former Michelle Renee Adkins. Myke was a star football player at Cardinal Mooney High School and later played collegiately at Bowling Green State University. Michelle attended South High School where she played tennis, was captain of the pom-pom squad, and served as secretary of her senior class. Married in their early twenties, Myke and Michelle quickly produced three sons—Michael Junior, Marcus, and Maurice.

Myke was an enterprising young man, a business professional with the state of Ohio as well as an entrepreneur with his own truck delivery service called Myke's Same Day Delivery. He also dabbled in local politics, and was an active member of the Trinity Baptist Church. But as with many unions between young men and women, the Claretts divorced before their eighth anniversary. It apparently was an acrimonious split with Michelle wanting her children to have nothing more to do with their father other than benefit from child support payments. As a result, Myke lost any influence he might have had to stop his youngest son from traveling down the meanest of streets.

"In that environment, you're really trying to grow up as fast as you can," Maurice said. "When I was eleven or twelve years old, I stole a car and ended up getting caught. I went to juvenile detention for a few days, and when I got back, everybody thought that was cool. Like getting locked up is cool or some rite of passage.

"Later, I got locked up again, this time for getting into a fight at a skating rink. There was a big fight and they just locked up everybody. When I got in front of the judge, he said, 'If I ever see you again, I'm sending you to the state detention center.' So, I stayed out of trouble for a couple of years, playing football and running track, trying to find something positive where I could focus myself."

But the dark side pulled him back. A friend talked Clarett into robbing a house, but during the process of the late-night break-in, the occupant woke up and confronted the youngsters.

"To make a long story short, we got arrested and taken down to the juvenile detention center," Maurice remembered. "When I was down there, I met a corrections officer named Roland Smith, who said to me, 'I've seen you play football and other sports. I also know your mother and father, so let me see if I can talk to the judge and get you and your life redirected.' I was put on house arrest for the summer, but I was allowed to leave for weight training and conditioning with him."

From that point, Clarett said he adopted a new mindset. If athletics was going to be the ticket out of his particular mean street, he was going to punch it.

"I began to realize I was playing from a different space," he said. "Most people don't want to admit it, but when you live in an environment with murders and drugs and gangs, you're scared, so you take on a mentality that you really don't want to take on. But you do it to fit in. You do it to survive. So, when I hit the football field, that was the first place I could channel that emotion in a different direction. Our neighborhood, from 1991 to at least 1998, was just out of control. Murders, home invasions, pistol whippings, all type of madness. You do what you have to do to get out of there."

Clarett threw himself into the sport of football, creating as many head-on collisions for himself as he could. Adopting the nickname of "Maurice The Beast," and with 200 pounds of rock-like muscle jammed into a barely six-foot body, Clarett quickly became the talk of Ohio high school football. His freshman season at Austintown-Fitch, located just west of Youngstown, was cut short when he broke his ankle. But after transferring a half-hour north to Warren G. Harding High School, Clarett's career began to take off.

"I never had any aspirations at that time of going to the NFL. My whole thing was getting to college and making something of myself," Maurice recalled. "In my mind, I thought if I took football seriously, maybe I could accomplish something. The transfer to Warren G. Harding was to compete with guys who were on a higher level."

As his power increased, so did his understanding of the game and his place in it. Attending summer camps at Notre Dame and the University of Indiana only reinforced that mentality. "I started to see players from other parts of the country," he said, "but as I competed against them, I thought—and maybe it was just part of being from Youngstown—but I thought, 'I'm better than most of these guys.'"

At first, Clarett was leaning toward attending Notre Dame, the private Catholic university in northern Indiana that has produced nearly a dozen national championships in football. With its campus of stained glass, gothic architecture, and expansive greenery, it was about as far from Youngstown as a young man could get. But when Ohio State made a coaching change following the 2000 season, it forever altered Clarett's future.

The Buckeyes had fired longtime coach John Cooper and hired in his place Jim Tressel, the scion of a famous Ohio high school football coach and a former assistant at Ohio State under Earle Bruce. Tressel got his first crack at being a head coach when Youngstown State hired him in 1986, and over the next decade and a half, he led the Penguins to six Division I-AA national championship game appearances and won four of them.

Just when Clarett thought he was about to escape the grip of Youngstown, his hometown pulled him back in.

"Ohio State hadn't even offered me a scholarship," he said, "but when Coach Tressel became the head coach, he was already a legend in Youngstown because he had won so many national championships at Youngstown State. I guess one of his first phone calls as the new coach was to me. He said something like, 'I'm not only offering you a scholarship, I expect you to take it.' So, I was the guy who got the trend started of graduating high school early. I wanted to forgo the second half of my senior year so I could get a head start rocking and rolling at Ohio State."

Clarett was an instant star in Columbus. Arriving on campus as a prep All-American and the number one prospect in the country, he lived up to the hype. Despite some nagging injuries that limited his performance in some games and held him out of a handful of others, he smashed the program record for freshmen by rushing for 1,237 yards and sixteen touchdowns.

His five-yard touchdown in the second overtime of the Fiesta Bowl against the University of Miami provided the winning points as the Buckeyes won their first consensus national championship in thirty-four years. He was named to the All-Big Ten first team, earned conference Freshman of the Year honors, and was afforded mention on several freshman All-America teams.

What followed was a whirlwind offseason during which Clarett admittedly bought into his own hype. Celebrities from the worlds of entertainment, music, and sports suddenly had his cellphone number, and he found himself sharing a limousine with LeBron James and on stage with Grammy-winning rapper 50 Cent. He also found himself accepting the benefits of his newfound fame, something that ran afoul of NCAA rules governing active student-athletes.

Before his sophomore season in 2003, Clarett was suspended for receiving improper benefits worth

As a freshman, Maurice helped lead Ohio State to the 2002 national championship, the program's first in thirty-four years.

thousands of dollars, and he was eventually dismissed from the school. That led to a challenge of the National Football League rule requiring players to wait three years after their high school graduation before entering the draft. Some of Clarett's attorneys employed a scorched-earth policy, directing allegations of everything from misrepresentation to outright racism while arguing the case. The national media picked up on the allegations, putting Tressel, his program, and the university squarely in the crosshairs.

In the end, the case went all the way to federal court before it was dismissed. The firestorm gradually abated with Tressel and the Ohio State football program moving on, earning trips to the national championship game again in 2006 and 2007. Meanwhile, Clarett made several unsuccessful attempts to make it in the NFL before his life veered back onto the mean streets.

On New Year's Day 2006, one day before the Buckeyes were to play Notre Dame in the Fiesta Bowl, Clarett was charged with robbing two people at gunpoint in Columbus. That September, he was sentenced to seven and a half years in prison. (He served three and a half years.)

Understanding that something had to change, he began sharing his story during speaking engagements with high-profile college teams and other organizations. He used the money he received from those events to launch The Red Zone, a behavioral health and substance abuse agency in his hometown that services adults and children.

Clarett opened The Red Zone in June 2016, and the agency employs more than 100 people and services 700 kids and 300 to 400 adults. About sixty adult clients live in houses Clarett has bought and fixed up in and around the Youngstown area, and he also purchased a four-story building near the facility that offers medical services.

He rises at 4:30 a.m. each morning for meditation and exercise in the basement office of his home outside Columbus that he shares with his fiancée Ashley and their two children. In addition to crisscrossing the country for speaking engagements and mentoring sessions, he regularly makes the roughly 160-mile commute from Columbus to

Youngstown because he prefers a hands-on approach to The Red Zone.

"His heart was always there," says Coach Tressel, who returned to Youngstown State in 2014 as university president. "I remember when he first got to Ohio State, he talked about wanting to be a preacher, wanting to be a difference-maker in the urban areas. He's just a loyal guy to his roots."

Clarett says his mission is deeply personal. He wants to help others who face the same demons that once derailed him. "I want to talk about my life. I want to talk about what's next," he says. "OK, you fucked up. Shit happened. Own it. My life started once the game was over. Once you've lost everything, you don't fear failure."

One hole remains to be filled, however. Dismissed by most Ohio State fans and teammates in 2003 as a scowling, ungrateful pariah, Clarett has been trying to rebuild his relationship with the school and the football program. He returned in 2012 for a ten-year reunion of the national title team, a situation he described as "real funky" and "uncomfortable."

Since then, current university director of athletics Gene Smith has expressed his openness for Clarett to become more involved, albeit saying it is Clarett that will have to reach out. "If he called us," Smith says, "we'd embrace him."

Clarett met current Ohio State head coach Ryan Day in 2020 at a coaching clinic and came away more hopeful than ever that he could reestablish a connection with the Buckeyes. A return to the campus, and possibly completing his degree work, would enable him to close another unfinished chapter in his life.

"Look, what happened, happened," Maurice says, "but what I contributed to that place and what I made people proud of, it was from an eighteen-year-old kid who loved the place more than anyone could love anything else. What's done is done, brother. It's over. Now, how do we move forward?"

TED GINN JR.

OSU RECEIVER, KICK RETURNER 2004—2006

7

NICKNAME: Junior, Teddy

HOMETOWN: Cleveland, Ohio

HEIGHT: 6 ft 0 in **WEIGHT**: 180 lb

ALL-AMERICAN: 2006

NFL DRAFT: 2007, Miami Dolphins

The old saw about the difficulty of having a father as a coach might not have been coined by Ted Ginn Sr., but he certainly perfected it. His son, Ted Jr., was quite likely the most gifted athlete to grace an athletic field at Ohio State during the mid-2000s. Had he chosen to run track, the younger Ginn most certainly would have made a run at an Olympic gold medal in hurdles. On the football field, he had uncanny instincts to go along with blinding speed that made him a threat to go all the way each and every time he touched the ball.

Yet while most observers simply sat back and marveled as Ginn time after time displayed his generational gifts, his father shrugged as if to say talent means nothing without knowing how to use it. "Ted was a hard worker," Ted Sr. once said. "Not so gifted in the beginning, but he worked hard to be gifted. Above all, he is a team guy, a service guy, a blue-collar guy."

Not many blue-collar guys earn national high school championships, own seven Ohio State and Big Ten records for punt and kickoff returns, and score more than sixty touchdowns during a fourteen-year NFL career. And even that impressive résumé doesn't include the fact that Junior's ankle quite likely changed the career trajectories of two national championship coaches.

"I never really felt comfortable in the spotlight if that's what you want to call it," he said. "I just wanted to be one of the guys. You know, work hard, fit in, just help my team win. I never cared about all the other stuff."

Theodore Ginn Jr. was born April 12, 1985, in Cleveland to a pair of high school sweethearts. Ted Ginn Sr. and Jeanette Casey had graduated from Glenville High School just one year apart, and were married just fewer than two years when Ted Jr. came along. He would attend the same high school as his parents, and become an honor student as well as a legendary athlete there. But many years before that, Junior struggled with academics. In fact, he was such a slow learner that he failed first grade at St. Agatha-St. Aloysius in Cleveland.

"That hurt. No question," he remembered. But that was nothing compared to what awaited the youngster when he reported for school to begin the fourth grade. He was told by an administration official that the school could no longer accommodate his needs. He needed extra tutoring, and that was something the school either could not or did not want to provide. So, little ten-year-old Ted was ushered to the curb in front of the school so that his father could pick him up. By the time his father arrived, the little boy was crying his eyes out.

By the fifth grade at his new school, he ran into classroom trouble again when a teacher asked him to spell a word. "I told him I couldn't," Ted said. "He kept badgering me, so I just shut down. Didn't say anything. Finally, he got mad and told me, 'Your life is going to be nothing but flipping hamburgers at Burger King.' I was so embarrassed."

It wasn't until he was an eighth-grader when Ted was finally diagnosed with a learning disorder. But because it was not a classic disorder such as dyslexia, it took some time for the school to devise a learning system to fit Ted's needs. Tutors were assigned for certain subjects while he attended special education classes for slow learners.

"Teachers could never cope with how I learned so slowly," he said. "I just need more time. If it takes you two weeks to read a book, it will take me four. Or it might take three or four times of you explaining something to me. But I kept working. I didn't give up. By the time I got to high school, things had begun to turn around. For the first time in my life, I finally felt comfortable in a classroom."

Meanwhile, his father had changed career paths, and in 2001 began working as a security guard at his high school alma mater. A short time later, he became in charge of the football and track programs at Glenville, and would eventually lead the Tarblooders to six state track championships, including five in a row from 2003 to 2007. It was no coincidence that run of excellence coincided with his son's presence on those first two championship track teams.

Glenville won the 2003 state title chiefly because of the efforts of Ted Jr., who was responsible for more than half of his team's total number of points. He won the individual hurdle events at 110 and

300 meters, was a member of the championship 4x100-meter relay team, and finished second in the individual 200 meters. His personal-best times in the 110-meter hurdles, 200 meters, and 400 meters were each considered to be world class, and there was a time that he envisioned putting off any kind of college career for a chance to make the United States track team for the 2004 Summer Olympics in Athens, Greece.

More than fifteen years after his college career ended, Ted still owns seven OSU and Big Ten kick return records.

At the time, he said, "The Olympics is kind of a dream for me. It's been in the back of my mind for quite a while, and I want to take a shot at it. I probably won't get another chance."

It wasn't a pipe dream. While at Glenville, Ginn defeated future Olympic silver medalist Jason Richardson in a hurdles event and was a member of a squad that beat a 4x100 relay team anchored by eight-time Olympic gold medal sprinter Usain Bolt. "He was the anchor and I was the second leg on our team," Ginn said. "I opened up and gave us a lead that he couldn't get back. So, you know, I've run against the best of the best."

Lofty track credentials to be sure, but it was also difficult to overlook Ginn's exploits on the football field. During his senior year, he played quarterback and combined for 2,000 yards running and throwing. On defense, he grabbed eight interceptions and returned five for touchdowns, including one he brought out of the end zone for a 102-yard return. He scored more touchdowns while returning kickoffs and punts, and even handled his team's placekicking duties on extra points.

In the process of earning status as a world-class track athlete and highly sought-after football prospect, Ginn had become an honor student. "All of the special classes and special attention I got really paid off," he said. "It was a major turnaround from almost failing every grade to getting on the honor roll." He finished sixteenth in his graduating class with a 3.50 grade-point average.

The dream of winning Olympic gold eventually took a backseat to football, especially when every major college coach from coast to coast offered him every enticement (most legal, some not so much) to join their program. Perhaps the best thing Ohio State had going for it was proximity to home and the fact that head coach Jim Tressel was in the building stages of a pipeline from Glenville to Columbus. From the moment he first stepped on the practice field at the Woody Hayes Athletic Center, Ginn was alongside such former Tarblooders as future All-America safety Donte Whitner and quarterback Troy Smith, the 2006 Heisman Trophy winner.

Originally signed to play defensive back for the Buckeyes, and perhaps play a dual role on offense and defense as Chris Gamble did during Ohio State's run to the 2002 national championship, the truth is that Tressel really didn't know how best to utilize Ginn. At a slight 6-foot-1 and 170 pounds, he had to prove he could hold up against opposing receivers to whom he'd be giving up thirty pounds or more. Meanwhile, on offense, although Gamble was off to an NFL career, the Buckeyes were still well-stocked with their stable of receivers, starting with future Super Bowl MVP Santonio Holmes.

As a result, Ginn rarely saw the field during the first five games of his college career. But after getting just eight touches (four receptions and four returns) in those first five games, the freshman finally had his first big moment for the Scarlet and Gray when he kicked off a week-six victory against Indiana with a 59-yard touchdown reception. Two weeks later, during a 32–19 win at Michigan State, it was officially The Ted Ginn Jr. Coming-Out Party when he scored touchdowns on a 17-yard run, a 68-yard punt return, and a 58-yard reception.

It was the beginning of what turned out to be an electrifying career that included a Big Ten-record six career punt returns for touchdowns, four of them coming in a single season, another conference record. Ginn also finished his OSU career with two kickoff returns for touchdowns, including the last time he ever touched the ball as a Buckeye.

On a warm January evening in Glendale, Arizona, undefeated and top-ranked Ohio State stood one victory away from a second national championship in five years. On the other side, the second-ranked and once-beaten Florida Gators, led by a coaching upstart by the name of Urban Meyer. The battle was billed as a clash between the Heisman Trophy-winning Smith and Florida's swarming defense, but it also pitted the kind football conservatism displayed by the 55-year-old, play-it-close-to-the-sweater-vest Tressel against the shoot-from-the-hip Meyer, then just forty-two.

Strategies quick went by the wayside, however, shortly after Ginn accepted the game's opening kickoff. Moving straight ahead behind a pair of blockers, he easily shed a would-be tackler at the twenty-yard line and made a move to his right. By the time he had covered another twenty yards, Florida defenders fell in line behind him, already realizing their chase was a futile one. Ginn raced down the visitor's sideline right past a stunned Meyer and his coaching staff, not stopping until his 93-yard return had given the Buckeyes a touchdown lead a mere sixteen seconds into the game.

Then almost as surely as lightning follows thunder, Ginn was injured during the touchdown celebration when all six-foot-three and 240 pounds of receiver Roy Hall came down on Ginn's ankle. The junior speedster later limped to the locker room, and in the aftermath, Ohio State's early 7–0 lead evaporated into a 41–14 embarrassment.

The Buckeyes would return to the national title game the following season, losing to Louisiana State University, but they would never again reach the sport's pinnacle under Tressel, who was dismissed by the university in 2011 due to NCAA improprieties. Meanwhile, Meyer won a second national championship at Florida in 2008, and a third in 2014 in his third season at Ohio State.

Had Ginn not been injured after the opening kickoff, might the outcome of the 2007 BCS title game been altered? And had the Buckeyes defeated the Gators in that game, would Ohio State have been so quick to dismiss a coach who had guided the program to a pair of national championships? Then would Meyer have ever been hired at Ohio State?

"That's a lot to unpack; a lot of ifs and maybes," longtime Ohio State football historian Jack Park said. "If you go back to that championship game, the Ohio State offensive line had so much trouble with the Florida defense, it's hard to envision many scenarios where a healthy Ted Ginn Jr. would have made that much of a difference. Then again, who's to say he wouldn't have returned a punt for a touchdown and somehow turned the tide?"

Ginn decided to forgo his final year of college eligibility and was taken by the Miami Dolphins with the ninth overall selection in the 2007 NFL draft. Making six different stops over fourteen seasons in the league, he amassed 15,742 all-purpose yards and scored 41 touchdowns, including seven on kick returns. Two came during a 30–25 win against the New York Jets in 2009 when Ginn had 100- and 101-yard returns in the third quarter. It marked only the eighth time in NFL history a player had returned two kickoffs for scores in the same game, and just the second time anyone had accomplished the feat in the same quarter.

When he announced his retirement in July 2021, Ginn expressed his gratitude for being able to play the game he loved for so long. But when someone asked him about his long-ago track career, a smile crossed his face.

"I'm proud of my track career," he said. "If I hadn't gone on the route I took as far as football, then maybe I'd have some regrets about track. But I don't. Football gave me and my family a great ride. It sure beat flipping burgers."

MALCOLM JENKINS

OSU CORNERBACK 2005–2008

2

HOMETOWN: Piscataway, New Jersey

HEIGHT: 6 ft 1 in **WEIGHT:** 201 lb

ALL-AMERICAN: 2007, 2008

NFL DRAFT: 2009, New Orleans Saints

Malcolm Jenkins is a self-described introvert. Back when he was playing with younger brothers Martin and Myles under the towering pine trees in the friendly confines of the fenced-in backyard of his New Jersey home, Malcolm dreamed about becoming a professional football player. Never once did those dreams include becoming a social activist.

In a world of canned clichés, Jenkins was always a bit of fresh air on the Ohio State football beat, responding to reporters' questions with more thoughtful, erudite answers than most. After he landed in New Orleans just five years after Hurricane Katrina had ravaged the area and delivered impoverished pockets of the city with a particularly hellish brand of devastation, he was determined to make an impact in the community. He had just finished his rookie NFL season with the Saints in 2010 when Malcolm and his mother, Gwendolyn, started a charitable foundation focused on youth in underserved communities. That same year, Malcolm, who was still only twenty-two, became involved in tackling the issue of gun violence in New Orleans.

Six years later, after moving to the Philadelphia Eagles through free agency, Jenkins, who never set out to become one of the sports world's most visible social activists, nevertheless found himself thrust into the spotlight in the aftermath of the shooting deaths of Alton Sterling and Philando Castile, each man an African American shot and killed by police officers.

Sterling was shot and killed on July 5, 2016, by two Baton Rouge, Louisiana officers responding to the call of a man threatening people with a gun outside a convenience store. The owner of the store later said Sterling was "not the one causing trouble." One day later, Castile was fatally shot during a traffic stop in suburban St. Paul, Minnesota. Each incident resulted in successful wrongful death cases, and triggered nationwide protests that spilled over into the NFL when San Francisco 49ers quarterback Colin Kaepernick first sat and then kneeled during the playing of the national anthem.

"All of a sudden, I found myself in a place where I was prepared to step up," Malcolm said. "I was just like, 'OK, enough is enough. I don't want to just tweet, I don't want to wear a T-shirt.' And that came about because of a lifetime of, you know, people planting seeds and people pruning me. I found myself ready to be a leader, not only on the field, not only for myself, but for the community. I credit that to everybody who has been a part of my upbringing."

The decision to step from the shadows into the activism spotlight inspired some and infuriated others. And Jenkins, who has often said the most surprising thing is that it doesn't come naturally to him to be in the spotlight, readily admits that everything he has tackled off the field can be "quite frankly draining." He began seeing a therapist on a weekly basis in 2016 when he became a leading voice in the campaign toward racial equality and social justice because he was putting a lot of pressure on himself to be a superman of sorts on the field, in his business ventures, at home, and in the community.

"It's a lot easier for me to be a leader and vocal on the field," he said. "That's where a lot of my personality comes out. I've been a captain on every team that I've been on since I started this game. But stepping out more into the public eye and being kind of a voice in that regard definitely took a lot of preparation—and really, I think, courage.

"Just to fight my own battles, to unlock or free my own mind, to detach myself from the criticisms that we're 'just athletes' and don't have anything to contribute to the conversation or that we're not the experts, we don't know enough…It took me a minute to break out of that."

Not that he was blind to his surroundings before. Born Malcolm Damari Jenkins on December 20, 1987, in East Orange, New Jersey, he grew up in the working-class Arbor neighborhood of Piscataway. His father, Willie Lee Jenkins Jr., who prefers being called by his middle name, made sure his eldest son knew the value of being on time and delivering on a promise.

Lee would load Malcolm into the passenger side of his Yukon Denali and roll it through the neighborhood picking up all the kids for youth football practice. He wouldn't let his son quit when the going got toughest, and he didn't want any of the other kids to have an excuse for missing practice. Along the way they would stop at Dwayne Gratz's house. Gratz went on to play college football at the University of Connecticut before a four-year NFL career mostly with the Jacksonville Jaguars. Next up was Steven Miller, a running back who played his college ball at Appalachian State before a couple of seasons with the Detroit Lions.

"That was my first example of seeing someone give back," Malcolm said. "He literally took the whole neighborhood. Some parents couldn't take their kids or didn't know the importance of it. So he would sign them up and transport all of us—and I'm talking about the whole neighborhood."

Malcolm's mother, the former Gwendolyn Hardwick, covered the academic side of the coin. An honors student from North High School in her native Phoenix, Arizona, Gwendolyn went cross-country to earn a degree in Business Administration from North Carolina Agricultural & Technical State University. That was followed by twenty years in public service as an honored New Jersey Superior Court Executive.

By the time Malcolm reached high school, he had become a star in football as well as track. He played receiver and defensive back, earning all-state honors as a senior, and helped the Chiefs win three consecutive state championships. He also won a state track title in the 400-meter dash as a junior, took third place in the 200 meters as a junior, and placed third in the hurdles as a senior at the state meet.

Although the campuses of Piscataway High School and Rutgers University are separated by fewer than five miles, Malcolm never seriously considered attending his hometown college. In those days before membership in the Big Ten, the Scarlet Knights were struggling members of the Big East Conference without a winning season since the early 1990s. He never really eliminated the possibility of attending Rutgers, but during a visit to an Ohio State football camp the summer before his senior year, everything began to tilt toward the Buckeyes.

Always eager to improve his game, Malcolm returned to New Jersey after the camp with a few new defensive tricks up his sleeve thanks to then co-defensive coordinator and secondary coach Mel Tucker. "Coach Tucker pointed out things I didn't know I was doing," Malcolm recalled. "He taught me some difficult bump-and-run coverages and how to better defend a fade route. I left camp liking the way OSU's staff was teaching its players, which helped me make a decision to go to Ohio State."

Tucker said Jenkins was like a sponge when it came to coaching. "I remember he was eager," the coach said. "And some of the stuff we were showing him, we didn't show to just anybody. Only the elite guys got to see that, and Malcolm certainly fit into that category."

There was just one problem on the horizon. Tucker announced just before National Signing Day that he was leaving Ohio State to join the coaching staff of the Cleveland Browns. But Malcolm never wavered. "I wanted to play for Coach Tucker," he said, "but I still felt like it was Ohio State as a whole that wanted me. I loved the campus and I liked the coaching staff, so it just felt like the right place for me."

What followed was a four-year college career with the Buckeyes that included three years as a starting cornerback in what was considered one of college football's most ferocious defenses. Living up to its "Silver Bullets" nickname, the Ohio State defense ranked third in the nation with 21 interceptions while helping the team to the 2006 national championship game and then led the nation in total defense and scoring defense the following year. Jenkins was the tip of the defensive spear at the cornerback position, grabbing four interceptions (including one he returned for a touchdown) as a sophomore in 2006 and matching those totals a year later.

Malcolm capped his career in 2008 with three more interceptions, earning his third berth on the All-Big Ten first team as well as his second consecutive first-team All-America honor and the Jim Thorpe Award as college football's most outstanding defensive back. He graduated from Ohio State with a degree in communications and was the fifteenth overall pick in the 2009 NFL draft.

Through the 2021 season, he had started 191 of his 199 career games and had two Super Bowl championship rings—one with New Orleans for a 31–17 win against the Indianapolis Colts in Super Bowl XLIV, the other with Philadelphia for a thrilling 41–33 victory against the defending champion New England Patriots in Super Bowl LII. Along the way, he has been named to three Pro Bowl teams, won the NFL Players Association's Byron "Whizzer" White Award in 2017 for his community efforts, and was the Eagles' Walter Payton Man of the Year nominee in 2019.

In addition to his social activism, Malcolm has become a successful entrepreneur, beginning his own fashion line of bow ties, and he runs youth football camps in New Orleans, Columbus, Philadelphia, and Piscataway. The camps include standard stretching routines and scrimmages, but also offer parents informational sessions on concussions and symptom recognition, sudden cardiac arrest, common injuries, and nutrition. Educating the parents early, Malcolm said, could help them make more informed decisions. "It was my mom's idea," he said. "As a parent, she knows the importance of being educated. She was one of those moms where, when I grew up through football, there weren't as many resources. There's a lot of things you don't know as a parent. A lot of times people don't know where to look."

Still, most of his off-the-field energy is channeled toward what he described as a "passion for the greater good."

Jenkins has focused on solutions to end the cycle of incarceration to help ex-convicts move beyond their criminal records. The issue is personal for Malcolm, who has witnessed his younger brother struggle for years after being found guilty of marijuana possession in high school.

"His record has stopped him from getting jobs and providing for his family," Malcolm said. "It has been frustrating to watch him fight to better himself to be a productive citizen, only to be constantly denied the opportunity because of the exposure from the criminal justice system. He will own everything that has come from his decision, but it doesn't change the fact that it's counterproductive."

In June 2017, Jenkins joined former Buckeyes Chris "Beanie" Wells and Raekwon McMillan in signing a letter to Ohio state senators in support of Targeted Community Alternatives to Prison (T-CAP), a program that diverts low-level offenders from state prison into community treatment programs. The program drew only mixed reactions from state officials, but Jenkins remains unfazed.

"We'll keep after them," he said. "Alternatives that are community-based such as substance abuse treatment and mental health support have been shown to reduce the recidivism rates for low-level offenders. Instead of locking people up in jail for minor violations, we could funnel resources into stopping the cycle and provide a fighting chance for them to become contributing members of our communities."

Perhaps still nearest and dearest to his heart is the Malcolm Jenkins Foundation, still run by his mother with the guiding mission of Project REWARDS (Reinforcing Education with Activities, Recreation, and Developmental Supports).

Malcolm knows his work is far from over. It will last long after he is finished playing football and perhaps will even outlive him. But he remains encouraged.

"If people know me more for what I do off the field than on the field, I think that's a win for my life," he said. "Don't get me wrong. I take a lot of pride in being a damn good football player. The impact on the field I have is very important to me and it's what I love to do. I love this game, love playing it, and want to play it as long as I'm able. But if it comes down to being known more for my contributions to society than to the game, I'm actually very OK with that."

RYAN SHAZIER

OSU LINEBACKER 2011–2013

HOMETOWN: Fort Lauderdale, Florida

HEIGHT: 6 ft 2 in **WEIGHT**: 230 lb

ALL-AMERICAN: 2013

NFL DRAFT: 2014, Pittsburgh Steelers

2

It often takes a life-altering experience for some to choose a path of leadership and sacrifice. Others are simply born into it. The son of a preacher, Ryan Shazier was already in the latter category when confronted by his own life-altering experience, an injury sustained on the football field that not only ended his career but threatened to make him a paraplegic.

But for a young man who had already overcome so much before his thirtieth birthday, leveraging his injury as another way of proving his faith and fortitude wasn't much of a surprise for those close to him. Then after a grueling rehabilitation period during which he regained the use of his legs, Shazier redoubled his efforts to inspire others, becoming a living embodiment of the biblical verse from Philippians 4:13 already tattooed across his left arm: "I can do all things through Christ who strengthens me."

It was Shazier who changed jersey numbers as a sophomore in 2012 and then played the game of his life to honor the manager of his high school team who had recently succumbed to muscular dystrophy. It was Shazier who pleaded with head coach Urban Meyer to be excused from practice to join teammate Curtis Grant, who was returning to his Virginia home following the death of his father. And it was Shazier who changed his jersey again during his senior year, donning teammate Christian Bryant's number after Bryant suffered a season-ending ankle injury.

"All my life," Ryan said, "people have been helping me in all types of situations. It's only right to pay it back. When you see someone in need, it's only right to help them."

Ryan Dean Shazier was born September 6, 1992, in Lauderdale Lakes, Florida, to a pair of native Floridians who grew up less than ten miles from one another. Vernon James Shazier was raised in the spring break mecca of Fort Lauderdale, where he attended Boyd Anderson High School as a seemingly good-natured, athletic youngster who went by the nickname "V-Dog." But his easy and ready smile belied a difficult upbringing exacerbated by his parents' bitter divorce. His mother took Vernon and his three siblings, escaped the abusive relationship, and moved to Fort Lauderdale's projects.

Vernon had played football, basketball, and baseball, but gave up any hope of an athletic career in order to work and help his mother put food on the family table. Upon graduation, he enlisted in the U.S. Navy, where he knew he would get the discipline he had needed throughout his young life and a steady paycheck, most of which he would send home.

Eight miles to the west of Fort Lauderdale, Shawn Renata Dean was growing up in the sprawling city of Plantation, site of a failed rice plantation in the early 1900s. Shawn was a pretty but shy teenager, but her shyness masked an inner confidence and fortitude that has allowed her to wage a quiet battle with Crohn's disease as an adult. The inflammation in her digestive tract brings on a variety of symptoms, and once landed her in the hospital at Christmastime. But Ryan says his mother always finds light no matter the situation, describing her as "a God-fearing walking advertisement for the Golden Rule."

"I got introduced to a bunch of different sports to see what I'd like. I was too fast-paced for basketball—too aggressive, always committing fouls. Baseball? I had no hand-eye coordination. Track? That was way too much running if you weren't chasing after somebody holding a ball. Football, though? Love at first sight."

—Ryan Shazier

Despite their devoutness and strength of character, Vernon and Shawn Shazier's little boy grew up with a bit of a mean streak. Some of that was derived from the insults Ryan had to endure when his hair began to fall out in clumps at the age of five. The problem was diagnosed as alopecia areata, a polygenic disease that attacks the hair follicles and causes hair loss on the scalp, face and other parts of the body. But as the little boy agonized as he lost even his eyebrows, he had to endure such taunts as "Cueball," "Patches," and "Chia Pet" from his so-called friends. One even asked him if he was dying of cancer.

"Try explaining what alopecia is to children in the classroom or on the playground," he said. "Let me tell you: Kids can be mean."

About the same time, seeking to ease some of his son's distress about his condition, Ryan's father decided to immerse him in athletics.

"I got introduced to a bunch of different sports to see what I'd like," Ryan remembered. "I was too fast-paced for basketball—too aggressive, always committing fouls. Baseball? I had no hand-eye coordination. Track? That was way too much running if you weren't chasing after somebody holding a ball. Football, though? Love at first sight."

Unlike most youngsters who want to throw the football or run with it, Ryan was drawn to the controlled mayhem on the defensive side of the ball. "I lived for the big hit," he said. "That kind that's heard through the stadium, the kind that forces a collective gasp from the stands. You feel that *thwack* of body on body, and then you stand over your opponent and you can almost see the self-confidence leave his body."

By the time Ryan reached middle school, Vernon Shazier received what he termed as "a calling" and packed up his family, which now included Ryan's younger brother Vernon II, and moved it to Waco, Texas, so that he could attend seminary. It was there in Central Texas that the elder Shazier realized he had a football prodigy on his hands. One day, a director of the league in which Ryan was playing pulled his father aside and said, "Some of the parents are complaining that Ryan tackles a little too hard." Vernon's pragmatic response? "What do you want me to do? Tell him not to be so rough? This is football."

After three years in Texas, the Shaziers returned to Fort Lauderdale where Vernon became assistant pastor at Mount Bethel Baptist Church. Meanwhile, Ryan became a football star, first at Blanche Ely

High School, where his father had been defensive coordinator before entering the ministry, and later at his mother's alma mater in Plantation. At six feet tall and a muscular 180 pounds, Ryan flourished as a defensive end too quick for opposing linemen to block. He turned in twenty-two sacks as a junior, and followed that with nearly twenty more the following season earning prep All-America status in the process.

As with any highly rated Florida prospect during the early 2010s, the University of Florida was an attractive college destination. Head coach Urban Meyer had guided the Gators to three division titles and two national championships during a four-year span that featured forty-eight wins in fifty-five games between 2006 and 2009. Meyer recruited Shazier, now six-two and 210 pounds, to play linebacker for him beginning in 2011, and the young prospect quickly accepted the scholarship offer.

But when Meyer abruptly resigned following the 2010 season, Ryan rescinded his commitment to Florida and signed instead with Ohio State, joining the Buckeyes for spring practice after graduating early from high school. Unfortunately, just five months later, OSU head coach Jim Tressel was forced to resign and defensive assistant Luke Fickell took over as interim head coach.

"Before a single snap of my collegiate career, I'd committed to two teams whose coaches had both stepped down," Ryan said. "What a way to start out. Coach Fickell, who I loved, would serve as interim head coach, but the Ohio State program was in total disarray. I had to figure out how to make it work for me."

It didn't take him long. Making an initial impact as a bone-jarring tackler on special teams units, Ryan got his chance at extended action late in the season when regular linebacker Andrew Sweat was sidelined with a concussion. Shazier started each of the final three games of the 2011 season, beginning with a game against Penn State during which he recorded fifteen tackles. He finished the regular season with eight tackles against Michigan despite playing with a bad knee, and then totaled ten more tackles against Florida in the Gator Bowl despite playing at less than 100 percent. He finished with a total of 57 tackles, the most for an Ohio State true freshman in fifteen years.

And he was just getting started. In a twist of fate, Meyer took over head coaching duties at Ohio State in 2012 and led the Buckeyes to an undefeated season. Part of the credit for that record was an unrelenting defense spearheaded by Shazier, who led the team with 115 tackles as a sophomore, including five sacks among his seventeen tackles for loss.

A year later, Ryan upped his production to 143 total tackles—the highest total for a Buckeye in twenty-six years—as Ohio State again made a run at perfection, winning its first twelve games before stumbling in the postseason. But despite a loss in the Big Ten Championship Game to Michigan State, and a Fiesta Bowl defeat against Clemson, Shazier did about all he could do. He had a team-high twelve tackles against the Spartans and made nine stops in the bowl loss.

Following the season, he was named a consensus first-team All-American after which he decided to forgo his senior season and made himself eligible for the NFL draft. The Pittsburgh Steelers selected him with the number fifteen pick of the first round in 2014, and he became a mainstay at inside linebacker for the Steelers defense beginning in his second season.

After being elected to the Pro Bowl for the first time in his third season, Shazier was headed for another Pro Bowl assignment in 2017 when during a Monday night game in early December against the Cincinnati Bengals, he zeroed in on Bengals receiver Josh Malone, who had just caught a checkdown pass from quarterback Andy Dalton. Just before making the tackle, Malone turned and Shazier's head made contact with the receiver's left hip. He dropped to the turf, feeling what he described as a burning sensation in his lower back. And he couldn't move his legs.

The injury was later diagnosed as a spinal contusion, an injury that typically provides only a three-percent chance of walking again. Three days later, Ryan underwent spinal stabilization surgery to secure the injured section of his spine and to aid in his recovery. The innovative procedure was deemed a success, but Ryan's odds of walking again had increased only to twenty percent. The surgery was followed by weeks of frustration, panic, and depression before an aggressive rehabilitation program, one that began with Ryan struggling just to sit up in bed.

Along with an army of therapists were Ryan's parents, cheering every small victory. Vernon Shazier even began marking the hurdles cleared as "first downs."

"Once there were other people in the room, and I motioned for Dad to come in close for a secret," Ryan said. "He leaned over me and I whispered, 'I think I shit myself.' Dad didn't miss a beat. 'That means you can feel something, Son,' he said, before calling a nurse to get me cleaned up. 'Your body is waking up. Thank you, Lord, for this first down.' Yeah, my Dad actually thanked the Lord because I crapped the bed."

Just ten days after the surgery, Ryan had made so much progress that he made his first public appearance since the injury. He was wheeled out on the field during a Steelers playoff game against the New England Patriots to a thunderous ovation.

Four grueling months later, Ryan and his fiancée Michelle walked hand in hand onto a stage at AT&T Stadium in Arlington, Texas, to announce Pittsburgh's first-round selection in the 2018 NFL draft. A year later, on May 3, 2019, Ryan danced at his wedding to Michelle. One more important walk across a stage came in December 2020 when he accepted his diploma during commencement exercises at Ohio State.

While his injury ended his football career, he has channeled his efforts into charitable work and philanthropy as well as spending as much time with Michelle and their sons Lyon and R.J.

"I view each day with them as something to cherish," Ryan said. "When you've been told that you only have a twenty percent chance of ever walking again, you literally feel God's presence in every step you take. It's funny. I used to be obsessed with being strong and fast. Now, I am humble and so very grateful every time my foot hits the pavement."

BRAXTON MILLER

OSU QUARTERBACK, RECEIVER 2011–2013, 2015

HOMETOWN: Springfield, Ohio

HEIGHT: 6 ft 2 in **WEIGHT**: 215 lb

NFL DRAFT: 2016, Houston Texans

5

What if Chic Harley had chosen to go to college anywhere other than Ohio State? Would Ohio Stadium ever have been built? What if World War II had never happened and Paul Brown remained head coach of the Buckeyes into the 1950s and 1960s? Would anyone have ever heard of the Cleveland Browns or Woody Hayes? What if Art Schlichter had never thrown that interception at the end of the 1978 Gator Bowl? How much longer might Hayes have been head coach at Ohio State? What if Jim Tressel's teams had won the national title games in 2006 and 2007? Would the university have been so eager to cut loose a three-time national championship coach just three years later?

There are so many "what if" scenarios within the history of the Ohio State football program; scenarios that, had they gone another way, would not only have altered the program's path but of college football itself. But if there is a king of "what ifs," it must certainly be Braxton Miller, the star-crossed quarterback-turned-receiver who might have been the most athletically gifted player to wear the Scarlet and Gray over the past half-century.

The talented prospect graduated high school early in order to join the Jim Tressel-led Buckeyes for spring practice in 2011 only to watch the head coach get consumed a few months later by a tattoos-for-memorabilia scandal that cost him his job. Miller played the following season under interim head coach Luke Fickell and the succeeding two with Urban Meyer as his head coach, setting records and earning awards by the bushel. But the pounding he took as a dual threat to run or throw eventually took its toll, leaving hardy fans and casual observers with that lingering question: What if?

Braxton Miller was born November 30, 1992, in Springfield, Ohio, the second child to Kevin Miller and the former Kelly Deanne Huffman, following sister Bailey, who was three years older. Young Braxton's outward personality was so laid-back and quiet that he was once described that he "often seems to have just awoken from a nap." But behind that placid exterior beat the heart of a competitor always seeking to challenge anyone who challenged him.

When he was just four years old, and his family had just moved into a new neighborhood in Springfield, some older kids were playing basketball. They looked at the new kid and quickly decided he was too young to play with them. Braxton refused to accept that verdict and plunked himself down in the middle of the action.

"He got kicked off the court," his father recalled. "That's one we laugh about a lot."

Another time, Braxton and Bailey were playing kickball in their backyard. Braxton kicked the ball, and Bailey threw him out at first base by hitting him with the ball. "He got so mad that he chased her around the yard for five or ten minutes. He didn't think it was fair. I knew right then he was competitive," Kevin Miller said, before adding with a laugh, "but I was hoping he didn't have an anger management problem."

Blessed with an abundance of God-given gifts, there weren't many times growing up from sandlot to perfectly groomed stadium field when Braxton wasn't far and away the best player on his team. He was so gifted that he often didn't have to showcase his wares at one hundred percent efficiency when eighty was plenty good enough to get the job done. As a result, he earned something of a reputation as a "lights-on guy." In other words, he had a tendency to coast unless prodded with some kind of worthy competition.

An eighty-percent Braxton Miller was usually better than anyone else at full capacity, and that was on full display when he moved with his family from Springfield and began his prep career at Wayne High School in Huber Heights, a suburb of Dayton located at the intersection of two interstate highways that make it an ideal hub for the freight trucking industry. It was also an ideal destination for a quick, young freshman who wanted to hone his quarterbacking skills and perhaps follow in the footsteps of such other notable Wayne alumni as former Ohio State and NFL defensive back Will Allen, former OSU linebacker and current Notre Dame head coach Marcus Freeman, and a host of other pros in football, basketball and soccer.

Although he dabbled in basketball and track at Wayne, there was never any doubt that football was Braxton's premier sport. He started as a freshman for longtime Warriors head coach Jay Minton and was under center—or more accurately, accepting snaps in a shotgun formation—for more than thirty victories during his high school career. With each passing season, the recruiting crush from prospective college coaches became more and more intense, and the youngster quickly tired of the constant barrage of offers. By the time he had finished his junior season, Braxton was a lithe 6-foot-2, a sinewy 200 pounds and routinely produced jaguar-like speed, routinely turning in sub-4.5 times in the forty-yard dash whenever anyone produced a stopwatch.

With offers climbing near the two hundred mark, and destinations such as Alabama, Florida and the University of Southern California targeting him as their number one priority, with Nick Saban, Urban Meyer and Pete Carroll among those promising to tailor their offensive attacks to the youngster's unique talents, Braxton ended the speculation the summer before his senior year began and selected Ohio State.

Minton, who spent three decades as a high school head coach, more than twenty of those at Wayne, knew what his young quarterback was getting into, but he wondered if Braxton himself truly knew the expectations that would come with a commitment to play for the Buckeyes. "When I found out, I said, 'Now listen. You're going to the in-state school, and the people are very passionate about it,'" Mintor recalled. "I knew the slightest blips were going to be disappointments, and the successes were going to create more expectations. I knew there was going to be more scrutiny. Whether Wayne fans or fans of the team we were playing, I knew they'd want to see the guy going to Ohio State. I knew there would be more eyes on him, and it was up to him to be able to handle that."

His coach needn't have worried. In fact, Braxton saved his best high school performances for his senior season as he led the Warriors to the Division I state championship game. Along the way, he accounted for 284 total yards and four touchdowns during a thrilling overtime win against Centerville, and then did almost everything he could against Lakewood St. Edward in the state title game, throwing for 200 yards, rushing for sixty-four and scoring four touchdowns in a 35–28 losing effort.

A few months later, Miller graduated from Wayne early in order to enroll at Ohio State in time for spring practice. Normally, he would have walked into a program coming off a twelve-win season capped by a Sugar Bowl victory with a loaded roster featuring star quarterback Terrelle Pryor returning for his senior season. Instead, the Buckeyes were enveloped in turmoil with head coach Jim Tressel squarely in the NCAA crosshairs of an investigation into his players exchanging memorabilia for free tattoos.

"When I first got there, and all the stuff about tattoos and Coach Tress and all that other stuff was going on, I did my best to try and block that out," Braxton said. "I had other stuff on my mind like trying to learn the plays. I didn't even know half the players. I was just trying to keep my head above water."

Tressel was eventually forced out after ten years at the helm, replaced on an interim basis by linebackers coach Luke Fickell, while Pryor left school in the wake of the NCAA investigation. That left Miller to battle fifth-year senior Joe Bauserman for the starting quarterback job in fall camp. Bauserman began the 2011 season with an excellent game in the opener against Akron, but his performance fell off steadily over the next few weeks and Miller was the team's starter beginning in week four.

That 2011 season produced some lofty peaks, including a last-second comeback win vs. No. 15 Wisconsin, as well as several deep valleys such as blowing a 21-point, third-quarter lead in a loss at Nebraska. But the Buckeyes went into their regular-season finale at Michigan with a purpose. "You talk every year about how that game can make your season," Braxton said. "That was the only thing on our minds when we went up there in '11. Beat them and nobody cares what else happened."

Ohio State was working on a seven-game winning streak in the series, but were eight-point underdogs to Michigan in a game that was supposed to turn the tide in the ancient rivalry. Brady Hoke was in his first season as head coach of the Wolverines, and he had already wiped away most of the despair connected with the three years of futility under predecessor Rich Rodriguez. U-M was on its way to an 11–2 record in 2011, its best in five years.

But the Wolverines were clearly not ready for Miller, who guided the Buckeyes to a touchdown on the game's opening possession, putting an exclamation point on the drive with a 54-yard scoring pass to receiver Corey "Philly" Brown. That triggered an entertaining back-and-forth afternoon that featured enough big plays and momentum swings for an entire season.

Michigan appeared to gain the upper hand in the second half and led by as many as ten points at 37–27 with 8:32 remaining in the game. But Miller engineered an 80-yard touchdown drive in only five plays, and then when tailback Dan "Boom" Herron scored from the Michigan four, Ohio State had pulled back within three points at 37–34 with 7:09 to go. The Wolverines responded with a possession that lasted more than five minutes and culminated in a field goal, but they left 1:59 on the game clock for Miller and the Buckeyes to pull off a comeback.

It appeared for a time that something magical was in the works, especially when Miller barely converted a fourth-and-six with a successful dive for the first-down marker. But four plays later, on another fourth-and-six, the clock struck midnight on the fairy tale ending when Miller's throw to DeVier Posey bounced off the receiver's fingertips and into the arms of Michigan cornerback Courtney Avery for the game-clinching interception.

"I thought we were going to win that thing," Braxton said. "Right up until the end, I thought we were going to win it. That last pass to DeVier, it was a tough pass but one I still should have made. There are a lot of passes over my career that I'd like to have back, but I'd put that one at or near the top of the list." Nevertheless, he accounted for 335 yards from scrimmage in the game, rushing sixteen times for 100 yards and a touchdown while completing 14 of 25 passes for 235 yards and two more scores.

Miller was the incumbent in 2012 when Urban Meyer took over for Fickell, and the sophomore flourished in Meyer's wide-open attack, establishing a new program record with 3,310 yards of total offense that included 1,271 rushing yards, a new single-season standard among Ohio State quarterbacks. The following year, he again rushed for more than 1,000 yards, eclipsed the 3,000-yard mark in total offense, and was named the Big Ten's Most Valuable Player for the second season in a row. But all of that running, not to mention absorbing the punishment from being sacked an incredible eighty-eight times during his first three seasons, took its toll.

Early in the fourth quarter of the final game of the 2013 season, the Orange Bowl played in Miami, Florida, Miller endured a wicked shot from Clemson linebacker Spencer Shuey while throwing a touchdown pass to give the Buckeyes a 35-34 lead. Shuey lowered his head and drove Miller into the ground, landing his full 6-foot-3, 230-pound frame on the Ohio State quarterback, a play that was flagged for a roughing-the-passer personal foul. Clemson retook the lead a few minutes later, leaving Miller to try to engineer another comeback.

But on a third-and-thirteen play near midfield with 3:06 remaining, Miller was blindsided by Clemson cornerback Bashaud Breeland. The crushing hit, delivered just under the quarterback's throwing shoulder, caused a fumble and effectively ended the Buckeyes' chances. It also effectively ended the quarterbacking career of Miller, who underwent surgery on his labrum during the offseason and then reinjured the shoulder on a short pass during a practice session one week before the 2014 season-opening game.

Miller was replaced in the starting lineup by J.T. Barrett, who was injured during the Michigan game that year and subsequently replaced by Cardale Jones, who piloted the Buckeyes to the national championship. By the time Miller returned for his final collegiate season in 2015, his throwing shoulder, held together surgically by pins and wires, forced him to move to a receiver position.

The injury might have ended his days as a quarterback, but it didn't rob him of his play-making abilities. In the season-opening game, he made a diving catch for his first collegiate reception and later tiptoed down the sideline for his first touchdown as a receiver. But it was his third-quarter touchdown run of fifty-three yards that underscored the reason why highlight reels were invented.

Taking a direct snap from a running back position, Braxton quickly moved to his left, darting toward the line of scrimmage, retreating and then heading to his left again. While running away from two defenders and getting a key downfield block, his escape route appeared sealed off when a pair of Virginia Tech players closed in. That's when the God-given gifts were unwrapped. Braxton planted his right foot in the turf, performed a pirouette that would have made Anna Pavlova jealous, and motored away toward the end zone untouched.

It was the kind of performance that announced to the world that Braxton Miller was back and that a shoulder turned to spaghetti was not going to hold him back. He became accomplished enough at the receiving position that the Houston Texans selected him in the third round of the 2016 NFL draft, and he played two seasons in Houston as a receiver and punt returner.

Still, one is left to ponder what kind of career Miller might have had if not for the shoulder injury. Would Ohio State still have won the 2014 national championship? Would his talents as a dual-threat quarterback translated to the NFL where single-callers exhibiting the temerity to stray outside the pocket have always been an endangered species?

The lingering question with regard to Braxton Miller will never have to do with his talent. It will always be summed up in just two words: What if?

URBAN MEYER

OSU HEAD COACH 2012–2018

HOMETOWN: Ashtabula, Ohio

BIG TEN TITLES: 2014,2017, 2018

NATIONAL CHAMPIONSHIP: 2014

Before a stunningly ugly flameout in the National Football League, before a lapse in judgment with regard to one of his assistant coaches, and before an inoperable brain cyst forced him into the second sabbatical of his coaching life, Urban Meyer was a revered figure in Buckeye Nation as the man who saved Ohio State football.

The program was literally on the precipice in 2011, rocked by an NCAA investigation into illegalities that occurred on Jim Tressel's watch as head coach of the Buckeyes. Through the prism of 20/20 hindsight, the infractions that included players exchanging memorabilia they received from playing in a bowl game for free tattoos seem trivial. But at the time, they ignited a full-fledged firestorm that eventually resulted in Tressel's forced resignation and the suspension of a half-dozen players, including star quarterback Terrelle Pryor.

The successful ten-year reign of Tressel, with its 2002 national championship, seven Big Ten titles including an unprecedented six in a row, and program-record six consecutive seasons with ten or more victories, had abruptly ended with fewer than three months before fall camp for the 2011 season was to begin.

Luke Fickell, the team's co-defensive coordinator and assistant head coach, took over as interim head coach. But with no previous experience at running his own program, Fickell was admittedly in over his head. Meanwhile, with other members of the coaching staff wondering what their future might hold, the team tried its best to adopt a business-as-usual mentality.

The 2011 season began with a feel-good 42–0 romp against the University of Akron, an undermanned opponent from the Mid-American Conference. But the following week, against another perceived weakling from the MAC, the Buckeyes struggled before finally winning a 27–22 decision from the University of Toledo. Cracks that had begun to show in that game became full-blown leaks when Ohio State lost three of its next four games, including a 34–27 defeat at Nebraska in a game the Buckeyes had led by twenty-one points early in the third quarter.

By the time the 2011 season ended with a 24-17 loss to the University of Florida in the Gator Bowl, Ohio State had finished with a 6-7 record, the first losing mark in twenty-three years. It also was the first time the program had suffered seven losses in a single season since 1897.

The program had experienced disappointing seasons in the past, but something felt different this time. There was a nagging notion the Buckeyes were on the brink of joining a college football landscape littered with once-proud programs whose self-inflicted stumbles had led them to obscurity.

And then Urban Meyer rode into Columbus, revitalized from a one-year coaching sabbatical to bring Ohio State back from the brink. The supposed kinder, gentler version of the then 47-year-old coach who had wrecked his health during a six-year stint at Florida that included two national championships began with laying waste to his new players' egos and assuring them there were two paths they could take—his way or the highway.

The legendary stories of first contact between Meyer and his new team became legendary. There was something called the "dawn patrol," the punishment for tardiness that required a detailed cleaning of the team's weight room equipment, always before dawn and always in complete silence. "Attention training" required outside workouts in sub-freezing temperatures while wearing T-shirts and shorts. And there was the new coach's personal assessment of the receiving corps as "an absolute clown show."

Somehow, whether by brute force, luck, or skill—probably some combination of all three—the members of the 2012 team bonded with their new coaching staff to become one of only six teams in program history to record a perfect season. That kicked off a seven-year tenure for Meyer that included eighty-three victories in ninety-two games (a ridiculously spectacular .902 winning percentage), a division title or co-title each year, a pair of Big Ten championships, and the 2014 national title.

The way Meyer ran his program was equal parts meticulous and ruthless, and that kinder, gentler approach he promised himself and his family when he took the Ohio State job gradually faded to the point that the coach developed an inoperable brain cyst that caused blinding headaches and eventually was a contributing factor to leaving the Buckeyes following the 2018 season. It was the second time in a few short years that Meyer's balls-to-the-walls, take-no-prisoners mentality had forced him to walk away from the game to which he devoted much of his adult life.

Perhaps to know what molded Meyer into such a tunnel-visioned fanatic with an uncompromising predilection for perfectionism, one would have to understand that he came by those character traits honestly.

Born July 10, 1964, the middle child to Urban Frank Meyer Jr. and the former Gisela Maria Gumpert, Urban Frank Meyer III came into the world in Toledo, Ohio, the city on the westernmost tip of Lake Erie much closer to the campus of the University of Michigan than to Ohio Stadium. But Meyer grew up with sisters Gigi and Erika some 175 miles east of Toledo in the hard-knuckle, blue-collar town of Ashtabula.

Those lacking in a grindstone work ethic simply lived somewhere else. When Meyer was growing up in the late 1970s and early 1980s, Ashtabula was an important port on Lake Erie where raw materials were refined and shipped across the country. The town, named for an Iroquois word for "river of many fish," was populated by hard men—largely immigrants from Italy, Ireland, Germany, and Scandinavia—who worked in the factories, railyards, warehouses, and dockyards.

The population hovered around 25,000 from the 1950 census through 1980, and the football at St. John High School was just as strong and gritty as the town during that time. The Heralds advanced to back-to-back state championship games in the mid-1970s, but were unable to bring home the title trophy either time. Still, St. John dominated the Ashtabula City Series throughout young Urban's high school career, beating such rivals as Ashtabula High, Harbor High, and Edgewood High.

"People ask me why St. John was so good back then," said Rick Pugliese, a schoolmate of Meyer. "Those were second-generation kids. They went to a Catholic school. Those kids were raised different than kids now are. They were tough kids."

Young Urban fit that mold perfectly. The namesake of a chemist everyone knew simply as "Bud," the youngster was pushed to excel from the beginning. Bud's parental methods could generously be described as strict, while others might seek a stronger adjective.

When watching one of his son's sporting events, Bud would carry a tape recorder and take oral notes on Urban's performance. Once the game was over, Urban would return home for his father's recorded critiques. Small monetary rewards accompanied good plays while mistakes carried fines. Once, when he struck out to end a baseball game, Meyer had to walk from Cedarquist Park to his home on Lake Road West, a distance of more than six miles north along the river, west past St. Joseph's Cemetery and by the Harbor Golf Club.

"His dad pulled no punches," Pugliese recalled. "You knew where you stood with him. His dad didn't want him hanging around screw-ups and goofballs. He just didn't."

Bud's influence was evident on more than just the playing field. Poor grades were not tolerated, and the results showed. "I don't think Urban's dad gets enough credit," Pugliese said. "He was as strict on academics as he was on sports. People always wonder, how did Urban make it when some of these guys end up a failure at a sport and then that's it? His dad was as strict with his academics as he was with sports."

Still, it would be a misinterpretation to simply label Bud Meyer

Urban became a three-time national championship coach when the Buckeyes rolled to the title in 2014.

as a myopic disciplinarian. His support was unflagging to his son as well as sisters Gigi and Erika, and he attended almost every event in which his children took part. Years later, when Meyer went into coaching, Bud and Gisela traveled several hours each way just to watch him on the sideline.

Gisela, who was a gourmet chef, is often said to have provided the honey to her husband's vinegar. "Urban's mom was just the nicest woman," Pugliese said, but her resolve as a refugee whose family left Soviet-occupied Germany meant sympathy was something in short supply within the Meyer household.

Not that Urban needed or wanted it. He became a self-starter, always looking for some edge against his competition. After reading about how many pushups and sit-ups Heisman Trophy winner Herschel Walker did each day, Meyer adopted the same routine. He gradually worked himself from a scrawny middle-schooler to a two-sport star with football and baseball scholarship offers coming his way. His baseball skills were such that the Atlanta Braves drafted him as a strong-armed shortstop with the ability to hit, and his reputation as a hard-hitting defensive back eventually led him to the University of Cincinnati.

"I think he got to the point where he didn't need to be pushed anymore," said Bill Schmidt, Meyer's high school baseball coach. "He was very unique. He was a kid that once he was told something, that's what he did. He followed directions. He was not a kid I had to scream at and say, 'You're dogging it today.' He was always doing what he was told and trying to make himself a better ballplayer."

That meant when his high school friends were hanging out at a local restaurant or at the beach on Lake Erie across Lake Road from Meyer's house, Urban was often inside his family's two-story Cape Cod.

"It was not a façade, either," Pugliese said. "He was driven at that point. He just never messed around. It's not like he ever looked down on the rest of us, but he just wasn't into that. I'm sure that was part of the discipline from his dad. He just wasn't into messing around."

The youngster's hard-nosed determination was perhaps best suited for the football field. He lined up as a slot back in the St. John run-and-shoot offense, and played strong safety on the other side of the ball, often calling out defensive signals to his teammates. But what really got his competitive juices flowing was coming downhill and delivering a hard tackle on an opposing ball-carrier.

"He would come up and knock your head off," said Joe Pete, who was a freshman at St. John when Meyer was a senior. "He loved to hit people, man. He's one of the most physical safeties I ever saw. He was just a tough, tough guy."

Meyer was also a team leader. Elected a co-captain his senior year on what was known as the "God Squad," Meyer pushed his teammates verbally and by physical example to get better. "He spent every day in the weight room," Pete remembered. "He had all of those leadership qualities even in high school. He was a really good guy, but a no-nonsense person. He wasn't into anything bad. He really was a great role model for a young guy like me."

While Meyer was inspiring his teammates with his leadership skills, he also became keenly aware of the demanding style longtime St. John football coach Paul Kopko brought to bear on his team. Almost every week, the Heralds did battle against a school two or three times its size, a challenge Kopko not only welcomed but relished.

"I remember I played freshman year with Urban," Pugliese said, "and I remember Coach Kopko at two-a-days coming in and motivating the team so much that the place was going crazy. And that was just at two-a-days. I think that's where Urban got a lot of his coaching philosophy."

Kopko seemed cut from the same cloth as Meyer's father. The team practiced on a rough patch of grass near the school where the coach ran drills that fit the stereotype of what an old-school coach would devise. Tackling and live contact were givens along with one-on-one drills such as "bull in the ring," a contest of strength between two players while their teammates formed a circle around them. One teammate recalled it was a favorite of Urban's because "he would just knock your socks off."

Kopko said the drills were tough by design. "We always felt that we were a physical football team," the coach said. "We felt to be that way, we had to practice that way and have that type of mentality. We had to have a little bit of a chip on our shoulder, and to do that, I felt we had to push the kids sometimes. Not to the point of hurting them or anything, but I think that was our mentality going in. We thought we had to be physical, and that's what we were."

From Ashtabula, Meyer's path is well-chronicled. After playing his college football at Cincinnati, he began his coaching career as a graduate assistant on Earle Bruce's staff at Ohio State. Several assistants' jobs followed before he accepted his first head coaching assignment in 2001 at Bowling Green. Successful stints followed at Utah and Florida before Meyer took what he described as his "dream job" at Ohio State.

Ongoing health scares, coupled with a brief suspension due to the messy way he handled off-the-field behavioral issues of assistant coach Zach Smith, led Meyer to resign as Ohio State head coach following the 2018 season. This time, he remained sidelined for two years before taking over as head coach of the NFL's Jacksonville Jaguars, signing a five-year contract reportedly worth between $50 million and $60 million. However, it didn't take long to discover Meyer's rough-and-ready style didn't mesh with present-era professional athletes, and the coach was fired just thirteen games into his first season.

So, will Meyer ever coach again? His prospects would seem to be limited, especially after his tenure in Jacksonville imploded so quickly. But those who believe they've seen the last of Urban Meyer patrolling a sideline would do well to remember growing up in a hard-working, blue-collar town teaches a lifelong lesson. Never say never.

EZEKIEL ELLIOTT

OSU RUNNING BACK 2013–2015

15

NICKNAME: Zeke

HOMETOWN: Alton, Illinois

HEIGHT: 6 ft 0 in **WEIGHT:** 225 lb

NFL DRAFT: 2016, Dallas Cowboys

It was called *Deuces Left Zin 99 Coke*, and it didn't look like it was going to work. Clinging desperately to a 34-28 lead in the fourth quarter of the 2014 College Football Playoff semifinal game against Alabama, the Ohio State offense was looking for a jumpstart and the engine simply wouldn't turn over.

A pair of touchdowns, one each from the offense and defense, had allowed the Buckeyes to erase a 21-20 halftime deficit, but the powerful Ohio State offensive attack had done nothing but spin its wheels since the middle of the third quarter. The cold, hard truth was that the wheels were actually spinning in reverse. The Buckeyes had a paltry thirty-five yards to show for their previous twenty plays, with their last two possessions netting negative yardage. Now, they were at their own fifteen-yard line, head coach Urban Meyer and offensive coordinator Tom Herman frantically trying to come up with a play that would work against a hard-charging, fast-pursuing, steam-snorting Crimson Tide defense.

What Meyer and Herman agreed upon was *Deuces Left Zin 99 Coke*, a fairly simple zone read play in which quarterback Cardale Jones has to make a split-second decision. Does he hand the ball to running back Ezekiel Elliott or does the defensive alignment dictate the quarterback fake the handoff and run the ball himself? Jones assessed the situation and handed the ball to his powerful running back, an assessment that immediately looked like the wrong decision.

Elliott began to sprint to his left and saw nothing but maroon marauders walling off his escape route. But then it happened. Left guard Billy Price pulled in front of Elliott, and sealed off the corner with help from tight end Nick Vannett. That opened the tiniest sliver of a hole for the 6-foot, 225-pound sophomore, who squeezed into the gap just outside left tackle Taylor Decker. Then, as Elliott planted his left foot to turn upfield, wide receiver Evan Spencer cracked back on Alabama linebacker Shaun Dion Hamilton with such force that Hamilton toppled to the ground and rolled into fellow linebacker Trey DePriest, knocking over the Tide defender as if Spencer had converted a 3-6 split in a bowling alley.

After that, in Elliott's words, "It opened up like the Red Sea." The Scarlet-and-Gray wrecking ball suddenly turned into a runaway freight train, and it didn't stop until crossing the goal line some eighty-five yards in the distance. Ohio State had chopped down top-seeded Alabama, the upper crust of the college football elite, on its way to the program's first national championship in a dozen years.

And while Jones, who began the season as the team's third-string quarterback, gets much of the credit for sparking the title run, it was Elliott who rushed for 220 yards and two touchdowns against Wisconsin during a Big Ten Championship Game blowout, 230 yards and two scores versus Alabama in the national semifinal, and 246 yards and four touchdowns in the championship game against overmatched Oregon.

All from a guy nearly told by Meyer to go elsewhere to play his college ball.

Ezekiel Elijah Elliott was born June 22, 1995, into an Alton, Illinois, family that was the very definition of sports-minded. His father, Stacy, was a linebacker at the University of Missouri in the early 1990s, playing on mediocre teams that only served to stoke his competitive fire. Zeke's mother, the former Dawn Huff, was a high school champion in three sports at tiny Mount Ayr High School in southern Iowa, and later became a member of the Missouri women's track team. Dawn's father, Leon Huff, played basketball at Drake University and was named to the program's all-decade team of the 1970s, and his brother Shawn played professional basketball in Finland.

Still, when it came to providing opportunities for Ezekiel and his younger sisters Lailah and Aaliyah, Stacy and Dawn Elliott steadfastly placed academics ahead of athletics. That meant raising their family in a modest, two story house on a shaded corner lot, and reliable vehicles meant for transportation rather than status.

"Dawn and I sacrificed to provide a high quality education for Ezekiel and his sisters," Stacy said. "We were a middle-class family trying to provide an upper-class education and lifestyle for our children. Ezekiel went to private school for his academic career through high school. So, we didn't drive the best cars and we didn't go on fine trips or live in big houses. Most of our money went to the children. Our family vacations were AAU national track championships held in places across the country."

By the time he was ready to enter high school, Ezekiel was more than willing to attend Alton High School, only about ten minutes from his house. But despite an already burgeoning athletic pedigree, he was enrolled at the more academically driven John Burroughs School about thirty miles away in suburban St. Louis. It was the beginning of an ideal atmosphere of learning inside the classroom and achieving on the athletic fields of play.

Zeke was a three-sport standout in football, basketball and track, and even spent some time on the school baseball team. He played running back for the Bombers football team, coached by former NFL quarterback Gus Frerotte, and helped lead the team to three consecutive appearances in the state championship game. During his final two prep seasons, Zeke rushed for nearly 4,000 yards and 74 touchdowns.

He was even better on the track. With a two-and-a-half-hour span at the state track meet, he captured four individual titles, winning the 100- and 200-meter dashes as well as the 110-meter high hurdles and 300-meter low hurdles.

The blend of power and speed, an armload of national awards, and a relentless work ethic made Elliott one of the most sought-after prospects of the 2013 recruiting cycle. Virtually every big-name coach found his way to John Burroughs School, the Elliott home, or both although it seemed all but one was fighting an uphill battle. Missouri had just departed the Big 12 Conference for the prestige of becoming a member of the Southeast Conference, and longtime Tigers head coach Gary Pinkel had made signing Ezekiel Elliott his top priority.

That didn't seem too much of a hurdle for Pinkel to clear with Zeke's parents each proud Mizzou alums. Every year, Zeke, Lailah and Aaliyah attended Missouri's spring football game, which also serves as an annual reunion of sorts for former players. Some of Zeke's earliest memories are of running around Faurot Field after the spring game while his father chatted up former teammates.

But when it came time for a commitment, Zeke and his family went with their heads rather than their hearts. Urban Meyer had returned to coaching after a one-year hiatus, and the two-time national championship coach had taken up residency at Ohio State. In addition to his aggressive, innovative offensive mind-set, Meyer took with him to Columbus his take-no-prisoners approach on the recruiting trail, immediately targeting Elliott as his number one priority at running back. Meyer's rare combination of compassionate coach and hard-selling closer convinced Stacy and Dawn Elliott that Ohio State was the best place for their son, and Zeke offered his verbal commitment to the Buckeyes in April 2012—four months after Meyer's return to coaching and four months before Zeke's senior high school season was to begin.

Still, the tug of Mizzou lingered. Stacy kept peppering Meyer with questions about how he'd use Ezekiel, referring to an article sent to him by the Iowa coaching staff that noted a Meyer team had never produced a 1,000-yard tailback. Meyer did his best to assuage the father, but grew increasingly impatient with the incessant badgering.

During an in-person winter visit to the Burroughs School to watch Elliott play basketball, a flu-stricken Meyer had finally had enough. Zeke appeared to be going through the motions against inferior competition, his father was chewing on the coach's ear again, and the proverbial camel's back couldn't take any more.

"I'm sick as a dog and putting up with people questioning how we're going to use him," the coach recalled. "I almost got up and walked out of the gym and said, 'You like Missouri so much, I'll tell you what: You guys go to Missouri.' I was that fed up."

OSU running backs coach Stan Drayton, likely watching his coaching life pass before his eyes at that very moment, was sitting beside Meyer and reminded his boss what kind of talent he was passing up if he left the gym. Meyer wound up staying, of course, later saying, "I'm really glad we didn't leave."

The relationship between Meyer and Zeke's father, a pair of alpha males by every description, remained strained for a while. "When Ezekiel signed with Ohio State, I thought, 'Urban, where'd you come from, man?" Stacy recalled. "You just changed the course of history for my family. Why? Why'd you have to come out of retirement?"

But once Stacy moved to Columbus and got a job with the Columbus Urban League working with gangs, similar to the social work he'd done in St. Louis, the relationship between father and coach gradually improved. It got to the point where Meyer had Stacy speak to the parents of incoming freshmen to help ease their fears about sending their sons off to play football at Ohio State.

Meanwhile, any question about how Zeke's talents would be utilized became moot. During his freshman year in 2013, he apprenticed behind Carlos Hyde, who became Meyer's first 1,000-yard running back when rushed for 1,521 yards and fifteen touchdowns. A year later, Zeke became the second and already had eclipsed the 1,000-yard mark before embarking upon his postseason tear. Despite somehow garnering only an All-Big Ten honorable mention, he finished the 2014 season with 1,878 yards and eighteen touchdowns.

Ohio State fell just short of a chance to repeat as national champions in 2015, a 17-14 loss at home in late December to Michigan State robbing the Buckeyes of another Big Ten Championship Game appearance. The game against the Spartans was an odd one, played in a steady light rain before an Ohio Stadium record crowd of 109,975. The Buckeyes took a 14-7 lead into the fourth quarter, but couldn't hold off Michigan State, who got a game-winning field goal on the final play. But it was the OSU game plan, with Elliott getting only twelve carries, including only two in the second half, that left fans scratching their heads.

The Buckeyes went on to finish the season with statement victories against archrival Michigan and Notre Dame in the Fiesta Bowl to close out a record of twelve wins in thirteen games. Zeke topped off his junior campaign with 214 yards and two touchdowns against the Wolverines and 149 yards and four scores versus the Fighting Irish. That gave him 1,821 yards for the season, the only time in OSU history a running back had rushed for 1,800 or more yards in back-to-back seasons.

His three-year totals at Ohio State included 3,961 rushing yards, which still ranks third all-time in program history behind Archie Griffin and J.K. Dobbins, and 46 rushing touchdowns, tied for fourth all-time. He also had a string of 15 consecutive games in which he ran for 100 yards or more, the second-best streak in OSU history behind Griffin, who had 31. But Zeke was much more than just a dominant runner. He totaled 58 pass receptions during his college career and also returned an occasional kickoff or punt. But perhaps his most accomplished skill was one that usually went unseen.

"He's the best blocking running back I've ever coached and it isn't even close," Meyer once said.

Ohio State running backs coach Tony Alford continually added to a highlight tape throughout Elliott's career—not one of his long touchdown runs but rather one Alford called *Zeke's Greatest Hits*. For example, during a double-overtime victory at Penn State in 2014, Elliott was lead blocker on a fly sweep when he lowered his shoulder into Nittany Lions safety Marcus Allen so hard that Alford exclaimed, "Damn near breaks his femur!"

Included on the highlight reel is Elliott capsizing an Indiana safety some fifteen yards as well as throwing not one but two key blocks on Braxton Miller's famous spin play during the 2015 season opener against Virginia Tech. Zeke's own personal favorite came during his freshman year when he was on the kickoff coverage unit. During a 56-0 manhandling of Purdue, Elliott sprinted downfield and crushed a returner with such brute force that he tumbled five yards out of bounds, rolling to stop at the feet of the Boilermakers cheerleaders.

Watching the video on YouTube, Zeke's eyes twinkled when he pointed out a final indignity for his opponent. "There's a cheerleader," he said, "laughing at him on the sidelines."

JOEY & NICK BOSA

OSU DEFENSIVE END JOEY 2013—2015, NICK 2016—2018

HOMETOWN: Fort Lauderdale, Florida

HEIGHT: Joey 6 ft 6 in, Nick 6 ft 4 in

WEIGHT: Joey 275 lb, Nick 263 lb

ALL-AMERICAN: Joey 2014, 2015; Nick 2017

97

Joey and Nick Bosa are the yin to one another's yang. While Joey has a bit of a short fuse, Nick's personality features what his mother describes as "a gentle being." Joey is the more intense of the two, Nick a little more laid-back. Nick is the extrovert while Joey prefers quiet time and solitude. Joey played piano as a kid, Nick was more into electronic dance music. Joey barely has a social media presence while Nick enjoys nothing more than mixing it up about a variety of topics on Twitter. Where Nick is unabashed where his views on politics are concerned, Joey couldn't care less. Joey's chiseled face and classic Roman nose favors his father and his Italian heritage. Nick's rounded features and easy smile more resemble that of his pretty blonde mother.

Born a little more than two years apart, the Bosa brothers would seem to be cut from different fabric altogether. That is, until anything of a competitive nature enters the picture. That's when Joey and Nick morph into the same kind of beast, the ones who initially look for a crack in the opponents' armor and then set about exploiting it with brute force. It was that kind of mentality that led the brothers to All-America careers at Ohio State and top-three selections in the National Football League draft.

Joseph Anthony Bosa was born July 11, 1995, and brother Nicholas John Bosa followed October 23, 1997, in Fort Lauderdale, Florida. To say they were destined to play football would be understating the obvious. Their father, John, was an All-America linebacker at Boston College and a first-round selection by the Miami Dolphins in the 1987 NFL draft. Meanwhile, the boys' mother, the former Cheryl Layne Kumerow, grew up in an athletic family of her own in suburban Chicago. Her brother, Eric, was an All-American quarterback at River Forest High School in Oak Park, and then became a fixture in Ohio State's defensive lineup who was twice named to the All-Big Ten first team as a linebacker. He, too, was a first-round NFL draft pick, selected by the Dolphins in 1988.

Despite the obvious gridiron lineage, Cheryl and John Bosa did not set out to make their sons follow the family tradition. They had other ideas for their boys, more mundane activities such as baseball, soccer, tennis, golf, and skiing. "I tried to keep them away from football as long as I could," John said, "but they begged to play, so we let them give it a shot."

Joey was just eight at the time, and it was only a couple of years later when his father knew the sport was going to be his elder son's calling. "I saw him walking onto the field one day as a fifth-grader," John remembered, "and it was like his practice uniform just fit. I was like, 'Oh, yeah, he's done. He's a football player.'"

Meanwhile, his younger brother didn't understand why he couldn't join Joey on the football field. "He threw a fit," Cheryl said. "I mean, a full-blown temper tantrum. I remember him telling us, 'If you don't let me play, too, I'm going to die.' The kid slept with a football every night, so what were we going to do?"

Nick's first brush with organized football was at the age of seven. At his first practice, after spending some time with the offense, the youngster went up to his coach, tugged on his shirt, and asked to switch to defense like his dad and older brother. "He walked up to the guy totally on his own and asked to play defense," his mother said. "That's bizarre stuff. At seven, how do you even know?"

The attitude of doing whatever the other brother was doing, and then trying to outdo one another, began at an early age. Ping-pong, video games, pool, darts, even juggling. Joey would start a new hobby

Joey is one of only three players ever to win Big Ten Defensive Lineman of the Year honors in back-to-back seasons.

and Nick would follow right behind. "Every time I think I'm better than him at something," Joey says, "he just flies right by me."

There was one activity at which neither brother seemed able to gain a clean advantage. When Joey and Nick were still in grade school, their father bought a trampoline with mesh walls for the backyard of the family's Fort Lauderdale home. The boys enjoyed the beach and water sports their Southeast Florida locale afforded, but bouncing around the miniature palm trees and towering Florida pines while perfecting belly flops and backflips quickly became their most favorite pastime. Soon, afternoon sessions devolved into something less gymnastic.

The boys devised something they called *Kill the Man With the Ball*, a game whose rules were as simplistic as its name. Involving three to four players—Joey, Nick, and one or two brave neighbors—one boy would grab a small red-and-blue football, and the others attacked him until he coughed it up. Once, Nick attempted to flip over the oncoming assailants and broke his nose on a trampoline support bar. There were no official winners in the game, just relative levels of survival. "We would go at each other for hours," Joey recalled with a certain fondness. "I actually miss that."

Suffice to say, Joey quickly outgrew *Kill the Man With the Ball*. His father operated a pair of gyms in the Miami area, each called the Gridiron Club, and Joey became a workout fiend. When he was a sophomore at St. Thomas Aquinas High School in Fort Lauderdale, he filled out to about 240 pounds. His potential became crystal clear to college talent scouts when he attended summer camp at the University of Alabama where, after watching the youngster shed would-be blockers and blanket tailbacks on passing routes with equal ease, Crimson Tide head coach Nick Saban tendered Joey a scholarship offer on the spot.

It was the first offer he had received, and Joey was tempted to quickly agreed to a commitment, asking his father later, "How could I do any better than that?" But his father preached patience, and they decided to let the process play out. By the time he was a senior at St. Thomas Aquinas, he was a one-man wrecking machine, racking up nearly thirty tackles for loss for the state champion Raiders. He won every conceivable all-state honor as well as first-team All-America status while his college offer list reached nearly the century mark.

Joey had always been interested in his uncle Eric's alma mater, but Ohio State's coaching situation had been in a state of flux when he received that first offer from Alabama. However, when Urban Meyer was hired in 2012, and led the team to an undefeated season that first year, Joey began looking at the Buckeyes with a renewed interest. Saying yes to Meyer's pitch was the easy part. Informing Saban, who had left a scholarship spot open for two years, of his decision was decidedly less so. How did he ultimately say no to the Alabama coach? "I didn't," Joey said. "I just didn't tell him yes."

An immediate fixture in the Ohio State defensive starting lineup, Joey earned freshman All-America honors in 2013 and then became one of the team leaders for the Buckeyes as they marched to the 2014 national championship during his sophomore year. As a junior, despite working against constant double-teams and occasional game plans that designated three players to try and contain him, Joey finished with sixteen tackles for loss, pushing his career total past fifty, a total attained by only four other Buckeyes in program history. He also became the first OSU defensive end since Mike Vrabel in 1995 and 1996 to win consecutive first-team All-America honors.

The San Diego Chargers made Bosa their first-round selection in the 2016 draft, taking him with the third overall pick behind quarterbacks Jared Goff and Carson Wentz and just one pick ahead of Ohio State teammate (and roommate) Ezekiel Elliott. Joey went on to win NFL Defensive Rookie of the Year honors from *The Associated Press*.

Any lingering sorrow Ohio State fans might have had from Joey's departure were salved when Nick arrived in Columbus in 2016 as a five-star prospect from St. Thomas Aquinas. Like his older brother, Nick had led the Raiders to a state championship and made an immediate impact during his freshman year with the Buckeyes.

By the time he entered his junior season two years later, Nick was the reigning Big Ten Defensive Lineman of the Year and had already earned first-team All-America status. Unfortunately, that 2018 season was cut short when he suffered a core muscle injury during a week three win against Texas Christian University.

Missing the majority of that season didn't deter the San Francisco 49ers from making Nick the second overall pick of the 2019 draft, just one selection after Heisman Trophy-winning quarterback Kyler Murray. And just like brother Joey, Nick was named by the *AP* as the NFL's Defensive Rookie of the Year.

As Joey and Nick have continued to excel with their professional careers, their parents have stayed relatively level-headed, determined not to get caught up in the hype. Cheryl and John divorced when Joey was in junior high school, but the boys have remained their priority while John balances a number of business interests, including commercial real estate, and Cheryl enjoys a thriving career as a luxury real estate broker. They say they would have provided the same support no matter what careers their sons chose to pursue.

"It didn't matter," Cheryl says. "It's their passion."

When Joey and Nick were in high school, their father would wake them at five for breakfast and their morning workout and they never complained. "Not one single time,"

Nick inherited his father's work ethic, and trying to meet or exceed his older brother's accomplishments further fueled his drive.

John said. "And football is the worst sport to practice. Baseball practice is a blast. Football practice is a grind. But these guys embraced it. You can't teach that. Parents who push, push, push...I've seen it and the kids go the other way. If it's not in their heart, it's just not going to work out."

John also discounts the theory that he is getting to live the professional football career he didn't have through his sons. During his second pro season in Miami, an opposing guard dived at his left knee (a legal move at the time) and John was left with torn anterior cruciate, posterior cruciate, and medial collateral ligaments. He returned for two more pro seasons, but was never the same player.

"I was an overachieving guy. No one outworked me," he says. "But I didn't have the total package that (Nick and Joey) have. I didn't have that type of athleticism. I was more of a grinder. Those guys have the talent and they worked hard to refine it. If you want to say they got some of their work ethic from their father, I'd be OK with that."

As a result, Nick followed Joey, in effect copying his older brother. But Joey followed John and he felt some responsibility. "My dad came from nothing," he said. "He made a name for himself in the NFL and that's motivation for me. I had the talent; it's important for me to do something with it. I just want to do something to make (my parents) proud."

Despite averaging nearly ten sacks for each of his first six seasons in the league, and earning Pro Bowl nominations four times, Joey remains unsure if he will ever reach the goal of making his parents proud, at least in his own mind. "I hear that little voice in the back of my head," he said, "and it keeps saying, 'You're never going to be good enough.' That's just another difference between the brothers because if Nick, who has been to the Pro Bowl twice in three seasons, ever suffers from self-doubt, he doesn't show it.

There's no way to know what they would be like if Nick had been born first, and it likely doesn't matter. The Chargers are fortunate to have one Bosa brother, the 49ers are fortunate to have the other, and Ohio State is fortunate to have had them both.

J.T. BARRETT

OSU QUARTERBACK 2014—2017

HOMETOWN: Wichita Falls, Texas

HEIGHT: 6 ft 2 in **WEIGHT**: 220 lb

16

Jim Garfield was in his pickup truck, somewhere along the three-hundred mile stretch between Austin and Wichita Falls, driving back from a football camp at the University of Texas. Long truck rides are a given in Texas, which boasts more than 683,000 miles of paved roads and highways, far and away the largest number in the United States and nearly twice as many as California.

Garfield was certainly no stranger to lengthy trips. It was 2011 and he was a little more than a year removed from leaving his job as head football coach at Flour Bluff High School in the Gulf coast city of Corpus Christi and taking a job five hundred miles to the north at S.H. Rider High School in the Texas-Oklahoma border town of Wichita Falls.

As the truck neared its destination, a passenger in Garfield's truck suddenly sat up and asked his coach a question. "You know what, Coach Gar?" the young quarterback said. "I know I'm Wichita Falls good, but I want to be nationwide good. Do you think I can be nationwide good?"

Garfield looked out at the North Texas scrubland whizzing by as he pondered the question. But if he could have had the benefit of an oracle into the future, the high school coach would have seen a record-setting college career for his passenger, a career marked by multiple setbacks and agonizing losses always followed by triumphant comebacks. Garfield would have seen J.T. Barrett become not only one of Ohio State's most prolific quarterbacks, but the winningest starting quarterback in program history.

With its proximity to the massive Sheppard Air Force Base, home to the U.S. Air Force's largest technical training wing as well as one of the world's largest training programs to produce combat pilots, Wichita Falls is not dissimilar to most other military towns in that it is more temporary stopover than final destination.

When it comes to football, however, Wichita Falls fits every stereotype of a typical Texas town. On the southwest outskirts sits Memorial Stadium with its two-tiered press box and seating capacity of nearly 15,000. It was the first high school stadium in Texas to feature an AstroTurf playing surface and serves as home to three area high school teams as well as Division II Midwestern State University, making Wichita Falls a sort of *Friday Night Lights* on steroids.

It also just happened to feature just enough of a small-town feel for a couple newly retired from active military duty to want to raise their family there. Joe Barrett was born in the tiny East Texas town of Buna near the Louisiana border, while Stacy Joubert grew up in Beaumont, the booming port city on the Gulf of Mexico where the flare stacks of oil refineries and chemical plants dominate the local seascape.

The Barretts were still stationed at Fort Sill, the U.S. Army post in Oklahoma when they welcomed the second of their three sons, Joe Thomas Barrett IV on January 23, 1995. Shortly thereafter, the family moved fifty miles due south and into a brick ranch house that sat practically in the shadow of Memorial Stadium on the corner of Springwood Lane and Spring Shadow Drive.

It was in the backyard of that house, along with the one of next-door neighbors Eddie and Beverly Zinni, that served as the first football field for J.T. and his brothers, Xavier and Stephen. "You don't know how many times I had to throw that ball back over the fence," Beverly said with her sharp Texas twang before adding with a laugh, "I'm a better thrower than he is, you know."

Each Sunday, the Barretts would head off to the red brick and white-steepled St. Paul Missionary Baptist Church, all the boys dressed alike. Discussions with their parents and neighbors were always polite, punctuated by "Yes ma'am" and "No, sir." The Barrett boys were also shown the values of giving back to the community, whether by volunteering at the Kiwanis Pancake Festival, mentoring kids at Jefferson Elementary, refereeing youth soccer games or working at the church, where J.T. served as an usher and somewhat-reluctant member of the youth choir.

By the time he reached high school, J.T. had become a star in football, basketball and track at Rider. As a junior, he rushed for more than 1,500 yards and passed for more than 1,600 as a dual-threat quarterback for the Raiders. The following spring, he helped his track team to a second-place finish in the 4 x 400-meter relay at the Iowa Park Relays, and then took an individual first place in the 100 meters with a personal-best time of 11.1 seconds.

Still, at just 6 feet tall and barely 200 pounds, J.T. wasn't getting much attention from big-time college programs. That was one of the reasons Garfield piled his quarterback in his pickup and drove him to the University of Texas campus in Austin for that summer football camp in 2011. Despite the fact Barrett was rated a four-star prospect by nearly every national recruiting service, Longhorns head coach Mack Brown wasn't biting and neither were many others. It didn't help that J.T. was in the same recruiting class as such other future NFL quarterbacks as Jared Goff, Baker Mayfield and Mitchell Trubisky, and many scouts believed his future was as a defensive back rather than a quarterback.

Tom Herman, just hired as new Ohio State head coach Urban Meyer's offensive coordinator and quarterbacks coach, had heard about Barrett through his contacts in Texas. Herman had spent the first decade of his coaching career in the Lone Star State, including his first two as a graduate assistant on Brown's staff at Texas. Herman watched Barrett work out a couple of times, and immediately began lobbying Meyer to sign the youngster.

There was one catch, though. Meyer was chasing Trubisky and Malik Zaire, a pair of Ohio-born prepsters, to groom as his next great quarterback. But when Trubisky decided to commit to North Carolina, and Zaire signed with Notre Dame, Barrett became the fallback solution and eagerly committed to Ohio State during the spring before his senior year.

"He was the first quarterback I ever signed who I didn't physically see throw," Meyer later said.

J.T. began his senior year with lofty aspirations of leading Rider to a state championship. In just four games, he had already accounted for more than 1,300 yards and 12 touchdowns before tearing his ACL in game five. Just like that, his high school career was over, a sobering experience for an admittedly full-of-himself kid who had known nothing but success to that point.

"I was committed to Ohio State, and I feel like I was ballin'," J.T. said. "Everything was going the right way. But I wasn't right mentally. I wasn't right with God, really. I was really thinking it was all about me. I wasn't disrespectful. I didn't really say things that were arrogant or cocky. But in my head, I had this blown-up confidence.

"Then I tore my ACL and I was low mentally. I was mad at God, really. I thought, 'God, what's up? What's happening? Why would you do this?'"

That was just the beginning. Barrett graduated in December and enrolled at Ohio State in January 2013. But when he arrived in Columbus, he made the wrong kind of impression.

"He hadn't been working out because he had knee surgery," recalled Herman. "He shows up fat and out of shape, he's 6-foot-nothing, and Urban's looking at me, going, 'This is *Ohio State*, bro. The quarterback in this offense at this place needs to be capable of going to New York City.' As in the Heisman Trophy ceremony."

Barrett did his rehab and returned to physical shape, all of which got him to square one from which every freshman begins. He awoke every morning at 5:30, tired, sore and homesick, thinking as he remembered, "Life cannot be like this. This is crazy. I'm exhausted. My body is telling me it doesn't want to do any of the things that I'm asking it to do. But what am I gonna do? I'm at camp. Am I going to just stay at the hotel and lock the door? They have a key to the room. What am I gonna say? I'm not going?"

He survived that brutal beginning and did mostly scout team work during the fall of 2013, taking a redshirt season. The following year, he was ready to battle teammate Cardale Jones for the backup spot behind starting quarterback Braxton Miller, the two-time defending Big Ten Most Valuable Player. But just a few weeks before the scheduled 2014 season-opening game against the U.S. Naval Academy, Miller let out a shriek and crumpled to the practice field turf outside the Woody Hayes Athletic Center. He had torn the labrum in his surgically repaired throwing shoulder, ending his season before it had begun.

"It was almost like a tornado came from Tornado Alley and came into your life," J.T. said. "It was like, 'Man, what are we going to do now?

We're not going to cancel the games. So, how do you want this to go? Do you want to be a guy watching on the sideline or do you want to be in a game making a difference?'"

Barrett started in place of Miller, leading the Buckeyes to eleven wins in twelve regular-season games. But in the fourth quarter against Michigan, he broke his right ankle and had to watch from the sideline as Jones took over the offense and led Ohio State to the national championship.

The following spring and fall, Jones took the majority of snaps at quarterback while Barrett rehabbed. Then, when it came time to name a starter for the 2015 season, Barrett simply had too much rust to scrape off and Meyer gave the reins of the offense back to Jones.

"I'm all about competition," J.T. said. "I'm a competitor. I wasn't mad at competing. If anything, I was more angry at myself because I wasn't playing at the level I knew I could play. When Cardale was starting, I wasn't mad at Cardale or mad at Coach Meyer. That wasn't the case.…I want (Meyer) to watch film and say, 'This is our guy.' I didn't allow that to happen the way I played."

Barrett kept working, and by midseason, he overtook Jones. In his first start, the Buckeyes cruised past Rutgers, 49-7. Ohio State had the next week off, so on Saturday night, J.T. kicked back, drank some whiskey and got behind the wheel of his car. Soon thereafter, he was being booked for operating a vehicle under the influence.

"I was like, 'Man, you could have *hurt* somebody,'" Barrett said. "I thought, 'You could have hurt yourself, which would have affected your family, how much they care about you. And also your teammates and all these different things. This is way bigger than you, brother. Let's be honest about it. It's bigger than you. You could have hurt somebody else. You could have hurt somebody's mother, father, son, daughter, auntie, uncle, brother, sister, all these different things that you don't even think about when you do that.'"

He served a one-game suspension and lost his summer tuition, but returned a changed man. Gone was any of the me-first attitude he had acquired, and in its place returned a God-fearing and community-minded leader cultivated by his parents back in Wichita Falls. "I'm actually glad that it happened," he said, "because if it didn't happen, I probably still would have been drinking and driving. Who knows? I could have killed somebody. I could be in jail. All these different things that could have happened. Fortunately, they didn't."

J.T. returned to the starting lineup and led the Buckeyes to a season-ending victory against Michigan and a Fiesta Bowl blowout of Notre Dame. The following two seasons with Barrett at the controls, Ohio State continued its winning ways with eleven victories in 2016 and twelve more in 2017. Along the way, J.T. established thirty-four program records, including most career passing yards, finishing with 9,434 and in the process smashing the old mark of 7,547 held by Art Schlichter for more than three decades. He broke the school and conference career record with 104 touchdown passes.

Additionally, Ohio State never lost to archrival Michigan during Barrett's five years on campus, and played in the five straight New Year's Six bowls, winning three of them. In both the 2016 Fiesta Bowl win against Notre Dame and the 2017 Cotton Bowl victory vs. the University of Southern California, Barrett was named the offensive player of the game. He was also named a team captain three times, another first in Ohio State football history.

So what made the kid from Texas the Buckeyes' version of The Little Engine That Could? What gave J.T. Barrett the drive to endure setback after setback—some self-inflicted—and return each time a better version of himself? Who better to answer than his college coach, who signed J.T. only as a last resort after other quarterbacks had turned him down.

"I get asked that question quite often and I'll never get tired of it," Meyer said. "J.T. Barrett is an elite leader that raises the level of those around him. He raises the toughness, of will to win, of practice habits, of the human spirit. I know he says he doesn't want to coach, but I'm not done trying to get him to coach because he should do that.

"God made a very special guy there. A very unique guy, and he has a skillset that I haven't come across very often."

J.K. DOBBINS

OSU RUNNING BACK 2017–2019

HOMETOWN: La Grange, Texas

HEIGHT: 5 ft 10 in **WEIGHT**: 217 lb

ALL-AMERICAN: 2019

NFL DRAFT: 2020, Baltimore Ravens

2

Consult any dictionary for the meaning of "perseverance" and you just might find a picture of J.K. Dobbins.

The list of adversities which Dobbins has had to endure in his young life is an extensive one. The result of an unplanned pregnancy. An undersized, overachieving running back prospect who broke his leg and missed his entire senior high school season. Got his first start in college only because the player in front of him was injured. Set Ohio State's single-season rushing record only to fall to near the bottom of the second round of the NFL draft. Despite rushing for 805 yards and finishing his rookie year with 160 yards against the Cincinnati Bengals, wasn't rated among the top twenty-five NFL running backs prior to the 2021 season. Tore his ACL in the final preseason game and missed the entire 2021 season.

Oh, yeah. And his father died in prison when he was just fifteen years old.

Still, when anyone brings up the word "perseverance," Dobbins sees nothing but new hurdles to clear, new challenges to overcome, and new critics to be proven wrong. "I'm not afraid to work hard for what I want," he said. "Hard work is how you make the most of an opportunity when it comes your way. I don't mind criticism. Never have. I use it as fuel. I've got to prove people wrong."

J'Kaylin Dobbins was born December 17, 1998, in Houston, Texas, to Lawrence Dobbins and his teenaged girlfriend Mya Sheree Grounds. He grew up in La Grange, the dusty blink-and-you're-liable-to-miss-it town located on State Highway 71 about midway between Austin and Houston. With the exception of being the subject of a highly suggestive song by Texas blues/rock band ZZ Top regarding one of town's "attractions," as well as the loosely-interpreted inspiration for a hit Broadway musical called *The Best Little Whorehouse in Texas*, La Grange hasn't been known for much of anything since Henry Kreische died in 1882 and his family brewery was shuttered two years later.

Lawrence Dobbins was a native of La Grange, the son of Connie Lee "C.L" Dobbins and the former Rita Smith, and he starred on the same high school football field where his son would make a name for himself nearly two decades later.

Like son, like father, as Lawrence was an outstanding running back for the Leopards who helped lead them to the 1997 Texas 3-A division semifinals in 1997. There, La Grange dropped a 24–14 decision to three-time defending state champion Sealy in a game played in the historic Houston Astrodome. Lawrence had a 70-yard touchdown run early in the game, his power and speed still available to witness on a grainy YouTube video as he broke a tackle at the line of scrimmage, hurdled over one Sealy defender and then outraced three more to the end zone. He scored another touchdown early in the fourth quarter, this one from 74 yards away to give La Grange a 14–11 advantage, but Sealy scored twice in the final minutes to secure the victory.

The following spring, Lawrence ran his way to a state championship in the 100-meter dash. As scholarship offers poured in, and he began to chart his path toward college, his girlfriend Mya broke the lifechanging news. She was pregnant and the baby would be born later that year.

At the time, they were both just eighteen with seemingly limitless futures. Mya was a standout volleyball and basketball player in her own right, and she entertained aspirations of playing in college. She thought about her options, including the brief contemplation of an abortion, before deciding to give birth to J.K.

But her determination to get a college degree and provide for her son remained steadfast. She commuted to the University of Houston several times a week and eventually earned a degree in finance.

At the same time, Lawrence's life moved in a downward spiral. He enrolled at Blinn College, a two-year junior college in Branham, Texas, about fifty miles east of La Grange. He went out for football but got frustrated when he didn't get immediate playing time, quit the team and dropped out of school.

Legal trouble along with long-term health issues followed and conspired to darken what was a once-bright future. Lawrence was convicted of a theft of property in 2012 and sentenced to serve two years in jail. At the same time, he was diagnosed with hypertension, a cardiovascular disease more prevalent in young Black men than any other ethnic group. Lawrence had apparently let his high blood pressure as well as ongoing heart problems go unchecked for many years until prison officials prescribed the proper medicine.

Still, the damage had been done, and on February 14, 2014, Lawrence Dobbins died of a stroke while an inmate at Bartlett State Jail just north of Austin. He was only thirty-three.

"J.K. was really close with his dad," his mother said. "The death of his dad just gave him that drive and discipline. He was competitive (before), but it seemed he was more focused and committed....He realized life is short, and let's make the most of it. It made a big impact on the way he handled himself."

"That was probably the turning point in my life," J.K. said. "I just had to grow up at a young age. My dad taught me a lot of things through actions and through words. Seeing what he was doing, and the trouble he got in, I didn't want to be like that and he didn't want me to be like that. So, that's how I see it. I didn't want to go there."

And go there, he did not. The following fall, the 5-foot-10, 175-pound ball of determination rushed for 2,243 yards and 37 touchdowns as a sophomore for La Grange. As a junior, he increased his yardage total to 2,740 with 35 touchdowns. "If there is a better back in the nation, I'd like to see him," La Grange head coach Matt Kates said at the time. "I know I'm partial to this young man, but he really does things that no one else in the nation can, I believe."

High-profile college coaches descended upon tiny La Grange with offers rolling in from Texas, Texas A&M, Baylor and Houston as well as Oklahoma, Notre Dame and Stanford. But somehow, Ohio State surged into the lead for J.K.'s services despite the fact he had never laid eyes on the OSU campus. The Buckeyes were only a year removed from winning the national championship, and much of the program's recruiting mail contained photos of Heisman Trophy running back Eddie George, whose jersey number 27 was the same as that worn by Lawrence Dobbins when he was breaking records at La Grange High.

"I would never say that was the only reason I committed to Ohio State," J.K. said. "But it didn't hurt."

Dobbins entered his senior season, still 5-foot-10 but now a muscular 200 pounds, ranked among the top three or four high school running backs in the country and seemed poised to justify that lofty rating in the first game of the season. He had already piled up 166 yards and two scores when he broke the fibula in his right leg, ending his senior season almost before it had begun.

"I had to stay in a cast for seven weeks," he said. "I had to miss my whole senior year. It was really tough on me."

But he took the dedication and work ethic he inherited from his mother and threw himself into an aggressive rehabilitation program. He graduated high school in the spring so that he could enroll early at Ohio State. Although admittedly still not 100-percent healthy, Dobbins was impressive during spring practice and carried that performance into fall camp where he was the talk of the coaching staff. But he was still locked on the depth chart behind incumbent Mike Weber, who was coming off a 1,000-yard season in 2016. But when Weber was slow to recover from a hamstring injury, J.K. found himself in the starting lineup for the Buckeyes during their 2017 season opener against Indiana.

Sharing a backfield with such veterans as fifth-year senior quarterback and three-time team captain J.T. Barrett might flutter the butterflies in the stomach of most true freshmen, but Dobbins made the most of his opportunity by rushing twenty-nine times for 181 yards, breaking the program's single-game rushing record for a freshman and helping the Buckeyes cruise to a 49-21 victory in front of a Thursday night nationwide television audience.

After the game, Ohio State head coach Urban Meyer had a succinct reply when asked if he was surprised a true freshman pressed into action could perform so well. "Not surprised at all," the coach said. "We've seen that since spring practice. I mean, he walked in here as a grown man."

What Indiana and the nationwide audience saw was but a glimpse of the running back Dobbins would become. Before his Ohio State career was finished after three seasons, he amassed 4,459 yards, second in program history only to the legendary Archie Griffin, who rushed for 5,589 yards in four years. Dobbins established the single-season record at OSU with 2,003 yards in 2019, and his 301 carries that season placed him third all-time behind Keith Byars, who logged 336 carries in 1984, and George, who totaled 328 attempts during his Heisman-winning season in 1995.

Despite all of those lofty numbers, Dobbins never finished higher than sixth in the Heisman Trophy voting, earned first-team All-Big Ten honors only once and had to settle for All-America status as an all-purpose player from the Football Writers Association of America. Then when his name was called by the Baltimore Ravens near the end of the second round of the 2020 draft, his competitive fire began to burn just that much hotter.

"I'm working like I didn't get drafted," Dobbins said during his rookie training camp, "like I'm not even on the team, like I'm a guy off the streets...working for a spot. That's how I'm approaching it." Then came his first season with the Ravens followed by the second catastrophic injury of his young career. Rehab is a long and arduous road, but those who have underestimated the resolve of J.K. Dobbins in the past have lived to regret it.

"I see a lot of his dad in him," his mother said. "But J.K. is more determined and more disciplined and more committed than his dad was. Hard times only seem to toughen J.K."

"Never give up," Dobbins said. "That's one of the things I've learned. It's just been a wild life for me. A lot of people don't see that, but that's what makes me the person I am. I've had to fight for everything. It never has come easy to me, but I see it as a blessing. I'm just thinking every day I lay my head down, my mind is racing about how to be the best. I want that. I truly want that."

CHASE YOUNG

OSU DEFENSIVE END 2018–2019

NICKNAME: The Predator

HOMETOWN: Upper Marlboro, Maryland

HEIGHT: 6 ft 5 in **WEIGHT**: 265 lb

ALL-AMERICAN: 2019

NFL DRAFT: 2020, Washington Football Team

2

From "The Old Lady of the Olentangy" to simply "The Shoe," Ohio Stadium has a number of nicknames to which it is referred with reverence by Ohio State football fans. The impressive structure, constructed using some 40,000 cubic yards of concrete and more than 4,000 tons of steel, opened in 1922 to accommodate the rapidly increasing popularity of the university's football team.

But what few of the millions who have passed through the stadium's iron gates over the years realize is that Ohio Stadium's unique horseshoe design was intended to intimidate opposing teams. Award-winning architect Howard Dwight Smith, himself an alumnus of the university, incorporated distinctive columns and a rotunda into the design, envisioning the stadium as a modern-day Colosseum where gladiators battled centuries before. Additionally, Smith rejected the idea of a bowl-like structure, designing the stadium in a horseshoe shape with upper decks hanging over part of the lower deck, thereby enabling the roar of the home crowd to roll down onto the field of play and bury opposing teams in a cacophonic avalanche.

The first time a player emerges on the field and looks up to gaze at rows upon rows of seats that seemingly rise into the clouds, there is no doubt the lump in the throat grows larger and stomach butterflies immediately transform into killer bees.

Of course, not every player is intimidated. Every once in a while, he is the one in charge of the intimidation.

It was a late July evening in 2016, and the Ohio State football program was hosting its annual Friday Night Lights camp for prospective players inside the Horseshoe. Temperatures had been kissing the 90-degree mark all week, yet there was a festive, party-like atmosphere in the stands as sweat-soaked fans filed in, eager to check out a host of elite high school standouts as they were put through a number of drills by Urban Meyer and his coaching staff.

Meanwhile, down on the stadium's artificial surface, the prep athletes did their best to showcase an array of talents, each trying to remain focused despite the sauna-like conditions, all the while cognizant of his intimidating surroundings.

And then there was Chase Young, barely seventeen years old but already a sinewy six-foot-five and 226 pounds. The five-star rated defensive end from DeMatha Catholic High School in Hyattsville, Maryland, was embarrassing fellow recruits in the north end zone of Ohio Stadium to the point that Meyer came over to watch next to defensive line coach Larry Johnson.

It was late in the evening, the stadium lights had been switched on to provide an ominous glow in the hot July night, and the camp was in its waning minutes when an overconfident offensive lineman called out Young to participate in a pass-rushing drill. With Meyer standing only a couple of feet away, Young exploded past the left tackle and pushed over the tackling dummy stationed in the backfield. A few seconds later, he repeated the exact same sequence. The defensive players watching the drill erupted while Meyer and Johnson looked at one another and smiled a knowing smile.

"A left tackle actually called me out because I guess he recognized me and knew how good I was," Chase said. "He called me out, so I had to beat him twice in front of Coach Meyer. I guess he thought I was going to be intimidated or something. I usually like to be the one doing the intimidating."

The youngster grabbed a towel, roughly ran it through his long braided hair, and made his way to the stands, where he chatted with his parents for several minutes. They were eventually joined by Meyer and then by Johnson. After about fifteen minutes, the conversation was over. Already armed with a multitude of scholarship offers from coast to coast, Young ended any suspense by committing to Ohio State before his senior season of high school had begun.

"I really just came in to put in some work," he said of his appearance at the Friday Night Lights event. "I didn't even know I was going to commit. But I had a feeling in my head that Ohio State was where I wanted to go, so I just made that choice. It just felt right, so I did it. My mom always told me to go with my gut feeling, so that's what I did."

The bond between Young and his parents has been a strong one ever since he was born April 14, 1999. The fact that he became an enforcer on defense didn't come by accident, either.

His father, Greg, was a tall, athletic youngster who went by the nickname of "Big Bird" while in high school and whose ambition was to become a pro football player. But he concentrated on basketball while attending nearby Bowie State University, after which he began a law enforcement career and spent more than two decades as a police officer in Arlington, Virginia.

One could say law enforcement is the family business. Chase's mother, Carla, worked in the Department of Transportation's Office of Investigations, which fights fraud and other crimes related to the DOT. His uncle, Bernard Joseph, put in twenty years in the county police department in Prince George's, Maryland, and two other uncles, plus two cousins, made careers of policing as well. Altogether, there are 144 years of law enforcement experience in the family, spanning an incredibly diversified list of agencies and every imaginable role—patrol cop, correctional officer, hostage negotiator, narcotics investigator, bailiff and college police chief.

Along the way, the family has seen the shift in race relations firsthand in a way few could fathom. In 1971, Chase's uncle Von was set to become the first black police officer in Lincoln, Illinois, with a hire date of April 1, but, as he was later told by his chief, city officials postponed his hiring by a day to April 2 because they feared citizens might consider it an April Fool's joke.

The long hours, hard work and discipline required for a career in law enforcement led to a number of unique ways in which Greg Young prepared his son for an athletic career. "When he was ten years old, I bought Chase a lawnmower," he said. "Then I took the self-propel cord and broke it apart, and I said put your football cleats on and push this now." When Chase got older, he began doing curls with 35-pound buckets of cement and even added boxing to his training regimen.

His father swears he knew his son would be good enough to earn a college scholarship while watching Chase run circles around fellow peewee leaguers at the age of six.

But when he transferred from St. Vincent Pallotti High School to DeMatha for his junior season, it was readily apparent that a budding superstar was in the making.

"When we got the kid, when we watched his work ethic in the weight room, it didn't take long to figure out he was going to be special," DeMatha defensive coordinator Deno Campbell said. "We just had to figure out a way not to screw him up."

The seriousness that Chase entered DeMatha surprised the staff. The culture of the all-boys school with its strict discipline, rigorous schedule, and rigid hair requirements sometimes proves difficult for first-year students. But Young seemed unfazed. Joan Phelan, the co-director of the academic support center, remembers how Young spent most of his pre-practice time doing homework. Wendy Norris, the athletic trainer, remembers how he understood the importance of recuperating in ice baths.

Mike Jones, the basketball coach, can recall how Young helped corral unruly students in public speaking class. "It wasn't fake either," Jones said. "He wasn't doing it because Coach is here. There was no B.S."

On the field, the new kid quickly asserted himself as one of the Stags' best players. He refused to take practices easy and often sneaked in extra reps with the scout team, exasperating his coaches by blowing up the offense. Chase learned power pass-rush moves to complement his natural speed, and as a junior, he registered nineteen sacks.

The team's coach, Elijah Brooks, remembered his star player didn't shy away from his success. He let everyone know how good he was and what the team needed to do to win—including opposing players or older teammates. "He never backed down from anyone," Brooks said. "If people have something verbal to say to him, or if they challenge him on the field, he's always going to be on time to address it. That's how alphas operate."

By Chase's senior year, he had already committed to Ohio State but refused to rest on his previous laurels. He totaled nineteen more sacks among 118 tackles, forced five fumbles and scored two defensive touchdowns during DeMatha's undefeated season in the Washington Catholic Athletic Conference.

After the season, Campbell told Chase the new style of football was "basketball on turf," and he needed to refine his speed as much as his strength to prepare himself for the next level. So, he signed up for the track team, running the 100- and 200-meter dashes and concentrating on his explosive first step out of the blocks. He had little experience on the track, but he was out there almost every day, honing one of the skills that would make him an elite pass rusher.

When he joined the Buckeyes in the fall of 2017, Chase joined a loaded defensive end position that featured such future NFL players as Nick Bosa, Sam Hubbard, Tyquan Lewis and Jalyn Holmes. Young saw action in 12 games as a true freshman and recorded only nineteen tackles. But he showed flashes of the force he would eventually become, registering three and a half sacks among his six tackles for loss.

The following year was a tumultuous one with Meyer suspended for the season's first three games and Bosa sidelined for the final eleven games after a week three groin injury. But those problems only seemed to add fuel to Young's competitive fire, and he became one of the Big Ten's most lethal pass-rushing weapons. Nicknamed "The Predator," he totaled ten and a half sacks, making him only the eighth Ohio State player in program history to reach double figures in sacks in a single season.

And the best was still to come. Despite often being double-teamed and also triple-teamed, Young established a new single-season sacks record in 2019, totaling sixteen and a half and besting the old mark of fourteen set in 2007 by Vernon Gholston. During a 38-7 win against Wisconsin, Young matched OSU single-game records with four sacks among his five tackles for loss.

A slew of postseason accolades came his way, including Big Ten Defensive Player of the Year and the Silver Football Award, presented annually by the *Chicago Tribune* to the conference's most valuable player. Additionally, he was named winner of the Bronko Nagurski Award and the Chuck Bednarik Award, each given to college football's top defensive player, and the Ted Hendricks Award for the best defensive end before being selected by the Washington Football Team with the second overall pick of the 2020 NFL draft. It took a couple of months before both sides could agree on financial terms, but when they did, Young was signed to a four-year deal worth in excess of $34 million.

Making the step from college to pros seemed effortless as Young started fifteen games for WFT, forced four fumbles, recovered three and totaled seven and a half sacks to win several Defensive Rookie of the Year awards. He also made the Pro Bowl during his first season, a rarity for NFL rookies.

Chase was primed to improve upon his first season numbers in 2021, but in week ten against Super Bowl defending champion Tampa Bay, he suffered a torn ACL in his right knee, ending his season. He immediately attacked an aggressive rehabilitation program with his normal intensity, vowing to come back better than ever. But he also joked that he could always fall back on his criminology and criminal justice degree from Ohio State.

"I know for a fact that if he doesn't have a long career in the NFL or playing football wherever that he will pursue law enforcement somewhere," his uncle said. "At a local level, sheriff's department or something. I do think that's something that he has the passion and desire to do."

Chase doesn't discount that possibility despite the fact he is looking forward to a long professional football career. And as far as the local level stuff, maybe that's a little too mundane for someone who might someday trade chasing down opposing quarterbacks for chasing bad guys down the street.

"I would want to be a special agent out in the street," he said. "Like a detective."

RYAN DAY

OSU HEAD COACH 2019–PRESENT

HOMETOWN: Manchester, New Hampshire

BIG TEN TITLES: 2019, 2020

Ryan Day will talk football with you all day. The intricacies of quarterback reads against different defenses, how many ways a slot receiver can be used as a primary target or decoy, the pros and cons of huddle versus no-huddle—if it's a topic on football you wish to discuss, Day is your man.

Until recently, however, getting Day to open up about himself or his upbringing was akin to the proverbial pulling of teeth. Everyone knew he grew up in Manchester, New Hampshire, the largest city in northern New England where church steeples still tower over the landscape, and was a high school and college star in his native state before embarking upon a coaching career. But before that?

Day never liked talking about his childhood because he harbored a secret about it. A secret that contained equal parts of sorrow, rage, and resentment. On a late January morning, when the coach was just eight years old, he found himself in his living room surrounded by sobbing family members and police officers. His father was dead, apparently taking his own life at the age of thirty-one. It was a tragedy apparently no one saw coming for the industrious young man with the easy smile, pretty wife, and three young sons.

It represented a complete dichotomy of the world into which Ryan Patrick Day was born on March 12, 1979, in Manchester. He was the first of three sons for Raymond J. Day and his wife, the former Lisa McGaunn, Manchester natives who grew up with the sturdiness of character and work ethic of traditional New Englanders. Raymond owned and operated a convenience store, while Lisa tended to their two-story Colonial on Bayberry Street with the leafy maple tree standing guard in the front.

Ryan's brothers Chris and Tim soon joined the growing family, and Raymond acquired a second convenience store in nearby Merrimack. "We were always so happy to see him when he got home," Ryan said. "He had the convenience store and he would bring candy to us. I do remember that."

While winters were filled with skiing and backyard snowball fights, summers found the family on weekend getaways at nearby beaches or a full-blown vacation at Walt Disney World in Florida. By all outward appearances, it was a typical American family growing up together in the decade of Reaganomics, the fall of the Berlin Wall, the AIDS crisis, and the advent of MTV and the first personal computers.

But that all changed on January 20, 1988.

"A police officer came to the house and let our family know," Ryan said. "I was in shock. I remember the shock on people's faces. That was one of those moments you obviously won't forget. What I remember is that he was on his way to work, and the next day, he was gone."

It was a pain from which the youngster tried his best to distance himself. "I don't want to call him angry, but he had a chip on his shoulder for a long time," said Ryan's wife, the former Christina Ourania Spirou, now known to everyone as Nina. "Ryan's ambition and intensity came from always wanting to be mentally tough and not show a lot of weakness."

Sometimes that manifested itself into silence. And then there were other times when it was channeled other ways. "We didn't talk about it at all really growing up," Ryan said. "Somebody made a comment to me, like making fun of me that I didn't have a father, and that ended up in a fistfight. I kind of had that edge. I would see somebody running up and hugging their dad after a game, and that was where I think the chip came from. It was like, 'OK, you've got a dad, but I'm going to beat you on the field.'"

That's when Day decided to make athletics his outlet. Sports had always played a large role in his life—"My dad liked baseball and I remember him pitching to us when we were little," Ryan remembered—and he starred in football, basketball, and baseball in high school. But football was the one that always held a special place.

He began his football life playing tight end and kicking in youth football. One day, a high snap led to a fumble. The kicker picked up the ball and threw a pass into the end zone for a touchdown. "The next game, I played quarterback," Ryan said with a smile. "That was it."

He often tells the story of someone mentioning the term "flea flicker" when he was kid and wanting to know what sport that was from. "That's from your grandfather's favorite sport," he was told. "Football." After that, Ryan continued to play basketball and baseball, but he lived football.

Paul McGaunn was a gregarious, larger-than-life figure whose bald head and disarming smile served him well during a career in the hospitality industry that lasted nearly a half-century. Known as "Papa" to his family, he loved to cook, tinker in his backyard, and once said he never had to make a bucket list because "I was blessed with more love and happiness than most."

But if McGaunn had an avocation over all the others, it was football. He had played the sport in high school, coached by Maryland prep legend Ray Riddick, and instilled upon Ryan and his brothers the life lessons that can be learned by playing the game. Ryan, Chris, and Tim each played quarterback, a position their grandfather loved because he knew that's where leaders were made.

"He always said football brought out the best qualities in a leader," Tim said. "It forced you to be a leader right out of the gate. And Ryan learned that at an early age with what we went through. And he ran with it."

Following the death of his son-in-law, Papa Paul grew even more important to Ryan. Each Sunday during the NFL season, he would accompany his grandfather to New England Patriots home games, and sit on his grandfather's couch to watch every road game on television. "I wanted to do well in that sport," Ryan said, "because that was his favorite sport."

Despite his own personal tragedy, as well as his attempts to suppress it, Day appeared to have a good time in high school playing the role of a local hero. He can be seen in the pages of his Central High School yearbook posing with a football as one of the "most athletic" members of the senior class, and then several pages later clowning among students named "most versatile." He also seemed to have a dry sense of humor, offering a quote beneath his senior photo that read, "Along the way you may stumble, but as long as you've had a good time, you'll be back for another taste." The quote is attributed to one Jackson Daniels, a likely take on the popular Tennessee sour mash whiskey.

Ryan also found time for membership in the National Honor Society, Foreign Language Honor Society, and Beech Street Buddy Program while serving as a member of the yearbook staff. But his passion was reserved for athletic endeavors. In addition to playing baseball and captaining the basketball team, he earned state player of the year honors in football. He never really thought about advancing his career at anywhere other than the University of New Hampshire. The campus at Durham was less than an hour away from home, Nina was already there, having graduated high school a year earlier, and the Wildcats had an innovative offensive coach on staff, future college and NFL head coach Chip Kelly, himself a product of Manchester Central High School.

Before he was finished at UNH, Day had established a handful of new program records, including those for career completion percentage and touchdown passes. Upon graduation, Day immediately got a job at his alma mater coaching tight ends and began a career that has taken him from Boston College, Temple, and Florida (where he and Nina were married in 2005) to Philadelphia and San Francisco in the NFL, and finally to Ohio State, where he succeeded Urban Meyer as head coach in 2019.

All along the way, Day tried his best to keep his past buried. "People would ask about his family," Nina said, "and I remember him saying, 'Don't say anything about my dad.'"

Day admitted he didn't want to face the reality of what had occurred. "I was eight when it happened, but it wasn't until I was about eleven when I found out what really happened. From then, it was a range of anger and resentment. I felt like he was a coward, that he left our family behind, and how could he do that? You have sadness, you have anger, you have guilt. You have resentment," he said. "And then as you get older, you start to recognize that maybe something was wrong. Maybe he was sick."

In 2018, during his second year as an assistant at Ohio State, Day was on a recruiting trip to the Perry Local School District near Lima,

Ohio. It was a trip that forced the coach to finally confront his past.

"I was with one of the high school coaches, and I walked through the hallway and nobody was in school," he said. "I asked the coach what was going on, and he said, 'We've had another suicide. It was the seventh of the year.' And I remember calling Nina and saying, 'Something is wrong. Why is this happening?' It was sort of an epiphany.

"I remember him saying to me over the phone, 'This has to stop. We have to get ahead of this thing. This is a crisis,'" Nina said. "That moment was a turning point in our lives because that was the point when he was like, 'I've been not talking about this, but now it's time to talk about it.' It's been therapeutic the last couple of years for him and for our family. The conversations about mental health have to happen."

It was the genesis for the 2019 founding of the Christina and Ryan Day Fund for Pediatric and Adolescent Mental Awareness in connection with Nationwide Children's Hospital in Columbus. Joining with the national "On Our Sleeves, The Movement for Children's Mental Health," the Day Family Fund helps support children and young adults living with mental illness.

At the time the fund was founded, Day said, "Growing up, I didn't quite understand what all went down. Then as I get older, I start to realize that it was a sickness and there are people out there that need help. And there is a stigma attached to it that I don't think is right. It was a stigma that maybe as a young person I bought into."

The coach didn't stop with simply putting his name on a fund and posing for some photos with his wife. The following summer, Ohio State replaced three part-time football staff positions with four full-time mental health professionals. One of the hires was Candice Williams, who holds a degree in psychology as well as a Ph.D. in counselor education. She came to Ohio State after five years as a member of the NFL Players Association Mental Health Crisis Team, providing case management and assistance to retired players in acute mental health distress.

"I knew it was important to him the day he stopped practice during training camp to introduce us," Williams said. "You have a coach who's bringing awareness to it to break that stigma, but then he's also bringing things into action."

Meanwhile, the Day Family Fund has not only helped bring awareness to mental health issues in young people, it has generated thousands of donations necessary to keep treatment available and affordable.

"We've received some great feedback from the foundation over at Nationwide," Ryan said. "They've received a lot of positive feedback and a lot of donations, which is really important for what they do there with the Behavioral Health Pavilion that really operates at a deficit. They don't make money on that, so they need those donations to be able to operate and serve the Central Ohio area.

"I've also gotten a lot of positive feedback. The whole idea was to bring attention and maybe help one or two people. Maybe it's more than that, but I just felt like the legacy of my father can now be felt in somebody in Ohio or across the country that asked for help or got help.

"Maybe somebody was able to help somebody that they loved or maybe they made a call about something that would have otherwise got pushed under the rug. It wasn't easy to do, but I feel better afterward and maybe it helped somebody out there."

Day added that he hopes bringing mental health issues to light can help remove any related social stigma attached to those issues. He understands that is perhaps the toughest hurdle to clear.

"Being aware of your thoughts and being aware of your mental health is important, and I can't say I always had that during my whole career," he admitted. "There are still a few guys on the team who are ashamed to go ask for help. I certainly don't force that on anyone, but it's just a regular conversation. You don't need to be in crisis to just talk to somebody and get something off your chest. Those things go a long way.

"Life is about ups and downs, and if you can work through those times when you're down low and things aren't going well, when you're going through those challenges and adversities, they can make you stronger."

C.J. STROUD

OSU QUARTERBACK 2020—PRESENT

HOMETOWN: Rancho Cucamonga, California

HEIGHT: 6 ft 3 in **WEIGHT:** 218 lb

7

To understand where C.J. Stroud is going and how he plans to get there, one must know where he's already been.

The youngest of four children from a home broken apart by drugs and the ongoing incarceration of his father, Stroud grew up a scrawny wisp of a kid in a sprawling Southern California city where the ever-increasing number of gated communities underscore the stark contrast between those who have made the most of their opportunities and those who perhaps have had no opportunity at all. Constantly told what was impossible for him to achieve, he developed an inner thermostat permanently set on high. "If you tell me I can't do it," C.J. would think to himself, "I'll make it my mission to prove that I can."

Always confident in his ability, Stroud began as a freshman getting in his high school coach's ear about starting at quarterback, something the coach resisted until C.J. was a junior. Then a virtual unknown on the recruiting circuit with a two-star rating, he somehow scored an invitation to a prestigious quarterback camp where he took home the most valuable player trophy. He received the same honor at another elite camp later that summer, and all of a sudden jumped to five-star status.

After spending the 2020 season redshirting at Ohio State, C.J. won a highly-contested battle to become starting quarterback for the Buckeyes. The early part of the 2021 season featured plenty of growing pains as well as physical pain from a lingering shoulder injury suffered in the season-opening game. At one point in the season, radio call-in shows were inundated with angry fans demanding head coach Ryan Day bench Stroud in favor of one of the other three highly touted quarterback prospects on the roster.

Yet, the youngster prevailed to turn in one of the most prolific seasons in Ohio State history. By the time he threw for a record-setting 573 yards during his team's Rose Bowl victory against the University of Utah, C.J. had already taken home awards as Big Ten freshman, quarterback and offensive player of the year, and enjoyed a December layover in New York City where he had been named a finalist for the Heisman Memorial Trophy.

"You don't know you're in a storm until you're in it," C.J. said of the whirlwind he encountered as starting quarterback for one of the premier programs in college football. "It's definitely something that I had to adapt to. I had to just continue being myself and stop people-pleasing. People are always going to talk good and bad, so you might as well just do you and remain faithful to God."

The young man's faith, both to God and in himself, have been threatened time after time but seem unshakable. Pensive and reserved in public, he is one of the most respected and well-liked players in the locker room. In the parlance of football, he sees the entire field. Once asked about his aching shoulder, C.J. shrugged off the question, saying, "It hurts, but life hurts. You just have to grind through it."

A grinder almost from the time he took his first breath, Coleridge Bernard Stroud IV was born October 3, 2001, in Rancho Cucamonga, California, a city of about 175,000 sitting at the foot of the picturesque snow-capped San Gabriel Mountains. Named for the Kukamongan Native Americans who around the year 1200 established a village on the city's present site, Rancho Cucamonga was once known only for its vast vineyards and being part of a running joke on comedian Jack Benny's long-running radio show.

With a dusty topography once dominated by farms, orchards and vineyards—Cucamonga is derived from a Native American word for "sandy place"—Rancho Cucamonga experienced a land development boom in the late twentieth century and now boasts regional headquarters for healthcare, pharmaceutical and retail corporations as well as myriad gated communities honeycombing the landscape.

When C.J. entered the picture, he was the fourth child born to Coleridge Bernard Stroud III and the former Kimberly Lee Moreland. When C.J. (a shortened version of Coleridge Junior) turned five years old, his father, a pretty fair athlete during his younger days at Fairfax High School in Los Angeles, had already introduced his youngest child to football and basketball.

The youngster's first love was basketball, a sport he could play with the rest of his family. But when his youth football coaches with the Alta Loma Warriors and Pomona Steelers were introduced to his gridiron skills, they suggested he might want to think about focusing on just one sport.

"That was horrible. I hated it because I wanted to play basketball so bad," C.J. recalled. But he already knew what he wanted to do at a young age. "I had to do what was best for my career," he said, "because I wanted to play professionally one day."

By the time C.J. was in middle school, he was beginning to flourish on the football field. However, his father was beginning to show signs of falling into old, self-destructive habits. Coleridge Stroud had served a prison term for a series of crimes committed during the late 1980s and early 1990s, including felony drug possession, receiving stolen property and armed robbery. He paid his debt to society, rebuilt his life, began raising a young family, and spent the next twenty years with no criminal activity.

But in 2015, something apparently snapped. He stole a car, and while released on bail following that arrest, turned up in San Diego, where he allegedly kidnapped a woman and forced her to drive him around the city looking for a place to buy drugs. During the course of the carjacking, Stroud allegedly assaulted the wom-

C.J. was named the Big Ten's freshman, quarterback and offensive player of the year in 2021.

an, and then after she managed to escape, he led law enforcement on a high-speed chase that culminated in his eventual capture after he had tried to elude police by jumping into San Diego Bay.

Under California's "Three Strikes" law, Stroud's third felony conviction carried with it a prison sentence of twenty-five years to life. Suddenly, C.J.'s father, mentor and best friend was taken away from him. He was still barely a teenager, angry and confused about the adversity his rough circumstances now presented.

"It's typical stuff, but it's hard. It's hard," he said. "People read about it and are like, 'Oh, that's a regular Black kid's story.' But it's not. It's not a story. It's real life and it's really hard. You go through things you don't want to do, and see things you don't want to see. You can't sleep, you can't eat. It's little things like that that people don't know.

"My life has been like a rollercoaster. It's been up and down. I've been through hell and back. I've been through so much in my life.... I was young. I was a kid when this stuff happened. I had to grow up early. I had to grow up really fast."

C.J. continued to stay as close to his father as the situation permitted—"I still love him to death," he says—but sporadic visits and occasional phone conversations didn't seem to help. His focus began to wane and his grades began to slip before the teen experienced a spiritual awakening.

Saying something inside him "snapped," he began reading the Bible more, going to church and praying every day. At a make-or-break time in his life, he believes faith is what kept him afloat.

"The only thing that keeps me grounded is God," C.J. said. "It's something that you can't really explain. You just feel it in your heart. He sends you signs and shows you things. Whenever I pray, my day doesn't go bad. That's why I'm so big on God because I could've been dead in a ditch right now. I could've been still in the streets and never been playing football. I could be in jail right now. You never know what could happen in a young Black man's lifestyle.

"But God, he won't tell you exactly what to do, but he'll open that door for you to be able to put your feet in the water and see what things are like. I think that's what he did with my life."

By the time he reached high school, Stroud had his choice of attending any one of four in the city. He chose Rancho Cucamonga, but then almost wished he hadn't. He dominated junior varsity competition as a freshman, and then expected to get a chance to compete for the varsity starting job as a sophomore. But there was a senior ahead of him on the depth chart, and C.J. wound up with only thirty-nine pass attempts that season.

"Me and the offensive coordinator kind of bumped heads," Stroud said. "I'm not playing, so of course, I'm frustrated. I feel like I'm the best quarterback. Me and him bumped heads with that."

When the head coach stepped down after that season, and was replaced by the offensive coordinator with whom Stroud had "bumped heads," many thought the young quarterback would transfer.

"Everybody thought I was going to leave," he said, "but you can't run from your problems your whole life. I knew from day one I got to Rancho I should've been playing. My junior year was like my coming out from a national aspect, but everybody in California already knew me."

And he was about to introduce himself to the rest of the country. A dazzling performance at a regional camp earned Stroud one of the coveted spots to the Elite 11 Finals quarterback camp. He was one of the lowest-ranked quarterbacks

Returning to his native California on New Year's Day 2022, C.J. set new Rose Bowl records for most passing yardage and TD passes.

to be invited to the event, but he stole the show. He was on the same seven-on-seven team with fellow Californian Bryce Young (the future 2021 Heisman Trophy winner from Alabama), but it was Stroud that led the team to a title in the championship game, earning him Elite 11 MVP honors.

His prospect rating immediately shot from two stars to four (it would later go to five by some recruiting services), and he went all the way from being ranked the 860th overall player in his class to the number two-rated pro-style quarterback in the country. Scholarship offers began to flood into Rancho Cucamonga, and he pulled a mini-shocker when he chose Ohio State over such other schools as Oregon, Texas, Baylor and Michigan as well as UCLA and the University of Southern California.

"I never even thought about playing for Ohio State when I was growing up," C.J. said, "but seeing the success Dwayne Haskins and Justin Fields had in that offense, that definitely played a part into my decision. I used to go to camps and people would think I played receiver because I was tall and Black. So, just seeing how Ohio State has a majority of African American quarterbacks the past several years…I'm really big on my culture. And that's not a disrespect of any other culture. If you can play, you can play. It doesn't matter. But I just saw how they treated us at Ohio State, so that really played a part into it."

Stroud served a one-year apprenticeship behind Fields in 2020, appearing in three games, including a 52–12 win against Michigan State during which he scored his first collegiate touchdown on a run of forty-eight yards. After Fields departed for the NFL, Stroud participated in a spirited battle for the vacated starting quarterback job with fellow five-star prospect Kyle McCord and four-star Jack Miller II. Quinn Ewers, yet another five-star prospect who skipped his senior year of high school, joined the fray in the fall.

Citing decision-making, leadership skills and accuracy, Ohio State head coach Ryan Day gave the starting assignment for the season-opening game to Stroud but stressed the quarterback's hold on the position would last only as long as he continued to produce. If Day thought he had to add that caveat for Stroud to maintain his focus, he needn't have bothered.

Beginning with a performance that included 294 yards and four touchdown passes during a 45-31 road win at Minnesota in the opener, Stroud finished the 2021 season with 4,435 yards and 44 touchdown passes, capping the year with his record performance in the Rose Bowl. His yardage total and scoring passes rank second all-time in program annals, trailing only Haskins, who threw for 4,831 yards and 50 touchdowns in 2018.

He will head into the 2022 college football season—most likely his final one before a National Football League career—as the leader of one of the most potent offensive attacks in the nation, and barring anything unforeseen, should again be a contender for the Heisman Trophy. After that, he has expressed a desire to honor his mother by starting a charity for single mothers, and seeks ways to show other kids who might be going through some of the same things as he did that there are success stories generated from dark times.

Above all, though, C.J. Stroud remains a singularly focused young man on a mission.

"I can't explain it, but I get chills whenever I'm competing," he says. "I get a grit to me. It's like, I'm at your neck and I don't care who's looking or who's watching. I'm not going to be disrespectful to nobody, and I'm going to always be a good teammate. But I'm a competitor. When you go through some things, it makes you scratch and claw. I look at it like this: If I can scratch and claw through life and the things that I've been through, football will take care of itself.

"People always seem to expect me to be angry. I'm not angry. Not at all. It's just that some circumstances in my life went the wrong way. But I wouldn't change any of this for anything. It taught me so much. It taught me how to not take things for granted. It taught me how to love people and taught me what compassion is. It taught me so much that I would never, ever want to go back. I've been through a lot, but I would never want to go another way."

BIBLIOGRAPHY

3-Time Champ Expects More Great Things, by Stacey Stathulis, Buckeye Sports Bulletin, April 30, 2005

After The Zone Blitz, The Deadpan Defense, by Holly Brubach, The New York Times, January 8, 2009

Baschnagel Recalls Prayer Being Answered, by Eric Loughry, Buckeye Sports Bulletin, November 18, 2006

Been Through Hell And Back, by Zack Carpenter, ElevenWarriors.com, February 8, 2020

Big Daddy Gets A Chance To Grow Into Something, by Liz Clarke, The Washington Post, July 16, 1998

Blue Plate Special, by Michael Farber, Sports Illustrated, April 25, 1994

Born To Be A Buckeye, by William Nack, Sports Illustrated, November 25, 1996

Borton Showed Why He Was OSU's Co-Captain, by Joe Scalzo, The (Canton) Repository, June 15, 2017

Buckeye Bumper Crops, by Bill Conley with J.C. Phillips, 2005

Buckeye Rebirth, by Bill Rabinowitz, Triumph Books, Chicago, Illinois, 2013

Busted: The Rise & Fall of Art Schlichter, by Art Schlichter with Jeff Snook, Orange Frazer Press, Wilmington, Ohio, 2009

Catch A Rising Star, by Larry Stone, The Seattle Times, July 28, 1996

Catching Up With Tom Cousineau, by Bill Syken, Sports Illustrated, November 10, 2002

Chase Young's Draft Prep Has Included Boxing, Cement Buckets, by Sam Fortier, The Washington Post, April 22, 2020

Chris Ward Is On A Mission, by Doug Harris, Dayton Daily News, August 28, 2005

Days of Yore: The Men of Scarlet and Gray, by Dan P. McQuigg, Stone City Press, Bedford. Indiana, 2020

Dick LeBeau: The Bengals' Man For All Seasons, by Mark Curnette, The Cincinnati Enquirer, September 7, 2001

Expanding Your Horizons: Collegiate Football's Greatest Team, by Donald Steinberg, M.D., Dauvid Press, Boynton Beach, Florida, 1992

Fanatic Francis: How One Coach's Madness Changed Football, by Brett Perkins, University of Nebraska Press, Lincoln, Nebraska, 2009

Fekete Should Not Be Forgotten, by Bob Hunter, The Columbus Dispatch, May 2, 2011

FGCU's Cobb Learned Toughness From Dad, by Seth Soffian, Fort Myers (Fla.) News-Press, November 21, 2016

For Glenn, Game Is The Easy Part, by Melissa Isaacson, Chicago Tribune, January 23, 1997

Forged By Fire, by Alex Tresniowski, People, January 27, 1997

Former Baltimore Colt Who Starred In NFL Playoffs As Running Back And Emergency Quarterback, Dies, by Mike Klingaman and Edward Lee, The Baltimore Sun, November 3, 2021

Game of My Life: Ohio State, by Steve Greenberg and Laura Lanese, Sports Publishing LLC, Champaign, Illinois, 2006

Ginn Can't Help But Wonder If He Could Beat Bolt Again, by David Newton, ESPN.com, August 10, 2016

Goodbye Columbus, by Austin Murphy, Sports Illustrated, September 9, 1991

Gradishar Reduced To Tears By Snub, by Mark Kiszla, The Denver Post, January 15, 2020

Growing Up Fast, by Rick Telander, Sports Illustrated, November 16, 1987

His Hugeness, by Bill Plaschke, Los Angeles Times, April 22, 1994

How a North Texas Town Raised an Ohio State Quarterback, by Bill Landis, Cleveland.com, January 15, 2015

How Ryan Day, Master Doodler, Turned His QB Brain Into Ohio State's Head Coaching Job, by Doug Lesmerises, Cleveland.com, August 30, 2019

Inside The Latest Chapter Of Former Ohio State Star Maurice Clarett's Life Turnaround, by Adam Rittenberg, ESPN.com, May 12, 2020

Jenkins Excited To Get Chance At Receiving, by Gary Housteau, Buckeye Sports Bulletin, February 12, 2000

Jones Was An Ohio State Football Star, by Berry Tramel, The (Oklahoma City) Oklahoman, September 4, 2017

Katzenmoyer Graduates 25 years After Enrolling, by Bill Rabinowitz, The Columbus Dispatch, December 22, 2021

Katzenmoyer Has One Small Season-Threatening Weakness: The Classroom, by Austin Murphy, Sports Illustrated, August 31, 1998

Kern and Otis Were Home Grown, Newspaper Enterprise Association, October 30, 1969

LeBeau Talks Titans, Christmas Traditions And More, by Andrew Maraniss, The (Nashville) Tennessean, June 12, 2016

Life In The Fast Lane, by Hugo Kugiya, The Seattle Times, August 30, 1995

Malcolm Jenkins: Buckeye, NFL Player, Community Leader, by Jessica A. Johnson, Ohio State Alumni Magazine, Fall 2017

Molding Meyer, by Jeff Svoboda, Buckeye Sports Bulletin, December 1, 2011

Never Give Up, by Bill Rabinowitz, The Columbus Dispatch, December 28, 2017

No Stretching Truth—Sutherin's Kick Was Huge, by Eric Loughry, Buckeye Sports Bulletin, September 15, 2007

Ohio State: 100 Years Of Football, by Marv Homan and Paul Hornung, 1990

Ohio State Athletics 1879–1959, by James E. Pollard, Ohio State University Athletic Department, Columbus, Ohio, 1959

One Family Witnesses 60 Years Of Change In Sports, America, by Ken Denlinger, The Washington Post, April 29, 1990

Oregon Finds Glory In Defeat, by Jim Murray, Sports Illustrated, January 13, 1958

OSU Walk-On Turned Into All-American, by Kevin Orr, Buckeye Sports Bulletin, September 21, 1991

Paving The Way For $$$, by Rick Telander, Sports Illustrated, August 30, 1982

Prep Lineman Can Fill Variety Of Spots, by Brent LaLonde, Buckeye Sports Bulletin, October 27, 1990

Saint Woody: The History and Fanaticism of Ohio State Football, by Bob Hunter, Potomac Books, Washington, D.C., 2012

Season on the Brink, by Bill Long, Columbus Monthly, September 15, 2017

Sister's Aid Helped Klaban Deliver In '74, by Eric Loughry, Buckeye Sports Bulletin, November 19, 2005

Snow Seeks Better Life, by Rob Oller, The Columbus Dispatch, January 26, 2019

Speedy Ginn Among Nation's Best Prep Stars, by Chris Hoppes, Buckeye Sports Bulletin, February 7, 2004

Still Alive and Kicking, by Ray Kennedy, Sports Illustrated, December 2, 1974

The Life and Career of Paul Warfield, by Ben Donahue, BrownsNation.com, April 21, 2021

The Long and Winding Road of J.T. Barrett, by Ivan Maisel, ESPN.com, October 12, 2016

The Official Ohio State Football Encyclopedia, by Jack Park, Sports Publishing LLC, Champaign, Illinois, 2001

The Patriot, by Charles P. Pierce, The Boston Globe, September 5, 2004

The Real Story of 'Suds,' by Steve Doerschuk, The (Canton) Repository, January 14, 2022

The Rest of the Iceberg, An Insider's View on the World of Sport and Celebrity, by Robert Smith, Inkwater Press, Portland, Oregon, 2004

The Suite Life of Malcolm Jenkins' Family, by Joseph Santoliquito, Philly Voice, October 8, 2017

The Zeke Squad, by Pete Thamel, Sports Illustrated, November 16, 2015

Two-Point Stance, by Chase Goodbread, NFL.com, April 16, 2020

Vrabel Molds Titans In His Own Image, by Marla Ridenour, Akron Beacon Journal, December 3, 2020

Walking Miracle, by Ryan Shazier with Larry Platt, Grand Central Publishing, New York City, New York, 2021

War As They Knew It, by Michael Rosenberg, Grand Central Publishing, New York City, New York, 2008

What It Means To Be A Buckeye, edited by Jeff Snook, Triumph Books, Chicago, Illinois, 2003

What Saints' Malcolm Jenkins Had to Overcome to Build Social Activist Legacy, by Mike Triplett, ESPN.com, September 26, 2020

Whoosh and a Zonk, by Tex Maule, Sports Illustrated, November 22, 1971

Woody Hayes and the 100-Yard War, by Jerry Brondfield, Berkley Publishing Corporation, New York City, New York, 1974

Woody's Boys: 20 Famous Buckeyes Talk Amongst Themselves, by Alan Natali, Orange Frazer Press, Wilmington, Ohio, 1995

You Win With People!, by Woody Hayes, Typographic Printing, Columbus, Ohio, 1973

Young Following His Family's Formula For Success, by Stephen Means, Cleveland.com, September 26, 2019

Young Gives Ohio State Another 5-Star Commit, by Ryan Ginn, Buckeye Sports Bulletin, August 2016

ABOUT THE AUTHOR

Mark Rea is Managing Editor Emeritus of Columbus Sports Publications, a Columbus, Ohio-based firm that publishes sports-related fan newspapers including *Buckeye Sports Bulletin* and manages the internet website Buckeye-Sports.com.

For more than forty years, Rea has been a writer, journalist, editor and columnist at newspapers and magazines for such companies as Scripps-Howard and McGraw-Hill.

Throughout the course of his career, Rea has won a variety of writing awards, including several national first-place honors from McGraw-Hill in 2002 and 2003, and national awards in 2004 for feature writing as well as in 2019 for column writing from the Football Writers Association of America. In 2009, he authored the book *The Die-Hard Fan's Guide To Buckeye Football,* and followed in 2014 with *The Legends: Ohio State Buckeyes—The Men, The Deeds, The Consequences.*

Rea has residences in Washington Court House, Ohio, and Marco Island, Florida.